The Resurrection of Jesus

Knowing the Transformative Message of the Resurrection from Burial to Ascension

The Resurrection of Jesus

Knowing the Transformative Message of the Resurrection from Burial to Ascension

"And if Christ has not been raised, then our preaching is in vain and your faith is in vain"
(1 Corinthians 15:14)

By Dr. Manuel Bello

Edited by Eliud A. Montoya

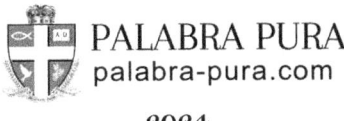

PALABRA PURA
palabra-pura.com

2024

The Resurrection of Jesus
Copyright © 2024 by Manuel Bello
ISBN: 978-1-951372-50-7
Paperback

Unless otherwise noted, all Biblical references are quoted from King James Version. King James Version – Public Domain.

ESV: The Holy Bible, English Standard Version® (ESV®) Copyright © 2001 by Crossway, a publishing ministry of Good News Publishers. All rights reserved. ESV Text Edition 2016.

NKJV: Scripture taken from the New King James Version®. Copyright © 1982 by Thomas Nelson. Used by permission. All rights reserved.
MEV: The Holy Bible, Modern English Version.

No part of this publication may be reproduced, distributed, or transmitted in any form or by any means, including photocopying, recording, or other electronic or mechanical methods, without the prior written permission of the publisher, except in the case of brief quotations embodied in critical reviews and certain other noncommercial uses permitted by copyright law.

Publishing house: Palabra Pura, **www.palabra-pura.com**
Edited in Frederick, OK

Design: Palabra Pura

CATEGORY: RELIGION / CHRISTIAN THEOLOGY / CHRISTOLOGY

Printed in the United States of America

TABLE OF CONTENTS

Synopsis / ix
Foreword / xi
Introduction to the Resurrection / 1

Chapter 1. Revelation of the Death and Resurrection of Jesus / 13
Chapter 2. The Burial of Jesus / 23
Chapter 3. The Day of Resurrection / 35
Chapter 4. The First Appearance of Jesus / 51
Chapter 5. The Guard's Report / 65
Chapter 6. The Testimony of Women / 81
Chapter 7 The Disciples of Emmaus / 95
Chapter 8. The First Appearance to His Disciples / 161
Chapter 9. Thomas' Disbelief / 185
Chapter 10. The Appearance in the Sea of Tiberias / 201
Chapter 11. The Appearance on the Mount of Galilee / 229
Chapter 12. The Ascension / 243

This work is dedicated to our Lord Jesus Christ, to whom I am deeply grateful for the great love with which he has loved me. I am thankful to him for humbling himself to death for my sin, loving me unconditionally, and showing such patience and grace throughout the years, to such a great sinner as I am.

SYNOPSIS

The resurrection of Jesus is one of the most important events found in the Bible. It is the event that separates Christianity from all other religions that exist, have existed, or will exist in the future. Although there are certain myths and religious beliefs that relate the resurrection of their leaders (ex. Krishna, Osiris, Quetzalcoatl, and others), none have the evidence that the Word of God demonstrates about the resurrection of Jesus. Even the fulfillment of all the messianic prophecies, and God's plan regarding Christ's birth, life and crucifixion were all fulfilled perfectly. If Jesus had never risen from the grave, Christianity today possibly would not exist, or, it would just be another story of a man who said that He was the Son of God. In such a case his disciples would have dispersed after Jesus' martyrdom, and Christianity would not exist.

The purpose of this book is to describe in detail every event immediately prior to the resurrection of Jesus: from his burial to his ascension to heaven, and in these events to observe the important interactions that he had with his disciples. We will follow a chronological order of all these events, reviewing the four Gospels and the book of Acts, and possible "contradictions" that could be found in such readings will be explained.

In this book we will carefully observe the great love of Mary Magdalene for her Savior; the great pain that Thomas felt when his Master was taken; the restoration of Peter for having denied Christ; the encounter of the Lord with the disciples of Emmaus, and many other interactions. Likewise, we will be able to see in perspective how us Christians can relate to these disciples, and perhaps how we see ourselves reflected in them (especially at a time when unbelief took over their hearts), and appreciate, at the same time, the beautiful grace and patience that Christ showed them.

I pray that this book impacts your life —as it has impacted me— and that it inspires your heart so that your eyes never stray from Christ, who rose from the dead to show everyone that He is the Author of life: the same one who has promised that one day all of us who serve him will also rise from the dead, to serve and reign with him for eternity

.

BIOGRAPHY

Dr. Manuel Bello is currently an internist and endocrinologist residing in the United States. He was born on June 10, 1985, in Boston, Massachusetts, and grew up in the Dominican Republic. He is a graduate of the Universidad Iberoamericana del Caribe (UNIBE) as a Medical Doctor, and did his specialty in internal medicine at Mount Sinai Medical Center in Miami Beach, FL. Subsequently, he also completed his fellowship in endocrinology at the University of Mississippi Medical Center. Manuel became a follower of Christ in 2005, at the age of 20. Currently, Manuel Bello is married to his wife Pamela, and they have three daughters: Amelia, Annabelle and Nicole.

Foreword

Before you start reading this book, I just want to confess that I am not a scholar of the Scriptures, nor a great theologian, nor one who has studied theology in the best universities in the United States, or anywhere in the world. I am also not a pastor of a church or an elder. I'm just a man who loves Jesus and his Word. I am just another human being unworthy of his grace and forgiveness; with struggles, sins, and temptations, one who seeks to be guided by the Word of God every day and to be changed by his love and grace.

I want to ask your forgiveness if something that is reflected in this book turns out to be inaccurate or wrong, because I confess that, although I truly tried to the best of my ability to base it on the Word of God, and I have made an effort to always remain faithful to his scripture, I am but a man, and like all men, fallible. However, it is my prayer that the words embodied here be as close as possible to the truth, because the last thing I have in my heart is to divert a believer from the truth of the Gospel.

I am not looking for titles, popularity, or flattery, or for my name to become recognized by this work. My greatest wish is simply that this book will help you know and love Christ more. My greatest longing is that its content helps you see more clearly the cardinal importance of the resurrection of Jesus, and that in this explanation you may find an application to change your life to be more like Christ. I pray that He will use this book, to touch not only your heart, but the hearts of many who need God's love and forgiveness so that they may you be encouraged to search the Scriptures.

I also pray that this book will transform your life, just as it transformed mine as I studied each passage, and that each day you and I will become more like Jesus. It is my hope that while you read you feel his resurrection as if you yourself had seen it with your own eyes, and may you feel identified with these men and women who saw him alive at that time; fallen and sinful human beings, but at the same time confronted by Jesus and by his resurrection. Men and women who were transformed and restored to bring the Gospel of salvation to the world after seeing him. After seeing the risen Jesus their lives were never the same again.

With the help of God, while we advance in the knowledge of the facts of his resurrection, we will see more clearly our Christ, just as if we had physically eaten with him as his disciples did; and may the reality and power of his resurrection be just as it was for them.

"Jesus said to him, 'Have you believed because you have seen me? Blessed are those who have not seen and yet have believed'" (John 20:29).

—Dr. Manuel Bello

INTRODUCTION TO THE RESURRECTION OF JESUS

No matter where in the world you live, if you take an introspective look at the world we live in, you will be able to realize the constant pain and suffering that prevails everywhere. No one escapes suffering while on this earth. Everyone who is born is already dying, and it is only a matter of time before death arrives. However, the human race was not conceived to die, but to have eternal life in the presence of God; that is why the idea of dying always shocks us, it is abhorrent to us; However, it is inevitable and whether we like it or not, it will surprise us one day; And if you don't believe it, just take a look at the statistics of the millions of people who die every year.

Suffering is present in every human being in one way or another. We see it in our parents, when they get sick or pass away; in that accident that took our child before their time, or due to terminal cancer. We see it in natural disasters, which claim the lives of thousands of people. Every day some 150 thousand people die in the world; that is around 50 to 60 million people each year; however, even so, we resist thinking about it; and this is reasonable to do so, since the truth is, dying has nothing beautiful or desirable. Death is, and will continue to be, something shocking, repulsive, repugnant, something that we naturally repel, because it is what deprives us of the people we love forever. Dear reader, one thing is certain: at some point death will knock on my door, but also on yours, who can be saved from it?

How can a world like this have any kind of hope? The sting of death will arrive, and everything we accumulated on this earth, whose will it be? No matter how hard we fight, our memories end with our grandchildren, and after that, we become perhaps one more name, one that perhaps no one remembers, because, after all, most of us will be forgotten. The truth is that this life is harsh and judgmental. From the moment we are born, we are already dying.

This world was created by God to be full of life and his presence. The Lord designed it to be a world without wars, without famines, without plagues or natural disasters; without hate or lies. A world devoid of quarrels, robberies, murders, sexual disorders, adultery, infidelity; devoid of all those dire ills that afflict humanity. God made a world without death for man; one in which each person would have loved each other deeply, and where the glory of God would fill every corner; one where all living would praise the one true God.

Death is nothing more than a perpetual reminder of the eternal consequence of sin. God wants to make it clear that life without Him has only one destination: death. Without Him, getting out of the grave is impossible, and outside of Him there is no hope. God wants all humanity to perceive this: death is inevitable, and no one will escape it.

"For the wages of sin is death, but the free gift of God is eternal life in Christ Jesus our Lord" (Romans 6:23).

Almost all the people who have passed through this earth have died, including the greatest men of faith. As we know, the patriarchs (Abraham, Isaac, Jacob) died. Moses, Joseph, Joshua, Elisha, Daniel, Ezekiel, Jonah, John the Baptist, Paul, Simon Peter, etc. also died. Also, modern-day men of God, such as Martin Luther, John Calvin, have died and the list could be endless. But the question would be: Are they really dead?

The Bible says that God is not a God of the dead, but of the living (Matthew 22:32; Luke 20:38; Mark 12:27). Those who die in faith only sleep, waiting to rise again on the last day, when Christ returns at his second coming.

The Word of God says that, from before the creation, before the heavens and the earth existed; before the sun, the moon and the stars were created; and before God created man, the world's condemnation by sin was already known to him. The entry of sin into God's creation was not something that took Him by surprise, since from eternity past He had already conceived a plan to redeem those He had proposed to love (Ephesians 1: 3-4).

Those who were shaped by his hand and were created in his image. Those to whom He gave everything they needed to survive. Those whom he gave life with his own breath. Those to whom He planted a beautiful garden and placed them there to take care of it; whom He gave authority over everything created on earth. For they are the most excellent creation of God that he had made since they were created in his image. This creation rebelled against Him, committing an act that would bring very serious consequences.

The disobedience of Adam and Eve constitutes the greatest symbol of rebellion and offense before God (a Holy God), something that brought about catastrophe onto this world, that is, death, something that still wreaks havoc on all creation until today. God had told Adam that the wages of sin was death (Genesis 2:17); thus, when he disobeyed God, his first death was spiritual, since the Lord separated himself from mankind (they were expelled from the garden where he had placed them, that is, from the continuous presence of God; and the relationship between God and man was broken). Also, eventually, they died physically.

Adam had sinned, he had not believed the voice of God, and this brought the condemnation of the world. His disobedience conferred death on billions of people who have been born through the centuries. Violence, lawlessness, and disease now reign over the world; while peace, goodwill, and obedience to God —things that were once the norm— would now be openly rejected. The image of God in man, although present, had been corrupted. Adam, because of his sin, though created to live eternally in the presence of God, died for his disobedience; and this seed of corruption from Adam and Eve passed to the entire human race.

> "Therefore, just as sin came into the world through one man, and death through sin, and so death spread to all men because all sinned" (Romans 5:12).

The only way to fully understand the resurrection is to understand the promise that God gave to Adam and Eve from the beginning. While still in the Garden of Eden, God promised that he would not perpetually condemn the entire human race to eternal death, but that there was a hope of life. God assured humanity that all was not lost. He promised that he would send a Savior to restore his image in man, the crown of his creation. A promise that would have its fulfillment through the seed of the woman, which would be his instrument to bring the Savior into the world.

> "And I will put enmity between you and the woman, and between your seed and her seed; he will bruise your head, and you will bruise his heel" (Genesis 3:15).

Adam believed this promise, which is why he named his wife Eve. After they caused the death of all their descendants, Adam named his wife Eve, which means "the one who gives life" or "mother of the living", since from her descendants would come the One who would once again give life to all the world. Since the fall of man, God began to reveal his redemption plan, a plan that culminated in the person of Jesus, who was God incarnated as a Man, who gave his life for us.

The resurrection of Jesus gives us security, certainty, and confidence that we truly have life in God. Death was totally abolished for all those who put their faith and trust in Jesus. The resurrection of Jesus Christ is our hope, and without it there would be no Gospel. Without the resurrection, the death of each of the apostles and disciples (and of all those who gave their lives for Christ) would have been in vain.

> "And if Christ has not been raised, then our preaching is in vain and your faith is in vain" (1 Corinthians 15:14).

His death and resurrection were a hidden mystery in the Old Testament, revealed little by little and in many ways through the centuries. It was a mystery because no one truly knew that God himself would take the form of Man to give life to the world by dying for humanity. This is a concept that is practically impossible to believe: that the Holy God would become a Man and would pay with his own sacrifice the great debt that we owed to Him. Although revealed, these prophecies were not clear until Jesus came into the world and died on the cross, a terrible and cruel death. Jesus came to save man from eternal damnation, and to restore man's relationship with God. He came to restore lives, change hearts, and show us how God wants us to live on earth.

In the Corinthian church, not everyone believed that the resurrection of the dead was possible. This seemed to be something implausible to them. That is why Paul wrote to them, explaining the importance of the resurrection. For Paul it was vitally important to believe in Christ, and in the Christ who had risen from the dead, without which, we would still all be living under God's judgment, and not under his grace (1 Corinthians 15:17).

The Corinthian church had doubts about the resurrection (1 Corinthians 15:12); yet Paul clearly tells them that without the resurrection of Jesus, the future resurrection of God's people and the Gospel itself are meaningless (1 Corinthians 15:14). Also, that if the resurrection of Christ had not occurred, none of us would be saved (1 Corinthians 15:15). If there is no resurrection, then this book has no meaning either. It would be better to go out, have fun and live our lives without fear of an eternal consequence for our sin and just enjoy each day until death comes. That is why Paul says then, that if there is no resurrection "Let us eat and drink, for tomorrow we die" (1 Corinthians 15:32).

However, in order for us to be resurrected, we first have to die. This earthly body that has been corrupted by sin must die to receive a spiritual body, which can dwell in the presence of God for eternity. Paul speaks clearly how we will be in this spiritual body.

"So is it with the resurrection of the dead. What is sown is perishable; what is raised is imperishable. It is sown in dishonor; it is raised in glory. It is sown in weakness; it is raised in power.

It is sown a natural body; it is raised a spiritual body. If there is a natural body, there is also a spiritual body" (1 Corinthians 15:42-44).

What does Paul mean by this? He is saying that there will be no more sickness and death in our incorruptible body; that there will be no more shame for sin (for he will rise us in glory); that there will be no more temptation, because this new body will rise in power. The spiritual body will not have the limits of a natural body, with which now we cannot see or appreciate the spiritual as we should. The blessing of the resurrection is that we will be equipped for eternity with a new body to live in the presence of a holy God. Hallelujah!

The day will come when God takes us into his presence. A day when those who died in Christ will rise from their graves, in the twinkling of an eye (1 Corinthians 15:52). Thus, our eyes will finally see Christ, the Lamb of God, and we will be with Him for eternity. I don't know about you, but I long with all my heart for this day to come. A Christian who truly knows his Savior should not be afraid of death, because this day will be the most beautiful day of our lives.

"For the Lord himself will descend from heaven with a cry of command, with the voice of an archangel, and with the sound of the trumpet of God. And the dead in Christ will rise first. Then we who are alive, who are left, will be caught up together with them in the clouds to meet the Lord in the air, and so we will always be with the Lord" (1 Thessalonians 4:16-17).

Paul's faith in the resurrection was such that he mocked death as if it were a bee that had lost its sting. He saw death as a bee that does not have the ability to defend itself or cause more pain. Death over us, believers, has already lost its power, and we have to know that, even if we die, we are already totally safe in Christ.

"When the perishable puts on the imperishable, and the mortal puts on immortality, then shall come to pass the saying that is written: 'Death is swallowed up in victory.' 'O death, where is your victory? O death, where is your sting?' The sting

of death is sin, and the power of sin is the law" (1 Corinthians 15:54-56).

When Christ came to earth, he showed us that the kingdom of God would be such that no more sickness, pain, or suffering would exist. A kingdom full of justice, peace, and joy. Jesus said in Matthew 12:28, "But if it is by the Spirit of God that I cast out demons, then the kingdom of God has come upon you" What then is the kingdom of God? What did Jesus mean by saying that the kingdom of God has come to you? Paul describes in a clear and precise way what the kingdom of God is.

**"For the kingdom of God is not a matter of eating and drinking
but of righteousness and peace and joy in the Holy Spirit"
(Romans 14:17).**
Paul clearly tells us that the kingdom of God is not tangible things such as food or drink. It is clear when saying how the kingdom of God is shown on earth, it is not through material or perishable things, but through the Holy Spirit. The kingdom of God does not become evident in my life because I do well at work, or because of the family I have, or because of the goods I have accumulated on earth; nor for any material provision that God has granted me.

The kingdom of God is evidenced in lives transformed by the power of his Word; lives that have decided to trust God and follow him, love him, and obey him with all their hearts, regardless of the circumstances they have to live on this earth. The kingdom of God on earth consists in the holiness of Jesus, in the justice and peace that are manifested through our belief in Him. Now in Christ, we also can enjoy the benefit of a life justified by his precious blood.

Let's analyze this a little more closely. What exactly does this mean that the kingdom of God is manifested in righteousness, peace, and joy?

The Kingdom of God is Manifested in Righteousness

When analyzing what divine righteousness means, and thinking about God's righteous judgment for our sin, this means that we should have been the ones murdered on the cross and not Jesus. The fair thing would have been for me to pay my debt before God; that I would be eternally condemned for the wickedness of my heart, and not that another person would pay for my sin and rebellion against God.

Our Lord and Savior was condemned for our wickedness. He was condemned for you and me. He was spat at, stripped of his clothes, tortured, disfigured, and nailed to a cross out of love for us. The crucifixion, the humiliation that Jesus went through, was the closest thing to hell here on earth that someone could endure.

The eternal debt we owed to God was a humanly unpayable debt, which demanded death and eternal damnation. This debt was the debt that Christ Jesus paid off with his own precious blood so that you and I would not have to receive just punishment for our sin. Divine justice fell on the only innocent who has walked this earth, and who voluntarily gave himself up for ungrateful people who hated and rejected him. People who continually —including many who profess to be believers— continue to dishonor God's name with their sin.

So why did Jesus have to die for us? Because of the total depravity of man, and because of our inability to save ourselves. If there were another way to save humanity, there would be no reason to believe in Jesus. If there was another way to get to God, then Jesus sacrificed his life in vain.

The Bible shows us that since the fall of Adam, the entire human race has sinned, and we have all turned away from God. The depravity and corruption of the human race was total, and there is not a single human being, except Jesus, who has not been a sinner. We all have the seed of Adam's sin in our being; even the holiest and most moral man on earth is worthy of damnation.

**"For all have sinned and fall short of the glory of God"
(Romans 3:23)**

Everyone who thinks they can save themselves has already been condemned because they have not believed the Word of God. If you believe that God may have mercy on you for your good works, kindness, or gifts, you have not understood the message of the Gospel. Christ Jesus is the one who has given his life so that the unrighteous may be held righteous before God. Christ Jesus took his own righteousness and bestowed it on us, and took our unrighteousness upon himself, paid the price by sacrificing his life that we might have eternal life in Him. This is the righteousness of the kingdom of God.

"For Christ also suffered once for sins, the righteous for the unrighteous, that he might bring us to God, being put to death in the flesh but made alive in the spirit" (1 Peter 3:18).

The Kingdom of God Manifests Itself in Peace

Why is it that the kingdom of God is manifested in peace? What does this mean? The righteousness of Christ given to us by his death brought man's reconciliation to God. Humanity has been at war with God since the fall of Adam, turning ourselves into enemies of God (Romans 5:10) by not wanting to honor him as the sovereign God. God's creation rebelled, turned away from the holy God, and was blinded by sin. Humanity has lived at war with God ever since, looking for different alternatives to have eternal life without honoring the true God. In this way, we have brought unto ourselves the just condemnation of the Almighty.

Humanity has adored animals, the stars, people; the sun, the moon, water, insects and many other things. Humanity has invented their own rituals, and their own way of seeking the spiritual, further blinding our eyes, and despising the God who created us. Today people worship movie stars, musicians, and other public figures. They put their trust and faith in another person only to be disappointed and let down by them time and time again. Mankind, professing to be wise, has become foolish in despising God's counsel (Romans 1:21).

Christ's justification by his substitutionary sacrifice is what brought me peace with God. His unjust death granted me undeserved justice which has allowed us to be forgiven by Him. Jesus' death appeased God's wrath towards those who believe in Him, and is what brings us peace with God, ending the war between God and those who believe in his Son.

This peace does not refer to being undisturbed while you are at home on a Sunday afternoon, for example; it is not the peace that you have when you are on vacation, without any worries; it is not living exempt from all pain or suffering. Rather, the peace we are talking about here is the reconciliation of God and with man. That is why the word says in Isaiah 53:5b "…Upon him was the chastisement that brought us peace…" This is the true peace that "…surpasses all understanding…" (Philippians 4:7). No one would think of giving their life for those who seek to harm them, who insult, defame, and outrage them, that is why this peace truly surpasses any comprehension or understanding that there may be.

This is the peace that should reign in our hearts: "For if while we were enemies we were reconciled to God by the death of his Son, much more, now that we are reconciled, shall we be saved by his life" (Romans 5:10).

Christ taught us how we should show others this reconciliation or peace that we have obtained. He is the model of how to love others. Christ said: "But I say to you who hear, Love your enemies, do good to those who hate you, bless those who curse you, pray for those who abuse you" (Luke 6:27-28); and we must do it because this is the way God has loved us.

It should come as no surprise that believers are called to be peacemakers. In Matthew 5:9 Christ said in the Sermon on the Mount: "Blessed are the peacemakers, for they will be called sons of God." We believers were called to bring the good news of the Gospel to the nations, in order to achieve reconciliation or peace between sinners and God, since, only through Christ, we have peace with God.

The Kingdom of God Manifests Itself in Joy

This righteousness that Christ has given me through his sacrifice, which has brought me peace and reconciliation with God, should be my greatest source of joy. It must be the source of inspiration that motivates me to live daily at the feet of Christ. It must be what guides every thought in me, so that my mind is restored and transformed by the power of his Word.

Knowing that we have an eternity assured at the foot of the great throne of God, to adore and praise him forever, thanks to his grace and love, must be the greatest reason we have to live joyfully every day. Therefore, we must get up in the morning giving thanks to God, because He, in his mercy, overlooked our sins; all by the precious blood of his Son Jesus.

When we lose our focus on Christ, the amazement, and enjoyment of such wonderful favor from God is lost, which then leads to the Gospel not bringing complete satisfaction to our soul. This is because we forget to be amazed every day at what we truly deserve and have not received; we forget the high price Jesus paid for our wickedness. It is then that, eventually, our heart hardens, and we come to be like the church of Ephesus, which, intellectually knew the truth of God, but her heart had strayed, and stopped loving him with all her heart (Revelation 2:4), this church then hardened her heart and eventually died and disappeared in time.

The joy of the truth of his Word had been lost in this church. Likewise, when someone loses the enjoyment that there is in obedience and in the presence of God, what follows is to fall into sin and we then face its consequences.

This joy does not mean always being happy in life. It does not mean that we will not cry, that we will not suffer, or have regret; nor does it mean that we should fake our joy before God. This joy is to be anchored in Christ that, although the circumstances of life bring pain and sadness, despite such circumstances, we know that our life has been made righteous in Christ, and that we have been reconciled with God. That, regardless of the difficulties, temporary ailments and earthly losses, our hearts are ultimately confident, resting joyfully in the God who will sustain us in the midst of all those difficulties.

This joy is not something that can be learned. Rather, it is a gift from God to his children; a gift given by his Spirit to his own.

"But the fruit of the Spirit is love, joy, peace, patience, kindness, goodness, faithfulness, gentleness, self-control; against such things there is no law. And those who belong to

Christ Jesus have crucified the flesh with its passions and desires" (Galatians 5:22-24).

I pray to our God that, through the study of this book, the reality of the suffering of Jesus and the glory of his resurrection can confront your life. May you be inspired by the beautiful revelation of his Word. May this book help you bring the life of Jesus into your mind and heart as we ponder the meaning and implications of his resurrection for each one of us.

CHAPTER

I

REVELATION OF THE DEATH AND RESURRECTION OF JESUS

The arrival of the Messiah was not an event that should have taken the Jews by surprise. They had been waiting centuries for the arrival of a supreme Redeemer; they waited for a man who would come to free them from political oppression, so that the Israelite nation could once again live the glory it had in the days of kings David and Solomon; days when they were an independent nation, and envied by other nations. They wanted to have God's material blessing, but they were not interested in spiritual awakening.

Despite knowing the prophecies about the Messiah, they did not expect one like Jesus. The prophecies of the promised Messiah say that He would be one who would preach good news to the downcast; that he would bind up the brokenhearted; that he would set the captives free and give sight to the blind (see Isaiah 61:1-3). They did not expect the servant of Jehovah who would bring about the spiritual restoration of Israel, but a leader whose restoration would be merely political and economic. Much less did they expect a suffering Messiah, as prophesied in Isaiah 53. The Israelites flatly rejected the idea of the poor Messiah, who would be numbered with the wicked and would bear the sins of all.

Rather, they expected a glorious king, born in a palace; one who fulfilled all Israel's desires for glory, and not a poor man, whose most of his life would have been lived in one of the least prestigious regions of all Israel, Nazareth. They did not want to be confronted by the Word, they were happy in their false religiosity; what they wanted was to continue pretending to be believers, living a life of sin.

"And this is the judgment: the light has come into the world, and people loved the darkness rather than the light because their works were evil" (John 3:19).

Was the death of Jesus something totally unexpected? Could men have fought with God and won by nailing him to the cross? In this chapter we will take a look at the prophetic evidence for the death and resurrection of Jesus. I think it is very important, before we dive into the details of the resurrection contained in the New Testament, that we analyze what the word of God says regarding the death and resurrection of Jesus in the Old Testament.

In the Old Testament the suffering and death of the promised Messiah had already been predicted. Regarding this, it is easy to look back, and with the knowledge we have today, blame the Jews for spiritual and intellectual closure for not understanding the messianic prophecies; but let us remember something: God was revealing the Scriptures progressively until the time of the apostles. Therefore, no one knew exactly who this Messiah would be or how he would be, nor the miracles circumscribed to his advent on this earth.

Seeing Jesus walking on this planet, working as a carpenter, and for 30 years living as a regular citizen (without performing a single miracle), but just waiting for his time to reveal himself to the world as God incarnate, was not something easy to believe. Even his own brothers did not believe in Him initially (John 7:5). However, the death of Jesus was predicted from the book of Genesis.

Genesis 22 tells the story of Abraham and Isaac. There God asks Abraham to sacrifice his son for Him. This was the son of promise, from whom Abraham would have countless and innumerable offspring, which would bring blessing to the whole world for all generations. Therefore, for God to ask him to sacrifice Isaac on the altar seemed totally irrational and devastating.

However, Abraham decided to put all his trust in God, the same one that he had miraculously given to Isaac, the son of the promise (since it was humanly impossible for Sarah to get pregnant, read Genesis 18:11). However, Abraham knew that God still had the power to raise Isaac from the dead (Hebrews 11:19). So great was the trust that he had in God, that he never hesitated to obey the voice of the Almighty. The result of his faith was this: just before Abraham plunged the knife into his son, a voice from heaven was heard that stopped him; and then, among the bushes, he found a ram (the male of the sheep) that he offered as a sacrifice, replacing Isaac (v.13).

What does God want to show us here? This story takes us to the cross. Abraham representing God, who is about to judge sinners with a just judgment. Isaac represents sinners, ready to receive just punishment for their sin. The ram represents the One who would one day come, the one who is called "the lamb of God, who takes away the sin of the world" (see Isaiah 53:7, John 1:29), who would lay down his life for us sinners. This innocent little animal did not deserve to die instead of Isaac, but Isaac's life was saved because of the shed blood of this sacrifice. The ram's horns caught between the thorns represented the crown of thorns that Jesus wore as a mockery and humiliation placed by the Roman soldiers (Matthew 27:29).

In the Old Testament the suffering of Jesus before his death is described. One of the prophecies says that his hands and feet would be pierced ("…they have pierced my hands and feet", Psalm 22:16b). It also mentions what would happen to his clothes: "they divide my garments among them, and for my clothing they cast lots" (Psalm 22:18). The prophet Isaiah —the messianic prophet— wrote more prophecies about Jesus than any other prophet in the Old Testament, and he clearly says how the Messiah would suffer for us. Around 700 years before Jesus was born, this prophet showed us the cruel, terrible, and unimaginable suffering of our Savior.

Isaiah prophesied that the Messiah would bear our diseases, bear our pains (Isaiah 53:4a), He would be "…but he was pierced for our transgressions; he was crushed for our iniquities; upon him was the chastisement that brought us peace, and with his wounds we are healed" (Isaiah 53: 5). He was going to be apprehended, unjustly tried, and then killed (Isaiah 53:8), and through all this suffering, He was going to pay for our sins and make us undeservedly righteous before God (Isaiah 53:11b).

Death did not take Jesus by surprise. He knew that he had come as that substitutionary Lamb to die for our sins. It is important to note that He did not hide from his disciples the death he would suffer. On multiple occasions Jesus predicted his own death (Matthew 16:21, Matthew 17:23, Matthew 20:19, Luke 13:32, Luke 18:33, Luke 24:7). In Matthew 16:21 Jesus declared to his disciples that he must go to Jerusalem to suffer and be killed and then rise again on the third day. In Matthew 17:22-23 He declared the same thing, although here he adds that He would be "delivered up" (Mattew 26:2)." In Matthew 20:18-19 once again he tells them about the same thing, although this time he says that they would condemn him to death, mock him, scourge him, and crucify him (this last time he talks about the way he was going to die, crucified).

"See, we are going up to Jerusalem. And the Son of Man will be delivered over to the chief priests and scribes, and they will condemn him to death and deliver him over to the Gentiles to be mocked and flogged and crucified, and he will be raised on the third day" (Matthew 20:18-19).

At no time did Christ say that he would only die; rather, He always declared his death along with his resurrection. The Son of God always claimed that he would be killed, but he also claimed his power over death. In this way the Lord consoled his disciples by telling them that death could not hold him; however, they did not understand this message yet. Perhaps they thought his resurrection would be at the last day (John 11:24), but Christ clearly said each time that He would rise on the third day. What man on this earth has ever had the power to make a statement of this magnitude and follow through on it? Only Jesus Christ.

Jesus prophesied his death not only to his disciples, but also to the Pharisees. Therefore, the latter, after the death of Jesus, asked Pilate to secure the entrance to the tomb so that no one would dare to steal the body and then say that He had risen (Matthew 27:63). The Pharisees knew exactly that a story like the resurrection of Jesus would make the Jewish people believe in the teachings He gave, and thus turn away from their teaching, taking away their religious power over the people.

THE RESURRECTION OF CHRIST

Not only the passion and death of Jesus was predicted in the Old Testament, but also, we see passages pointing to his resurrection. The book of Job speaks of a Redeemer who was going to die and then rise again. Job said, "But I know that my redeemer is alive and afterward he'll rise upon the dust" (Job 19:25 CEB). Even Jesus' visit to Sheol to announce his victory over death had already been declared in the Old Testament, for the Scriptures say: "For you will not abandon my soul to Sheol, or let your holy one see corruption" (Psalms 16 :10).

The prophet Hosea also prophesies the resurrection of Jesus when he says: "After two days he will revive us; on the third day he will raise us up, that we may live before him" (Hosea 6:2). Clearly the Old Testament says that death could not retain the Son of Almighty God, worthy of receiving power, honor, and glory forever and ever.

The other question we must ask ourselves is this: Why is it important that Christ rose from the dead? With this resurrection Christ has shown us that He has dominion over death. The condemnation of sin brings death to all human beings, and no one escapes from it; however, through Jesus Christ, we now have assurance that we will be alive in him, given he is the resurrection and the life (John 11:25).

During his ministry, Jesus demonstrated his power over death by bringing at least three people back to life (we have no Biblical evidence for other resurrections that Jesus might had performed). He restored life to Lazarus (John 11: 43-44), the daughter of Jairus (Matt. 5: 41-42), and the son of the widow of Nain (Luke 7: 11-17). So, when Christ said He was going to die and rise again, He had already given the evidence that supported what he was prophesying. And if Christ resurrected those people, and also, He himself, who am I to doubt the veracity of the Word when it says that we will rise with Him at His second coming? Well, let's remember that these resurrections were not symbolic or figurative, but literal, tangible and visible to all.

Jesus has told us not to fear death (Matthew 10:28), for He is our life. How could we believe in Christ as our Savior if He had not risen from the grave? How could you believe in Christ, that He is the resurrection and the life, if his remains were present today in a tomb in Palestine?

The tomb of Muhammad, the leader of the Muslim religion, is in Saudi Arabia and his remains lie there. The Egyptian pharaohs were considered gods and prepared beautiful tombs because they believed that one day they would return from beyond the grave. One of the most famous of these tombs is that of Tutankhamun, which was found in Egypt, in the Valley of the Kings, on November 1, 1922; and there laid the remains of this famous pharaoh. Mahatma Gandhi's tomb is in Delhi, India. The grave of Joseph Smith, the leader of the Mormons, is in Nauvoo, Illinois. The grave site of Jehovah's Witness leader, Charles Taze Russell, is in Pittsburgh, Pennsylvania. And so, we can mention many more names; but the tomb of Jesus has already been empty for 2,000 years; and it will remain so, because death will never again have dominion over him.

Another important point is that the perfect sacrifice of Jesus, that is, his death on the cross, was planned by God to happen at the time of his perfect will. It is impossible for man to kill God since God is eternal, that is, he has no beginning or end. On several occasions they tried to stone Jesus, or throw him off a cliff, but He always escaped these assassination attempts. Even robbed of his glory, vulnerable in this world, and in a corruptible body, Jesus always had power over his own life. No one took Jesus' life, but He gave it up voluntarily, and He also had the power to take it again.

"No one takes it from me, but I lay it down of my own accord. I have authority to lay it down, and I have authority to take it up again. This charge I have received from my Father" (John 10:18).

This is the reason why we must believe only in Christ. Anyone who says there is any way to get to God outside of Christ is condemned, and he is leading others down the same path. There is nothing to add and nothing to take away from the perfect sacrifice of Jesus. The Word of God clearly shows that only Jesus is "...the resurrection and the life. Whoever believes in me [in him] though he die, yet shall he live" (John 11:25).

So how can we prove that Jesus really did rise? What is the evidence we have of the resurrection? First of all, I must say that the most important thing to live the life that Christ offers is to have faith in the Word of God. The Bible says that without faith it is impossible to please God (Hebrews 11:6); therefore, the study of this wonderful subject requires faith in the powerful Word of God, and this is an indispensable ingredient. Well, for the world, the fact that someone has risen from the dead is crazy, something illogical; something that can't be proven by science, and if it can't be proven by science, then it doesn't exist. And in the case of the resurrection of our Lord, it is even more peculiar, since it is a unique fact and not replicable in all human history. Therefore, the resurrection is something that only the Spirit of God can show us and give us faith to believe in, because this challenges all human logic.

As for me, I don't need more evidence than what God has decided to leave us in the Bible to be convinced of the truth of the resurrection. His Word must be enough for those whom have truly believed in Christ. If I need something outside of the Word to be convinced of the resurrection of Jesus, then his Word is not enough for me, and this is serious, since I would be questioning the veracity of the God who inspired the Bible.

However, in the Scriptures (and outside of them) there are several arguments that satisfy our human logic into why we have faith that this truly occurred. How can I logically support the resurrection of Jesus? What historical evidence described in the Word of God leads me to believe that the resurrection is the only logical option? I want to mention four important pieces of historical evidence concerning his resurrection. (As we go through this book, I will add more information to each of them, for now, I'll tell you a few things preliminarily).

The Empty Tomb

First, we cannot deny the empty tomb. Very few times in history has a tomb been so protected from possible desecrators. This tomb had the seal of the authority of Rome, and no one could enter it without violating this seal, that is, without seriously breaking the law. If someone violated this Roman seal, dire consequences would result, possibly even being sentenced to death. The tomb was also guarded by soldiers, so that if anyone dared to try to move the stone that covered the entrance to the tomb, they would have been immediately stopped and the Roman soldiers had the authority to kill them. However, even with all this protection, God opened the tomb and placed an angel on the stone that covered the entrance (Matthew 28:2) so that no one would dare to close it.

The Roman Soldiers

The second important evidence of the Lord's resurrection was the testimony of the Roman soldiers (Matthew 28:11-15). These soldiers, the ones who oversaw the tomb, were generally unscrupulous people; Cold-blooded, and heartless. These men were impious, cruel, ruthless, and moreover, polytheists; they were not interested at all in the Jewish religion, much less in following Jesus. However, they fell unconscious with great fear as dead men when they saw the angel on the rock (Matthew 28:4). They then ran and told the priests what had happened and accepted a bribe to lie about what had happened, saying that the disciples had stolen the body. These non-believing men testified to having seen something supernatural.

The Eyewitnesses of the Resurrected Christ

The third piece of evidence is the eyewitness testimony of the resurrection. This is important because none of the followers of Christ believed that He would rise again. Absolutely all the followers of the Lord Jesus, including even Mary, his mother, did not believe that Christ would really rise on the third day. Rather, when Jesus died, all of his disciples (including his apostles) fled for fear of suffering the same fate as their Rabbi. However, after the resurrection, these same apostles of Christ were willing to die for the Gospel, and all of them lived a life of persecution for the love of their Lord, and almost all, with the exception of John, died as martyrs for the church.

By the way, these eyewitnesses testified to what they had seen, and carried the teachings of Jesus to the ends of the earth. They talked about what they had seen, touched, and heard; they were firsthand witnesses, and they did not rely on the experience of others, but of their own. This is why the apostle John begins his letter by saying: "That which was from the beginning, which we have heard, which we have seen with our eyes, which we looked upon and have touched with our hands, concerning the word of life" (1 John 1:1). Also, Peter, in his first sermon on the day of Pentecost said: "This Jesus God raised up, and of that we all are witnesses" (Acts 2:32).

The Death of the Apostles

The fourth important evidence of his resurrection is the death of the apostles. Who would think of dying for a lie? perhaps one, perhaps two or three of the apostles? There were only two possible options to explain the empty tomb: either the body was stolen, or Christ was resurrected. Suppose the disciples stole the body. The 11 apostles agreed to steal the body of Jesus, make up this story of the resurrection, and then flee in fear, enduring the dangers of persecution and death. Imagine! They did all of it with the sole purpose of creating a false hope in people that the Messiah was alive. Did they have any personal gain in it? No! If not the opposite. It is illogical that 11 men died for a lie that only brought them suffering for the rest of their lives.

Nevertheless, the truth of the matter is that these men did not have the courage to even be near a Roman soldier, and proof of this is that they all (except John) abandoned Jesus after his arrest. Then they gathered, but they were hidden, full of fear. They were afraid that the priests and religious leaders would also arrest them and crucify or stone them for being followers of Christ. None of these men had the strength, much less the courage to face a Roman guard and steal the body. The truth is that they probably didn't even know that there was a Roman guard guarding the entrance to the tomb. However, after seeing the risen Christ, all gave their lives for love of Him and for the Gospel. These incredulous and fearful men —because the word of Christ was not enough for them to believe in his resurrection— when they saw the living Lord, they were transformed to never again depart from Christ, and thus fulfill their command to carry the Gospel to the ends of the earth.

How Were the Apostles Martyred?

How did these apostles die after seeing the risen Christ? After having denied Jesus and fleeing from his presence; After being incredulous and shutting themselves up for fear of the enemies of Jesus, and after they were confronted by the truth of Christ's resurrection, their life was transformed. Mark was dragged through the streets of Alexandria to his death; Paul was beheaded in Rome, after having been a persecutor of the church; Luke was hanged in an olive tree.

Thomas was pierced with a spear and thrown into the fire; John was put in a cauldron of boiling oil and was banished to the island of Patmos, but eventually died in Ephesus of old age; Philip was scourged and crucified; Bartholomew was skinned alive and crucified; Matthew was beheaded; James was thrown from the roof of the temple and beaten to death; Thaddeus was killed with arrows; Andrew was crucified on a cross; James was beheaded, and Peter was scourged and crucified upside down.

My question is this: Did all of these (and many others) give their lives for a lie? I think this is one of the most compelling and exciting evidences of the resurrection, since none of these men ever recanted their faith in Christ or what they preached. Therefore, if all these men saw the risen Christ and gave their lives for the Gospel, I must thank God every day for them; since God wanted them to die as martyrs so that today I could be totally convinced of the reality of the resurrection; so that not a shadow of a doubt remained in me that Christ really rose from the dead and defeated death.

CHAPTER

II

THE BURIAL OF JESUS

From this chapter, and in subsequent ones, I will be talking about the resurrection story— ending with the ascension— starting with the burial of Jesus. Using the evidence from the Gospels, I will attempt to chronologically compile the events of Jesus' resurrection and go into some circumscribed important details. It is necessary to understand the burial as a preamble to his resurrection, since everything that happened prior to the resurrection of Christ is clear evidence of the impossibility that Jesus has not risen from the dead. Part of the evidence of his resurrection we see precisely in the events that occurred before the Sunday that Jesus rose from the grave.

How Did the Crucifixion of Jesus Occur?

This was an event never seen before in history and will never be repeated. This is where the God-made-flesh was nailed to a cross for our sins. This unique event, in which God himself —in the person of the Son— paid for our freedom with his blood, offering himself as a sacrifice once and for all (Hebrews 7:27), occurred during the Jewish Passover, between the months of March -April (which is the month of Nisan in the Jewish calendar), around AD 30-33.

The Passover was celebrated (and is still celebrated by the Jewish people) to remember the liberation of the people of Israel from slavery in Egypt (Exodus 12:41). In this feist, basically they focus on the last plague, the one in which all the firstborn of the Egyptians died. On that first Passover the Israelites sacrificed lambs, and the blood of these lambs was smeared with hyssops and placed on the two posts and on the lintel of the houses, and only those houses that had this blood were passed over by the angel of death (Exodus 12:23). Easter is a perfect representation of God's judgment and God's Grace. Those who have not believed in the Immolated Lamb, that is, in Jesus of Nazareth, will be condemned, but those who put their faith in Christ, their sins will be "passed over" [not taken into account] (John 1:29).

God established Easter in perpetuity, to be celebrated every year and thus remember the liberation of God's people. This party is so important that even the choice of the lamb for the sacrifice is fundamental. The day of the choice of the lamb was established in the Law of Moses, and it had to be the 10th day of the month of Nisan (Exodus 12:3). This very day —on which the lamb was chosen for sacrifice— was the same on which Christ entered mounted on a donkey at his triumphal entry; that was the day when everyone shouted hosanna! And they wanted to make him king over Israel.

"And the crowds that went before him, and those that followed, shouted, saying: 'Hosanna to the son of David, blessed is he who comes in the name of God, Hosanna in the highest'" (Matthew 21:1-10).

The word hosanna means save us! Salvation comes from the throne of God! But these same people who praised Jesus when he entered Jerusalem and asked him to save them (although not from their sins, but from the oppression of the Roman Empire), were the same ones who later shouted: crucify him! Just five days later.

Imagine the scenario: it was the time of the Jewish Passover, the lamb had to be chosen on Nisan 10th (the same day that Christ entered Jerusalem); therefore, there must have been thousands and thousands of lambs entering through those very doors to be sold. All of these were to be perfect young lambs without blemish or spots, specially prepared for the Passover sacrifice.

It is estimated that between 100-150 thousand lambs were sacrificed on a Passover. On the same day that the Jews bought or brought their sacrificial lamb, Jesus, the Lamb of God who takes away the sin of the world, the perfect lamb chosen and prepared by God, voluntarily entered to be sacrificed. God himself brought the sacrificial Lamb (One that was without blemish or spots), to be sacrificed for the sin of the world. So that, through his blood, the forgiveness of sins of all those who would put their trust in Him could be effected.

The Jews bought their lamb on the 10th (which should have been a Monday) and kept it until the 14th of Nisan (which should have been a Friday). This lamb was then sacrificed on Nisan 14th for the preparation of the Jewish Passover. Dinner was prepared during that day, before the sun went down, because on the Sabbath, which began after sunset on Friday (around 6 pm), they were not allowed to prepare food as this action was taken as a work on the Sabbath. The Sabbath for the Jews begins on the Friday night after sundown. The days in the Jewish time system change after the sun goes down, and not at 12:00 am (as it is for us in the time system used in the world today). For example, for them Monday begins on Sunday at approximately 6 pm.

Jesus is that Lamb of God who takes away the sin of the world (John 1:29). It is important to note that God always does things at the perfect time, it was so that Jesus was sacrificed as the Lamb of God the same day that the Jews gave thanks to Jehovah for having freed them from slavery in Egypt. While they shouted crucify him! While they spat on him, while they whipped him, and put the crown of thorns on him, while he carried his cross and then was nailed to it, while all this was happening, the Jews prepared the feast for the lamb's supper giving thanks to God for having brought them out of slavery in Egypt. On this very day, our perfect Lamb, sent by God himself, was sacrificed to set the world free from the slavery of sin, and he did it once and for all.

These lambs that the Jews sacrificed, which were beautiful, pure, clean, perfect, had no fault, that is, they did not deserve to die. It was not these little lambs that had to die, but the Jews who killed them, since they were guilty of their sin. They cruelly murdered these little lambs every year to cover up the sin they committed against God. They placed the blame on this little lamb and presented it as a substitute for themselves before God.

It was in this abusive, cruel, and unfair way that Christ was nailed to a cross, and being judged unjustly, he suffered a price that he did not deserve to suffer. This is how the perfect Lamb of God was sacrificed for the sin of the people whom he came to rescue.

> "He was oppressed and afflicted, but he did not open his mouth; like a lamb that is led to the slaughter, and like a sheep that is silent before its shearers, He did not open his mouth" (Isaiah 53:7).

The Romans were skilled killers. They had perfected the "art" of torture and death by maximizing the pain and agony of the victim. They had perfected the crucifixion, which probably inherited from the Medo-Persians and then from the Greeks. In this method, death was slow and extremely painful, but the Romans also knew when the executed person had already died. It was so that they, in the case of Jesus, had no doubt that He had died. Normally the Roman soldiers broke the legs of the crucified if they wanted to expedite the death process (as they did with the thieves who were next to Christ), but in the case of the Lord, they knew that he had already died, just six hours after being crucified. Still, so that there would be no doubt, a spear was thrusted on his side to confirm his death.

Joseph of Arimathea

Let us now see in detail what the Word says about the burial of Jesus and let us meet two characters who played a very important role in his burial. The burial of Jesus is described in Matthew 27:57-61, Mark 15:42-47, Luke 23:50-56, and John 19:38-42. I urge you to take a few minutes and read what these texts say to get a detailed idea of this important event.

This is a very important event since all four Gospels refer to it. The four evangelists understood the core importance of this story, which is why they included enough details, since these details are part of the biblical support of the narrative of the resurrection of Jesus. Let us take the reference from John to describe the burial of the Lord:

> "After these things Joseph of Arimathea, who was a disciple of Jesus, but secretly for fear of the Jews, asked Pilate that he

might take away the body of Jesus, and Pilate gave him permission. So, he came and took away his body. Nicodemus also, who earlier had come to Jesus by night, came bringing a mixture of myrrh and aloes, about seventy-five pounds in weight. So, they took the body of Jesus and bound it in linen cloths with the spices, as is the burial custom of the Jews. Now in the place where he was crucified there was a garden, and in the garden a new tomb in which no one had yet been laid. So, because of the Jewish day of Preparation, since the tomb was close at hand, they laid Jesus there" (John 19:38-42).

Who was this Joseph of Arimathea? All the Gospels mention him and some detail about him. Joseph of Arimathea was a prominent member of the Sanhedrin (Matthew 15:43); a man described as a disciple of Jesus (John 19:38); however, he followed the Lord in secret because he was afraid of the priests and religious leaders.

Joseph of Arimathea was sympathetic to the teachings of Jesus, but still, up to that time, loved his position in the council more than the Son of God. He was not willing to give up the benefits of being a prominent member of this "select" club called the Sanhedrin. The members of the Sanhedrin were respected religious people, many of whom had followers; they were usually wealthy, and whose businesses kept them in that oligarchy. They were people of knowledge and high prestige. Whereas, following Jesus would mean giving up his prestige, his comfort, being cast out of this select club, and forfeiting the confidence of his income and public respect. This was something the Pharisees were never willing to do. Joseph of Arimathea would be expelled not only from the Sanhedrin, but even from the synagogue if he identified himself as a follower of Christ.

He must have had a very good economic position, since he had enough to pay for a tomb dug on a rock; this type of tomb was very expensive. Also, it is possible that Joseph of Arimathea was an elderly person, since he had a tomb prepared for his own burial.

From John 19:38 we know that this man was a secret disciple of Jesus; however, after Jesus' death, he decided to make his decision for Christ public. The Bible says that he was filled with courage, that is, he put aside the fear that he had before. His fellow Sanhedrin members had tried and killed Jesus as a criminal, but he didn't care about himself now, or if he lost his livelihood, now he was willing to give up everything for Jesus Christ.

> **"Joseph of Arimathea, a respected member of the council, who was also himself looking for the kingdom of God, took courage and went to Pilate and asked for the body of Jesus" (Mark 15:43).**

Joseph of Arimathea ended up making his faith in the Lord public, since the Pharisees immediately found out where the body of Jesus was buried, and they knew on whose property he was laid for his burial. This man had the courage to go to Pilate, ask for the Lord's body, and thus be able to bury him with honor; Otherwise, the body of Jesus would have simply been taken down and thrown into the common grave of the crucified. Would we have the same courage that Joseph of Arimathea had? Would we be willing to risk everything we have for the love of Christ?

Each one of us has their own time in which God changes us truly to follow Jesus with no reserve, which is the moment we leave our own desires behind to truly follow Him. Joseph of Arimathea was a disciple of Jesus, but he did not follow him openly, because he was afraid of others; Likewise, there are those who believe that Jesus is Lord, but at the same time, they are afraid of suffering persecution because of Him. They fear being rejected at work, with their family or friends, etc., and for this reason they hide their faith. Others are embarrassed to let the world know they are believers; therefore, when they join unbelievers, they put their faith aside and do not speak of Christ.

However, a true disciple of Jesus cannot live this way. We can't be embarrassed or afraid to live out our faith, doesn't matter the circumstance. We are to be believers wherever we are in life. To truly live for Christ there must be a point in our lives that we act like Joseph of Arimathea. We must have the courage that he had. If you are now living a lightweight Gospel, a cold Gospel, a Gospel that wants to be right with God and with the world, I urge you to leave that life and decide once and for all to act like Joseph of Arimathea.

You cannot be a friend of God and at the same time be a friend of the world (James 4:4). Also, Jesus has said that whoever is ashamed of Him in this life, He will be ashamed of them in the last day (Mark 8:38).

Every true Christian will confess Christ before men. We are the ones who bring the Gospel of salvation to the world!

Joseph of Arimathea, out of fear, never openly followed Jesus and missed out on the blessing of walking with Him for years. However, at a time like that, a moment of great tension, where the religious of the time did not care about the body of Jesus, because they hated him; moment in which the other disciples —for fear— would never even dare to lower the body of their Lord from the cross; at that precise crucial moment, Joseph of Arimathea decided to risk everything: his entire life, his career, his social and economic well-being, to appear before the governor, Pilate, to request the body of his Master, and thus have the privilege of giving a proper burial to the One whom he loved with all his heart.

We don't know what happened to Joseph of Arimathea afterwards, but the Bible recognizes him as a man of courage and a disciple of Jesus. By this single action, his name was embodied for eternity in the Word of God. Jesus clearly said that in the world we would have tribulation (John 16:33), but he also said that everyone who was insulted or persecuted for his name would be blessed (Matthew 5:11). We should not be afraid of suffering the consequences of living the Christian life and showing others our faith in Jesus Christ.

Nicodemus

Another character who participated in the burial of the Lord is Nicodemus, who, by the way, is only mentioned in the Gospel of John. Nicodemus was a great teacher, scholar of the law, prominent among the Jews (John 3:1,10). Regarding this man the Bible says that he helped Joseph of Arimathea to bury the body and brought a hundred pounds of spices to anoint it for his burial (John 19:39). These were one hundred Roman pounds (which today would be about 70-75 pounds or 32-34 kilograms) —much more that was typically used in a common funeral— and according to Josh McDowell, these aromatic spices were so strong, that they would suffocate any living person (this is another proof that Jesus really died).[1] The manner in which Jesus was buried, with the quantity of aromatic spices with which he was

---

[1] Josh McDowell, *Evidence that Demands a Verdict* (San Bernardino, CA: Campus Crusade for Christ, 1972), 207.

buried, was the one typically used to bury kings (see 2 Chronicles 16:13-14).

Nicodemus was a disciple of Christ from the beginning of his ministry. He had with Christ one of the most impressive and lengthy conversations ever recorded in the Word of God. In John 3 Nicodemus is mentioned for the first time, and there, we can see that he was already convinced that Jesus came from God as a teacher. He was also afraid that the Jews would find out that he had begun to believe in Christ, and therefore, he came to Him at night (John 3: 2). The teaching that Jesus gave him on that occasion resonated with his heart, but it was in stark contrast to everything he had practiced and taught as a Pharisee.

In John 19 (where the apostle narrates the crucifixion and burial of Jesus), Nicodemus appears again. He is witnessing something impressive: the fulfillment of the prophecy of Jesus given to him, the one he personally declared to Nicodemus at the beginning of his ministry, that is, that the Messiah had to die, and by that death, everyone who believed in Him would obtain eternal life.

"And as Moses lifted up the serpent in the desert, so must the Son of Man be lifted up, that whoever believes in him may have eternal life" (John 3:14-15).

What a moment in the life of Nicodemus! The fulfillment of what Christ had told him was there before his very eyes. I imagine Nicodemus seeing Jesus being crucified and remembering the words He said to him that night: that he had to be raised up, so that everyone who had faith in Him would obtain eternal life. This powerful event was likely the trigger for him to become publicly a follower of Christ.

In John 3:14-15 Jesus was referencing the story in Numbers 21, where the people of Israel murmured against God and against Moses saying, "Why have you brought us up out of Egypt to die in the wilderness?" (v.5) because they did not have water or food to their liking. At that moment, they, with their attitude, separated from the God who created them, the One who through his power had brought them out of slavery. Therefore, God sent a plague of poisonous snakes to punish them, and many people died because of them (Numbers 21:6). The people then repented of their sin (Numbers 21:7), and God commanded Moses to make a bronze serpent. He told him to put it on a pole, and every person who had been bitten by one of these snakes, only had to turn to look at the bronze serpent, and he/she was healed.

Biblically, the serpent represents sin. This animal, created by God, was used by Satan in the Garden of Eden to deceive Eve, and bring death to the entire human race. Therefore, the serpent was condemned to crawl on the earth in perpetuity, as a reminder to mankind of the judgment that comes upon all who sin against God (Genesis 3:14).

Christ compares himself to this bronze serpent. Just as the bronze serpent was lifted, Christ was also lifted. Just as the bronze serpent saved those bitten by poisonous snakes, Christ would save those bitten by sin, bearing on Himself the sin of all of us. But every Israelite, who, bitten by a snake, refused to look at the bronze serpent, he or she would die inevitably. In the same way, the ones who do not come to Christ or seek salvation from the bite of sin (which is in all humanity), that person will not have salvation, because the poison of sin will lead him to eternal judgment (Romans 6:3).

That famous conversation between Jesus and Nicodemus in John 3 includes one of the most quoted verses of the Bible.

"For God so loved the world, that he gave his only Son, that whoever believes in him should not perish but have eternal life" (John 3:16).

In other words, Jesus said to Nicodemus: "I came to die for you, to heal you from the poison of sin, and if you put your faith in me, if you truly believe in me, then you will have eternal life; because this is the demonstration that I have loved you". All this conversation must have been echoing in Nicodemus's heart while he was bringing down the body of Jesus. He accepted Jesus as his King, for he bought the spices to anoint him as King at his burial (John 19:39).

Normally a crucified person could last days alive on the cross. Death on a cross was an instrument of torture, designed to cause a slow death of great suffering and shame. The condemned were raised on a wooden pole so that they could be seen by all. A certain death for the executed, who served as a warning and a fear tactic for those who dared to break Roman law.

Before handing over the body to Joseph of Arimathea, Pilate wanted to confirm with the centurion that Jesus was dead; and when they said yes, he was surprised that he had died so quickly. Jesus hung on the cross for about six hours, from 9 am (Mark 15:24-25) to 3 pm (Matthew 27:45). But Jesus did not die from the nails in his hands and feet, nor from the whipping, nor from dehydration, or from heart failure: Jesus himself was the one who gave up his life, and no one took it from him (John 10:18).

After taking him down from the cross, they wrapped the Lord in a clean linen sheet, and the spices of myrrh and aloe were thrown on him to preserve the body. In the area of Calvary, where the crucifixion occurred, there was a garden, and in this garden a new tomb that was carved out on a rock, which was never used before and belonged to Joseph of Arimathea (John 19:41).

They only had about three hours to take Jesus down from the cross, prepare the body for burial, take it to the grave, and be home before the Sabbath began for the Passover celebration that night; this was a hasty burial.

Since it was the day of preparation for the Jewish Passover, and it was already getting dark, the Sabbath was about to begin, and they would not be able to do any kind of work on Saturday until around 6 pm, there was not enough time for any other action regarding the burial of the Lord. Therefore, they put him in that empty tomb that was near Calvary (Matthew 27:60), rolled a large stone, and went to celebrate the Passover. Perhaps they were not realizing it, but we see here that Isaiah's prophecy was fulfilled.

"And they made his grave with the wicked and with a rich man in his death, although he had done no violence, and there was no deceit in his mouth" (Isaiah 53:9).

In addition to these two men, also present at the foot of the cross were Mary his mother, Mary Magdalene, Mary the mother of Joseph and James, Mary mother of the sons of Zebedee (John and James) and other women (Matthew 27:55-56; John 19:25). These women —of which Mark 15:47 identifies Mary Magdalene and Mary the mother of James and Joseph— followed Joseph of Arimathea and Nicodemus to see where they would lay the body of the Lord, and once the stone had been laid, they sat down before the sepulcher (Matthew 27:61); probably inconsolable for everything they had just experienced.

THE RESURRECTION OF CHRIST

After all this, we see the Pharisees go to Pilate to ask him to secure the tomb for at least the third day of his death. They knew very well the words of Jesus. He had said that he was going to rise again on the third day, therefore his enemies wanted to prevent his disciples from coming to steal his body. They thought that the disciples had that intention, to later say that He had risen.

> **"The next day, that is, after the day of Preparation, the chief priests and the Pharisees gathered before Pilate and said, 'Sir, we remember how that impostor said, while he was still alive, "After three days I will rise." Therefore, order the tomb to be made secure until the third day, lest his disciples go and steal him away and tell the people, "He has risen from the dead," and the last fraud will be worse than the first.' Pilate said to them, 'You have a guard of soldiers. Go, make it as secure as you can.' So, they went and made the tomb secure by sealing the stone and setting a guard" (Matthew 27:62-66).**

Only Matthew, who had previously worked for the Romans, records the Pharisees' request to guard the tomb. Perhaps his influence helped him learn about this situation. Jesus had previously declared to them about his resurrection, and these words would not be something that the religious Pharisees of the time would easily forget. The fact that a human being had power over death was something never before declared in such a way by any of the Jewish prophets.

> **"At that very hour some Pharisees came and said to him, 'Get away from here, for Herod wants to kill you.' And he said to them, 'Go and tell that fox, "Behold, I cast out demons and perform cures today and tomorrow, and the third day I finish my course. Nevertheless, I must go on my way today and tomorrow and the day following, for it cannot be that a prophet should perish away from Jerusalem"'. And after flogging him, they will kill him, and on the third day he will rise" (Luke 13:31-33; 18:33).**

They understood the great importance it would have in Israel if they found out that the body had disappeared, and the rumor of the resurrection spread through the town. They were afraid that the disciples would steal the body and then proclaim that He had risen on the third day as he said. It was for this reason that when Pilate provided them with the guard they wanted, they went, secured the tomb with a seal, and leaving the guards in front of it, they went home to celebrate Passover.

This protection, humanly speaking, could not have been easily defeated. We are talking about soldiers trained to torture citizens. These were masters of death and there were enough of them to effectively protect the tomb of Jesus. On top of that, the tomb had the Roman seal, and breaking it would mean open defiance against the authority of the empire, and his punishment could even be death itself. These guards were to remain in front of this tomb until the order was fully carried out. If they failed in their mission, the repercussions on them could be dire. Later we will learn more about these soldiers and about the testimony they gave to the Sanhedrin.

Chapter

III

THE DAY OF RESURRECTION

To recap, in the previous chapters we have been learning why Jesus had to die for us. We have learned about the impossibility of our own salvation and how we have all sinned by being descendants of Adam and Eve. Also, we learned that because of sin, we have all fallen short of the glory of God (Romans 3:23).

We have seen how Jesus predicted his own death multiple times, not only to his disciples but also to the Pharisees (Luke 13:31-33). Jesus, who perfectly knew the events regarding his death, also knew what these priests would do when they heard that prophecy from his lips. He knew that they would ask Pilate for soldiers to guard the tomb so that no one could go in or out; however, the guards that Pilate provided them, instead of helping the purpose of these Pharisees, were further evidence in favor of Jesus' resurrection.

Another important point that we have seen so far is that no one took Jesus' life, but He gave it up voluntarily. Jesus said in John 10:18 that no one would take His life, but He had the right to give it and the right to take it again; and that is what happened when he rose from the dead on the third day.

We know that Jesus is the perfect Lamb, immolated, prepared for the sacrifice for the sin of humanity, and how God brought him during the Passover Feast —in the perfect time— to be sacrificed for us, because in this way the prophecies that the Messiah would die, and that the punishment of our condemnation would fall on Him, would be fulfilled (Isaiah 53:5).

We have also discussed two disciples of Christ, Joseph of Arimathea and Nicodemus, who were both members of the Sanhedrin, and who, for fear of losing their social position, followed him in secret, but who after his death had the courage to bury him appropriate, publicly displaying their love and faith in Jesus. All this happened before the Sabbath began, so they were in a hurry to bury Jesus.

Finally, in the last chapter we learned about the Pharisees who asked Pilate for protection for the tomb, so that no one would steal the body of Jesus (Matthew 27:62-66); and about how they put up the Roman guard provided and sealed the tomb. These Roman guards were guarding the tomb of Jesus until Sunday, and we can be sure that no one entered or left this tomb until that day.

In this chapter we will learn about the importance of believing in God's faithfulness, the importance of believing in his word and the consequences of doubting it. It is important to emphasize that nobody, absolutely nobody believed Jesus, not a single person on earth thought that Christ was going to rise from the dead.

If you ever feel "proud" for believing in Christ, remember that these unbelieving men and women were the ones who eventually transformed the world by the preaching of the Gospel. There is no doubt that each one walks with God in different ways and different times in their life's, and they can transform your doubtful brother with little faith into a great man of God; likewise, God can also humiliate and shame those who are exalted due to their knowledge of the Bible. We must always remain humble no matter how much knowledge we think we have of the Word of God, because true wisdom comes from God, and not from us.

In these next chapters we will meet a woman who, before knowing Jesus, was full of sin, and controlled by seven demons. This was the person that God chose to be the first to see the risen Jesus. Her name was forever recorded in the Word of God to serve as an example to us; to show us that the Lord accepts and exalts even those who have led the worst lives, those we would consider unworthy, those who have been cast out of society.

The Bible teaches that before Adam was formed from the dust of the earth, God already had a redemption plan for humanity. God thought of us beforehand, even before creating the angels, the earth, the sun, the moon, all living beings, and the entire universe. Before creating us, he already wanted to save us. The eternal love of God conceived a redemption plan for his most special and unworthy creation: the human race. His plan of salvation had already been conceived in his mind, and in his omniscience, he knew we were going to sin and still decided to create us, knowing the cost he would have to pay for us.

"Even as he chose us in him before the foundation of the world, that we should be holy and blameless before him" (Ephesians 1:4).

This uncreated Being, infinitely holy, of incomparable beauty and majestic glory, created a being with similar but finite qualities, and placed his image in Him (Genesis 1:26); even knowing the perversity and depths of sin in which this created being would incur. He knew in advance of all our sins, of our impurity and wickedness, that we would become his enemy and come to blaspheme against him.

But God not only saw our sin, but also our impossible inability to return to Him with our own righteousness. God knew that, even if he sent prophets, judges, and angelic beings; that even if He himself would speak to man from heaven, our corruption and hatred of Him would never allow mankind to follow him wholeheartedly. He knew that even if he came himself (in the person of Jesus Christ), we would hate and reject him (John 1:11).

However, God (in the person of Jesus) took all our hatred towards Him. Thousands of years of mistreatment, countless transgressions, and our collective depravity; all the corruption that had been separating us from his presence, our unfaithfulness, and all our deeds worthy of eternal death, he took it all upon himself when he died for us on the cross. This plan of redemption was revealed to humanity even from the fall of Adam and Eve (Genesis 3:15): God promised He would send a Savior, and it was fulfilled in the person of Jesus Christ.

In the Gospel of Luke, we find the genealogy of Jesus from Adam to Joseph (Luke 3:23-38), which is the glorious fulfillment of God's promise to Adam and Eve. In The Church of Ireland, Archbishop James Ussher (1581-1656), calculated 77 generations from Adam to Christ using references found in 1 Chronicles 1 and Matthew 1; and he himself made a rough estimate of 4,000 years from Adam to Christ; and if we do a careful analysis, there are also 77 generations in the Luke reference. Therefore, the fulfillment of the messianic promise of Genesis 3:15 had its fulfillment 4,000 years after it was pronounced.

During this time God prepared everything on earth for the arrival of his Son, giving us a prophetic word regarding what He would be like. Like how he would suffer for us, that the Messiah would be God made man (Isaiah 9:6), etc. That Savior would have to bear the sin of the world, be unjustly judged, and die in our place.

"The saying is trustworthy and deserving of full acceptance, that Christ Jesus came into the world to save sinners, of whom I am the foremost" (1 Timothy 1:15).

The price Jesus paid for our sins is unmeasurable. The truth is that no one will ever know the depth, or the true cost of the payment of our debt towards God; no one will ever be able to weigh the true value of that debt, because the cost was too great. It is wonderful to think that I live here on earth free from that terrible eternal condemnation caused by sin, due to the forgiveness that Christ has given me. Now I know that when I die, I will go to dwell in the presence of God for eternity, Glory to God!

Neither you nor I deserve God's forgiveness, no one deserves it, and no matter how hard we scrutinize his Word, we will never understand fully God's wonderful forgiveness. I will never know the pain that Christ suffered on the cross, nor the pain of all those who die without Christ. Even if I imagine it, even if I read about it in the Bible, it won't ever be our reality as believers. Every day I give thanks to the Lord because I will never live that condemnation, because He bought us with the price of His holy blood, which has been the only true innocent blood that has passed through this world. This was the blood that was shed for me, and it is the only thing that could achieve my salvation.

> "Knowing that you were ransomed from the futile ways inherited from your forefathers, not with perishable things such as silver or gold, but with the precious blood of Christ, like that of a lamb without blemish or spot" (1 Peter 1:18-19).

This is the blood that took away the guilt of my sin, and through it, I have access to the throne of God. Now I can come to Him, and humble my heart, hear his voice, understand his Word, and know that He is a real God. A single sacrifice was necessary for the hope of salvation to reach the whole world.

In Israel millions of sacrifices were made to God through the centuries without these being able to appease the wrath of God until Christ came and gave His life. He was the perfect sacrifice to atone or erase the guilt of our sins. The idea of God's forgiveness through a surrogate victim was in the hearts of the Jewish people, yet they still failed to understand God's message.

> "For Christ also suffered once for sins, the righteous for the unrighteous, that he might bring us to God, being put to death in the flesh but made alive in the spirit" (1 Peter 3:18).

Jesus suffered a terrible, unimaginable death; He endured pain that only the one undergoing a crucifixion could know. The word to describe this pain in Latin is *excruciare* which means "extremely acute, maddening, to crucify or torment"; In other words, there was no way to describe such great pain, which is why the Romans invented this word to describe the suffering of the crucified.

That Friday night, after the death of Jesus, when the Jews celebrated the Passover, those who loved the Lord deeply mourned his death. This day must have been one of the most depressing and hopeless days in their lives. The women who followed Christ could not contain their tears, because they still had fresh in their minds the image of the Lord hanging from the cross and dying, the hope of having found their Messiah seemed to have been lost. The disciples had lost their Master and —so they thought— the hope of reigning with Jesus, when He would defeat the Roman Empire once and for all and when through his leadership, Israel would become an independent nation with a universal rule, was gone. The apostles and disciples of Jesus felt defeated.

The suffering of Mary, the mother of Jesus, must have been terrible. Mary saw her son disfigured and hung on the cross. She was not there on Sunday waiting for the resurrection, nor did she go with the women to the tomb in the morning when he was resurrected; she is not even mentioned until Acts 1:14, when the Holy Spirit descends on the disciples on the day of Pentecost. We don't know where Mary was in those days, perhaps she felt so devastated that she didn't have the strength even to face anyone.

On that particular Friday, as Passover was being observed (and for Christians, Easter), the dream of freedom from the Roman Empire appeared to be shattered, but that was not the end of it. The disciples of Jesus did not believe the words that Jesus gave about his resurrection; however, even if we do not believe his words, God is faithful, and he always fulfills what He promises. Even though the disciples had seen so many miracles in Jesus' ministry, they did not believe that He would rise again. The Lord had given sight to the blind; he made the mute speak, and the deaf hear; He had made the paralyzed walk; revived the dead; He calmed the storm with the word of His mouth, He walked on the waters, He was transfigured before John, Peter and James; He healed lepers and did many other miracles; however, the literal and bodily resurrection of Jesus did not cross their minds.

Perhaps Jesus' disciples were thinking like Martha, the sister of Lazarus: that Christ would rise from the dead at the last day. She knew of the last day resurrection but did not believe that Jesus had the power to raise Lazarus after four days of death (John 11:24). So, the disciples never imagined that on the third day Jesus was really going to rise again. Everyone doubted the words of Jesus, even after He told them this same thing on multiple occasions (Matthew 16:21; Mark 8:31; Luke 24:46).

These disciples doubted the words of Christ, and if I had been there, I would have acted the same way. We should never question what God has told us already in His word. The Bible mentions several examples of people who questioned the Word of God, and this never resulted in anything good, this is because it is a serious offense to God that we doubt His Word.

THE RESURRECTION OF CHRIST

Adam and Eve doubted the Word of God and therefore the entire human race was sentenced to death. Noah's contemporaries did not believe the flood warning, and an estimated two to four billion people perished. The Jewish people doubted the Word of God and did not obey Him, and for this reason, those of the Northern kingdom were taken captive to Syria, and those of the Southern kingdom to Babylon, and were in captivity for 70 years. After this, the Jews returned to their land, but they were not an independent nation until recently; from the year 587 BC to May 1948 AD (more than 2,500 years). Even after that date (1948), the promised land has been constantly invaded by other nations and they still only have a small part of the land that God had promised them.

The Jews doubted Jesus' words, rejected Him, and killed Him; thus, 40 years after his death, judgment came upon this nation, and the Roman emperor Titus, in the year 70 AD., destroyed Jerusalem, Herod's temple and persecuted the Jews. Since then, the Jewish people were nomads of the world for almost two thousand years.

Even today many doubt that Christ will return a second time, but the Bible says that He will return to rule on this earth, and that every eye will see Him when He returns (Revelation 1:7). Many people believe that there are many ways to get to heaven, and believe that by their good works they will be saved, they doubt the words of Jesus when he said:

"Jesus said to him, 'I am the way, and the truth, and the life. No one comes to the Father except through me'" (John 14:6).

But what happens when one decides to trust the word of God? What are the consequences of honoring and obeying the Almighty? Abraham became the father of faith by leaving everything behind to trust only in God. Joseph, after being sold by his brothers, enslaved, and made a prisoner, God made him second on the throne, after Pharaoh. Moses led over two million slaves, and through divine help, led them to freedom from Egyptian rule. Joshua broke down the walls of Jericho and led the people to the promised land. David killed a giant who defied the God of Israel with a single stone, and he became king of Israel. Daniel, being thrown into the lions' den, due to the tricks of his enemies, came out unharmed. Daniel's friends (Shadrach, Meshach and Abednego) were protected by God after being thrown into a burning fire oven, and their liberation was such that they didn't even smell smoke when they left there.

Why is it important to believe in the faithfulness of God's Word? Because to believe in the resurrection, I must first believe that what the Bible says to be true. The resurrection of Christ is an inexplicable miracle, a kind of miracle that has never happened before; and that it can only be accepted through faith in God's Word. The evidence presented before me in the Gospels only leaves me with three possible alternatives: either He was resurrected, or the body was stolen, or it is all a lie.

How Did the Resurrection Happen?

The truth is that no one was present inside the tomb when the resurrection occurred except Christ. Only God knows the exact time it occurred, but we know it was early Sunday morning, while it was still dark (John 20:1), probably between 6 and 6:30 in the morning. Paul describes the future resurrection as something that will happen in the twinkling of an eye. The duration of a blink of an eye is roughly three-tenths of a second; in other words, the resurrection of Jesus probably occurred in an instant.

"In a moment, in the twinkling of an eye, at the last trumpet. For the trumpet will sound, and the dead will be raised imperishable, and we shall be changed" (1 Corinthians 15:52).

The stone that blocked the entrance to the tomb was removed by an angel before dawn, not to allow Jesus to come out, but so that the witnesses could enter; so that they could see with their own eyes the empty tomb, that Christ really rose, because it was not possible for Him to be held by the death. If the stone had not been removed, no one would have been able to enter the tomb, much less with the Roman guards there. In fact, the tomb had to be left open, to the point that God sent an angel to sit on the stone, so that no one would dare of closing it again (as if nothing had happened).

How Did the First Appearance of Jesus Occur?

We can find the first appearance of Jesus to the women in Matthew 28:1-10; Mark 16:1-8; Luke 24:1-12; and John 20:1-10. It is important that you read these verses from the Gospels in order to fully comprehend what we will be discussing.

We have studied already that Jesus was buried on Friday afternoon, before the Sabbath began. These women gathered together on Saturday night, when the Sabbath had passed, and went to buy spices; and then, on Sunday, early morning, they all went to anoint Jesus at the tomb where he was buried.

> **"When the Sabbath was past, Mary Magdalene, Mary the mother of James, and Salome bought spices, so that they might go and anoint him" (Mark 16:1).**

They had not returned to the grave since the beginning of the Sabbath; therefore, they did not know that Roman guards had been posted to guard it, nor did they know that it would be virtually impossible to enter there to anoint the body of Jesus because of the seal placed by the Roman authority on the tomb. Under these circumstances, we see that the first person to appear at the tomb was Mary Magdalene, who arrived there while it was still dark (John 20:1). Later the other women arrived at dawn (Luke 24:1). The story is narrated in the four Gospels, but we will now review what the Gospel of Luke says:

> **"But on the first day of the week, at early dawn, they went to the tomb, taking the spices they had prepared. And they found the stone rolled away from the tomb, but when they went in they did not find the body of the Lord Jesus. While they were perplexed about this, behold, two men stood by them in dazzling apparel. And as they were frightened and bowed their faces to the ground, the men said to them, 'Why do you seek the living among the dead? He is not here, but has risen. Remember how he told you, while he was still in Galilee, that the Son of**

Man must be delivered into the hands of sinful men and be crucified and on the third day rise.' And they remembered his words, and returning from the tomb they told all these things to the eleven and to all the rest. Now it was Mary Magdalene and Joanna and Mary the mother of James and the other women with them who told these things to the apostles, but these words seemed to them an idle tale, and they did not believe them. But Peter rose and ran to the tomb; stooping and looking in, he saw the linen cloths by themselves; and he went home marveling at what had happened" (Luke 24:1-12).

Who Were These Women?

The Word mentions Mary Magdalene; Mary, the mother of James (on which I will comment on later, when we talk about the disciples of Emmaus); Salome, and Joanna, wife of Chuza (her husband was Herod Antipas's household manager, Luke 8:3). By the way, Salome was also present during the crucifixion of Jesus (Mark 15:40).

These women played a very important role in Jesus' ministry, as they were of great help for his support. They generously shared with the Lord their time, their love, their service, and their goods (Luke 8:3). Their love for Christ was unparalleled, and in turn, He revealed the true worth of women, a worth that remains unrecognized, even in modern times, let alone in the past thousands of years. Christ restored their lives, their families, and, above all, their relationship with God.

While all the disciples had fled (except John, who was present at the crucifixion, John 19:26), these women stood at the foot of the cross to the end and witnessed the death of the Lord (Mark 15: 40). They wanted to honor Christ at all times, even in his burial, and for this reason they followed Joseph of Arimathea and Nicodemus, to see where they would put the Master's body (Luke 23:55).

Among these devoted women —who were not afraid to show the world their love for Jesus— Mary Magdalene was probably the leader of the women's ministry group since in most of the verses where the women following Jesus are mentioned, she appears first (Mark 16:1;

Mark 15:40; Matthew 27: 56; Matthew 28:1); just as Peter is also mentioned first whenever the group of apostles is mentioned (Matthew 10:2; Matthew 17:1; Mark 3:16).

We know that Christ died around three o'clock in the afternoon on Friday (Matthew 27:45); that he was buried that same day (right before the Sabbath began, Mark 15:42); that the women went to see where Christ was buried, and then they rushed to celebrate Passover in the midst of all this that they had experienced. What happened after?

"After the Sabbath, Mary Magdalene, Mary, the mother of James, and Salome bought aromatic spices to go and anoint him" (Mark 16:1).

They waited for the Sabbath to pass, which was around 6 pm on Saturday, after which they went to buy aromatic spices so that, very early on Sunday morning, they could go to anoint the body of the Lord Jesus. It was probably dark or getting dark, so not an appropriate time to go to visit a grave. So, for that purpose, they bought aloe and myrrh, and set their hearts to anoint the Lord's body again very early on Sunday.

That day, as they made their way to the tomb, the last thing on their hearts was to find the risen Jesus. Normally, a dead body, without special preparation for its preservation, on the third day would be disfigured, smelly, full of liquid, and going through a process where the skin is disintegrating. But they wanted to honor Jesus until the last possible moment. However, they had a problem: the stone placed at the head of the tomb was large and heavy, and surely these women could not move it on their own, this was their concern; nevertheless, with everything in mind, they went to the sepulcher seeking to honor Christ.

In the Bible we see no indication that these women even had any idea of the existence of guards guarding the tomb (Matthew 27:62-66), nor that there was a government seal on it, since all this happened on Saturday, when the priests went to ask Pilate to secure the tomb for at least Saturday and Sunday (because as I already said, they feared that the disciples would steal the body of Jesus). If these women had known about how Jesus' tomb was protected, they probably would not have bought these aromatic spices, nor would they ever have intended to go to the tomb early to anoint the body of Jesus. They did not know that they wouldn't be allowed to enter the tomb, as only a high-ranking Roman official could break the seal.

But God already had all this planned forehand, from before the foundation of the world, so that there would be no doubt that his Son Jesus rose victorious from death. God took care that those women who came to honor the burial of the Lord could be the first witnesses to show that Christ had really risen. Then, before these women arrived, a great earthquake occurred, and an angel sent by God came down and rolled away the stone from the tomb and sat on it.

"And behold, there was a great earthquake, for an angel of the Lord descended from heaven and came and rolled back the stone and sat on it. His appearance was like lightning, and his clothing white as snow. And for fear of him the guards trembled and became like dead men" (Matthew 28:2-4).

This earthquake occurred before the women arrived at the tomb as these Roman guards fainted from fear, and then upon waking up, they surely fled the place because the Bible does not mention at any time that the women saw these guards; when they arrived, they were gone, and the stone had been rolled away (John 20:1, Luke 24:2, Mark 16:4).

Another question we must answer is this: did all the women arrive at the same time? To understand this story, we have to read the four Gospel accounts, because when we do so, then we will have a better understanding of the events that occurred at the resurrection.

In John 20:1 Mary Magdalene is mentioned alone; that is, the account seems to suggest that she reached the tomb first, before her friends, and arrived while it was still dark. However, by then the resurrection had occurred, so the stone had been rolled away from the entrance to the tomb. In John's account we can realize the love that Mary Magdalene had for Jesus. She was there early; for she had such a deep love for her Master, that she wanted to honor him as much as she could. Jesus, her Messiah, had been her deliverer and her healer, and she was, ever since the Lord did his miracle work on her, exceedingly grateful.

> **"Now on the first day of the week Mary Magdalene came to the tomb early, while it was still dark, and saw that the stone had been taken away from the tomb. So she ran and went to Simon Peter and the other disciple, the one whom Jesus loved, and said to them, 'They have taken the Lord out of the tomb, and we do not know where they have laid him'" (John 20:1-2).**

Mary Magdalene panicked when she saw the stone rolled away, and immediately thought that Jesus' body had been stolen. In John's account we can see that at that moment she did not see any angel, nor did she enter the tomb, but she ran to warn Simon Peter and John (the beloved disciple), and she did so at that very moment. She clearly thought that Jesus' body had been stolen, and that is what she told Peter and John. It must have been a terrible moment for Mary Magdalene as she thought that someone had desecrated the tomb of the Lord. Therefore, she did not even go to confirm whether the body was there or not, but simply assumed that the body was no longer in the tomb.

She knew —for some reason, perhaps because of how early it was—, that it couldn't be another disciple of Jesus, for example, Joseph of Arimathea or Nicodemus, who had entered the tomb. She was sure that it was not her friends or other disciples of Jesus who had done this. After she left, while Mary Magdalene was looking for Peter and John, her other friends arrived. Let us remember that Mary Magdalene arrived at the tomb while it was still dark, and now we see the other women arriving at dawn.

> **"And very early on the first day of the week, when the sun had risen, they went to the tomb" (Mark 16:2).**

They all went together to buy the aromatic spices on Saturday night (Mark 16:1), but Mark does not mention the arrival of Mary Magdalene at the sepulcher before the others, but rather John; he knew the story perfectly, because Mary Magdalene had gone looking for him. When the other women arrived, Mary Magdalene had already left. These women, Mary, the mother of James, Salome and Joanna of Chuza, when approaching the open tomb, saw an angel sitting on the removed stone, then the angel said to them:

"But the angel said to the women, 'Do not be afraid, for I know that you seek Jesus who was crucified. He is not here, for he has risen, as he said. Come, see the place where he lay. Then go quickly and tell his disciples that he has risen from the dead, and behold, he is going before you to Galilee; there you will see him. See, I have told you'" (Matthew 28:5-7).

After they entered, we can see that two of the Gospels have apparently different versions of the events. In Mark 16:5 it says that there was a young man sitting on the right dressed in white clothes, while in Luke 24:4 two men are described in resplendent garments.

"And entering the tomb, they saw a young man sitting on the right side, dressed in a white robe, and they were alarmed" (Mark 16:5).

"While they were perplexed about this, behold, two men stood by them in dazzling apparel" (Luke 24:4).

The discrepancy between these two verses is likely because it was one of the angels who predominated in the interaction with them, and Luke was more explicit in his description of this event. Mark's Gospel tends to summarize the events of the Gospels, and his stories are shorter and more concise; while Luke, being a historian, usually describes in more detail the events in his Gospel.

Let's see what these angels said to the women:

> **"And as they were frightened and bowed their faces to the ground, the men said to them, 'Why do you seek the living among the dead? He is not here but has risen. Remember how he told you, while he was still in Galilee, that the Son of Man must be delivered into the hands of sinful men and be crucified and on the third day rise.'" (Luke 24:5-7).**

These women immediately left the angels to tell the disciples what they had experienced when they went to the tomb. When these women had left, John arrived first, followed by Simon Peter, but John was afraid to enter the tomb; not so Peter, who when he had arrived immediately entered the tomb. Then John entered; and while they were inside, they saw the cloths placed where the body had been laid, and the shroud folded neatly. However, John's account does not mention that these two disciples saw the angels that had appeared to the other women (John 20:3-10). So, Peter and John saw the empty tomb, the linens, and the shroud, but even so, the resurrection did not cross their minds. They rather believed the theory of Mary Magdalene and thought that the body had been stolen (John 20:8).

This is one more piece of evidence that proves the veracity of Jesus' resurrection. If someone had thought to take the body, what was the purpose of removing the linens and the shroud (considering that this was already the third day since the death occurred)? And if so, it is irrational to think that these cloths would be neatly folded inside the tomb.

In Luke 24:12 it says that Peter went away amazed; and John 20:8 says that John also went home and believed. It does not say clearly whether they believed Mary Magdalene's assumption (that the body had been stolen), or whether they believed that Jesus had risen; However, in the next verse (John 20:9), speaking of Simon Peter and John, he says: "Because they had not yet understood the Scripture, that Jesus must rise from the dead." So, probably, this "believe" of John 20:8 does not refer to the resurrection, but rather, that the body had been stolen.

Until this moment Jesus had not appeared to anyone, but the evidence of his resurrection was already there. Just as it was on his birth, when he was heralded by angels, who witnessed his first arrival to earth given to his mother Mary —through the angel Gabriel (Luke 1:26-31)—, and then to the pastors; so also, his resurrection was announced by angels, and this announcement was given first to women.

We also have the evidence of the empty tomb, which was impossible for any man to open, (because it was guarded by the Roman guards); nevertheless, God himself opened it: he sent an angel to remove the stone, who, after doing so, sat on it so that no one would close the tomb again. This angel opened the tomb to show the world that the tomb was empty, and that Christ had risen. When opening the tomb, no body was found inside of it, and we have already seen the evidence of the Roman guards, who were not believers, and that, seeing the angel, the earthquake and the stone rolled away by the power of God, they filled with fear. In the next chapter we will see the first appearance of Jesus to Mary Magdalene and the other women.

Chapter

IV

THE FIRST APPEARANCE OF JESUS

In this chapter we will learn about those women to whom Christ chose to appear for the first time after he was resurrected. It is important to ask: why Christ decided to present himself first to a group of women and not to his male disciples? Of all the people to whom Jesus could have appeared alive, and of all the disciples whom He could have chosen, Christ chose those women whose testimony — before men— would be the least trustworthy during Jesus' time. He first introduced himself to a group of women, who, at that time, were considered to be second-class people, mere objects of property by many, and whose testimony was neither trustworthy nor valid in a legal proceeding. By the time Jesus was on earth, women had greatly lost their social value in many ways; and since Christ came to this world to restore humanity, part of this restoration consisted in restoring to women the true value they have as co-heirs of the grace of life (1 Peter 3:7), and their legitimate function within the body of Christ.

The woman was created to be the ideal helper for the man (Genesis 2:18), so that both would be an example of faith to the world. The woman, who was deceived by Satan (Genesis 3:13), had lost the trust of the man. Her word and her testimony had been broken, and her role as the perfect helper for man was reduced and belittled. The woman went from being someone in whom the man had to deposit his love (Ephesians 5:25), to being the object of mistreatment, abuse and contempt for centuries; she was seen only as a sexual object or as someone who only had the function of procreation.

However, Christ came to undo the works of the devil (1 John 3:8); He came to restore the credibility of women, to restore her and give her the value that she really has in Christ. Christ chose women to appear alive for the first time, and so that they were the ones to bring the message of Jesus' resurrection to his disciples. He chose women to restore their testimony, to show that He loves them as much as He loves men, and to put them back where they were before the fall.

The woman that Christ chose to manifest himself alive for the first time was, in the eyes of the world, the least worthy. A woman who was once filled with demons, with a horrible testimony before she came to Christ; a person despised by society, but who had had an encounter with the Savior: Christ had set her free! Therefore, this woman was aware of the many sins that Jesus had forgiven for her, and she had a deep gratitude towards Him, due to the deliverance she had received in him. Thus, the Lord's death was something extremely painful for her; she was torn, desperate, overwhelmed, and inconsolable due to the death of her Jesus.

This woman was the first to arrive at the tomb, and she came alone, at dawn, before sunrise, and she was the one who stayed crying in front of the tomb after John and Peter returned to their homes. They left her there, alone, amid her pain. This woman was Mary Magdalene, and we are now going dive into what the Bible reveals about her.

We can read a more detailed description of Jesus' first appearance in John's Gospel, but Mark 16:9 also confirms that this was the first time Jesus was seen after his resurrection.

In the previous chapter we saw how John and Peter returned to their homes, and how Mary was left alone. I also commented that they did not see the angels, nor Jesus; even Mary Magdalene hadn't seen these angels yet either. Not long ago, her friends had gone in search

THE RESURRECTION OF CHRIST

of the disciples to obey the order that God had given through the angelic messengers. Now let's read John 20:10-18.

> "Then the disciples went back to their homes. But Mary stood weeping outside the tomb, and as she wept, she stooped to look into the tomb. And she saw two angels in white, sitting where the body of Jesus had lain, one at the head and one at the feet. They said to her, 'Woman, why are you weeping?' She said to them, 'They have taken away my Lord, and I do not know where they have laid him.' Having said this, she turned around and saw Jesus standing, but she did not know that it was Jesus. Jesus said to her, 'Woman, why are you weeping? Whom are you seeking?' Supposing him to be the gardener, she said to him, 'Sir, if you have carried him away, tell me where you have laid him, and I will take him away.' Jesus said to her, 'Mary.' She turned and said to him in Aramaic, 'Rabboni!' (which means Teacher). Jesus said to her, 'Do not cling to me, for I have not yet ascended to the Father; but go to my brothers and say to them, "I am ascending to my Father and your Father, to my God and your God."' Mary Magdalene went and announced to the disciples, 'I have seen the Lord'—and that he had said these things to her." (John 20:10-18).

The first thing we might ask ourselves is, who was Mary Magdalene? and why did Christ present himself to her for the first time, and not to Peter? He was the leader of the disciples and not Mary. Probably Peter's testimony would have been more powerful for the disciples than that of the women; in fact, none of the disciples believed the testimony of the women when they affirmed that Christ had risen (Mark 16:11); however, they did believe Peter when Christ appeared to him alone, and later, he told the other disciples (Luke 24:34).

Mary Magdalene was a Jewish woman. Her name is mentioned thirteen times in the Gospels (more times than most of the apostles). The name Mary was one of the most common among women at the time of Jesus; It means "exalted, chosen, or beloved of God," and is a derivative of the Hebrew name Miriam, who was the sister of Moses (Numbers 26:59).

In the time of Jesus, it was not customary to use surnames or last names, so the second name was usually to associate this person with the city of their origin. Mary was probably from Magdala, which was a fishing town located on the northwest coast of the Sea of Galilee, halfway between Tiberias (which was the capital of Galilee), and Capernaum (where Peter was from).

We know that she traveled constantly with Jesus, and that she was probably a leader of the women's group; that is, possibly she oversaw the ministry for women. The reason why we might think so, as I already said, is because almost always Mary Magdalene is mentioned first when many women are mentioned as a group (Matthew 27:56; Matthew 28:1; Mark 15:40; Mark 16:1); just as Peter is mentioned first almost whenever the male disciples are mentioned as a group (Matthew 10:2; Matthew 17:1; Mark 3:16; Mark 9:2).

There is also the belief —among many Christians— that Mary Magdalene was a prostitute. Is this true? Why is this believed among Christians? There really is no Biblical basis to say that Mary Magdalene was a prostitute. This was a teaching that began to spread in the year 581 AD, with Pope Gregory I, when he confused her with Mary of Bethany (Luke 10:39), who was the sister of Lazarus; the latter was the one who washed Jesus' feet, dried them with her hair, and anointed them with a priceless perfume (John 11:2).

Mary of Bethany (who anointed Jesus with the perfume) is often confused with another woman who wept at Christ's feet on another occasion (Luke 7:26-49). That other woman is not mentioned by name, nor is it explicitly said that she was a prostitute, although, considering what the Pharisees said about her, it could be that she was. So, neither Mary Magdalene nor Mary of Bethany were prostitutes; however, this is where the confusion comes from.

The Word of God mentions that Mary Magdalene was freed from seven demons and was one of the people who financially supported the ministry of Jesus and his disciples (Luke 8:2-3).

"And also some women who had been healed of evil spirits and infirmities: Mary, called Magdalene, from whom seven demons had gone out, and Joanna, the wife of Chuza, Herod's

household manager, and Susanna, and many others, who provided for them out of their means" (Luke 8:2-3).

We could think from this that she was a woman of a good economic position. It is never mentioned if she had a husband, so she was probably single. The Bible does not give details regarding the sufferings that Mary Magdalene suffered due to the possession of these seven evil spirits, but we can probably conclude that she lived constantly tormented by them. Demonic possessions caused great physical and emotional disturbances.

We can see many examples in the Bible of what these demonic possessions caused in people, and get an idea of what Mary Magdalene might have been going through. These possessions could make a person mute (Matthew 9:33); cause people to live in torment (Matthew 15:22); can make people suffer epileptiform convulsions and lose their sanity (Matthew 17:15, Luke 9:41-43); can lead to supernatural strength, and irrational behavior (including mutilations and shouting, Mark 5:3-5), etc. The demons do not resist the presence of God (Mark 5:7), and they recognize the servants of the Most High God (Luke 4:41). Demons look for a body to rest in and subsist inside a person (Matthew 12:43). Sometimes they came out of people with great violence, shaking them strongly and shouting (Matthew 1:26). By the way, the Bible says that the spirit of divination is also demonic (Acts 16:16-18).

With all this said, we can get a better idea of what Mary was going through until the day Jesus set her free. This was a woman who was dominated by Satan and his spirits. She was a woman of perdition, of total depravity, which led others to stray from God. She was an empty woman, aimless and lifeless. She was a hopeless human being; one of those totally rejected by society. She lived in darkness, tormented, tortured, shaken, sickened by these seven spirits, which dominated her thoughts, her actions, and her life. She had no peace, she had no rest, and for months or years she suffered in this way without any hope of salvation. The Pharisees and religious people of the time surely rejected her and did not dare to approach her, judging her as a sinner.

When an individual is under demonic possession, their senses, thoughts, and heart are consumed by absolute darkness. Their whole life is dominated by immorality, and they are constantly given over to their soul-destroying sins. Likewise, when someone allows himself to be dominated by immorality, they expose themselves to having a heart filled with the things of this world, so that the unclean spirits see in them a suitable house to live in, where the depravity of their heart is the ideal environment to live. And being there inside them, invading their body, they intensify in that person the passion for sin and multiply the evil in their hearts, while bodily and mentally disfiguring the image of God due to the effects of their manifestations.

Demonic possession is nothing more than the most extreme expression of a life in which the Spirit of God does not dwell; a life where there is not even a ray of light in the heart. There, a life totally separated from God is observed: God has withdrawn all his protection from them and has given them over to be a house of demons. What does a person look like from whom God has withdrawn his mercy from them, and has given them over to their delights? Paul shows us what these people look like: they are given over to a reprobate mind. Many of us were in this same condition before we came to Christ.

> **"And since they did not see fit to acknowledge God, God gave them up to a debased mind to do what ought not to be done. They were filled with all manner of unrighteousness, evil, covetousness, malice. They are full of envy, murder, strife, deceit, maliciousness. They are gossips, slanderers, haters of God, insolent, haughty, boastful, inventors of evil, disobedient to parents, foolish, faithless, heartless, ruthless. Though they know God's righteous decree that those who practice such things deserve to die, they not only do them but give approval to those who practice them" (Romans 1:28-32).**

This reminds me of Isaiah 5:20 "Woe to those who call evil good and good evil, who put darkness for light and light for darkness, who put bitter for sweet and sweet for bitter".

When we were walking in sin and delighting in it, we find nothing but emptiness and sorrow at the end, instead of the joy that God gives by living by His Word and in righteousness before him. The world applauds fornication, sexual immorality, sex outside of marriage, etc., while chastity until marriage (or keeping oneself for God, even in the realm of thoughts) is an aberration. The world applauds adultery and says no to fidelity; approves of homosexual marriage, and rejects the idea of marriage instituted by God, and today the world is in chaos due to the fragmentation of the family.

I still remember many of the conversations I had before I became a believer; how fornication, sexual immorality, pornography, adultery were glorified; and while one talks with friends —all stupefied by alcohol— there was a feeling of joy and happiness; and thinking at the time how this was the most fun and pleasant thing on earth.

I have been in conversations, who, while speaking among men, they glorified themselves while discussing their infidelity to their wives. They bragged about their infidelities, and the more women they had out of wedlock, the better. And then when their wives find out, they break their hearts. And secretly and in the dark, they destroy their marriages, break up their homes, tarnish the vows they made before God, and desecrate the sanctity of what He instituted from the beginning of the world. True love cannot be faked or acted; that is why these men tend to be angry and take little interest in their wives and children. They are morbid, false, liars, and selfish. They only think about their carnal desires, and they don't care about their families, while they may profess this with their mouths, their actions show what is truly in their hearts.

In this world, the thoughts of human beings are deranged, and they take pleasure in being far from the truth of God. When we were in the world and they told us about changing our ways, and coming to God, all we saw in it was a waste of time, right? Our eyes were darkened by sin, and our understanding clouded; we could not perceive the reality, and the need for salvation from eternal condemnation. I don't know about you, but God called me many times before coming to the feet of Christ, and everything they said to me seemed totally absurd, and I flatly rejected it. I wasn't interested in the least, not even in knowing what it meant to be a Christian. In retrospect, I had no idea of the intense adoration I had for the worldly delights, nor the overwhelming darkness that consumed me.

> **"And this is the judgment: the light has come into the world, and people loved the darkness rather than the light because their works were evil" (John 3:19).**

This was the condition of Mary before she came to Jesus. A life of dense darkness, separated from God, in which loving the world more, rejected God's call to her life. She was deaf to the Word of the Lord, and she did not want to come to the light (because demons hate the light of God). But when she was not expecting it, nor was she searching for the light, Jesus came into her life, and she was transformed by his presence.

This transformation experienced by Mary Magdalene had been radical: from having been possessed by seven demons, she now lived free due to the powerful intervention of Christ! Due to this great event in her life, she now lived in immense gratitude. She felt a deep love for the Master, which was so great that not even the apostles themselves had it. She had been forgiven of her many sins, and because of this she loved him greatly. Because of this forgiveness, mercy, and grace towards her, she loved Christ with all her heart (Luke 7:42-47). The forgiveness and deliverance that she received was the most precious thing she could have received in her life. Since then, she followed him without looking back; she never stopped following the Lord Jesus Christ.

Can you now imagine the desperate anguish that Mary Magdalene experienced when her Lord died? The Scriptures describe this somewhat, although not in great detail.

Let us now return to the moment when Mary Magdalene was at the tomb. She had been left alone, those disciples whom she went to look for, Peter and John, instead of comforting her, left her there and went to their house; the other women that were to be there with her, also were not present. And meanwhile, the memories of her Master's death haunted her. Moreover, she could not continue to honor the Lord's memory on His grave at least one more time, for His body was not in the grave. Mary Magdalene cried thinking that she would not be able to say goodbye to her Lord. She had no hope, no comfort, no company, no friends, and no ease in her pain.

She thought that the Lord's body had been stolen. Can you imagine that moment in Mary's life? While she was crying on the outskirts of the tomb, disconsolate, the last thing on her mind was that she would see her Lord once again, and for her, it was even less likely that she would see Him alive in front of her.

> **"But Mary stood weeping outside the tomb, and as she wept she stooped to look into the tomb. And she saw two angels in white, sitting where the body of Jesus had lain, one at the head and one at the feet" (John 20:11-12).**

Simon Peter had not seen anyone inside the tomb, and neither had John. But even so, Mary, perhaps instinctively, or just to make sure for herself, entered the tomb. When she entered, she found two angels dressed in white. Then she, in her grief and still sobbing from her pain, did not recognize these beings as angelic. The other women immediately realized that these beings they found inside the tomb were angels; however, in the case of Mary Magdalene, her eyes were likely cloudy from crying so much she couldn't recognize them. It was at that moment that the angels asked her a question, an extremely interesting question.

> **"They said to her, 'Woman, why are you weeping?' She said to them, 'They have taken away my Lord, and I do not know where they have laid him'" (John 20:13)**

However, Mary did not understand what they were asking her. They knew exactly why she was crying (even though truly, there was no real reason to cry). She was crying because her Messiah had died, and she thought that his body had been taken to an unknown place. The angels knew exactly why she was crying; However, they still asked her: "Why are you crying?"

What was it really that the angels were asking Mary when they asked her why are you crying? What the angels were really asking her was this: "Mary, you have nothing to cry about. There is no reason to be sad. It is a moment of great joy! It is time to praise the Lord! Mary, remember the words of the Lord; Remember that He said that he was going to rise again. He has fulfilled it, Mary! Why are you crying? There is no reason to cry! Rejoice! Rejoice!"

We see that Jesus himself asked her this same question moments after the angels had asked her. At that moment she was inside the tomb, with these two angels in front of her, and when she turns around, she finds a Man who asks her the same question.

> **"At this, she turned around and saw Jesus standing there, but she did not realize that it was Jesus. He asked her, 'Woman, why are you crying? Who is it you are looking for?' Thinking he was the gardener, she said, 'Sir, if you have carried him away, tell me where you have put him, and I will get him'" (John 20:14-15).**

What an impressive moment! For Mary, it was a moment of great despair, suffering, pain, loneliness, and brokenness. Her friends (Peter, John and the other women) had gone, they had left her alone in the grave, crying in front of this apparent reality: that she would never see her Lord again. At this moment of tremendous anguish, while she is crying and longing to see her Messiah, Jesus appears to her and asks her the same question: "Why are you crying? Who are you looking for?". While Mary's eyes were darkened, clouded by her weeping, Jesus asks her these two questions, as if to say: "Mary, Mary, why are you crying? There is no reason to cry! I am alive! I'm here! I am the one you are looking for!"

At that moment, Mary was not able to recognize the voice of Jesus, and she thought he was the gardener. She was hoping that the gardener had moved the body of Jesus to another place. This was not at all strange that she wouldn't recognize him, since in almost all the appearances of Jesus the disciples could not recognize him because his physical appearance apparently was not the same, and they did not recognize him until he opened their understanding (Luke 24:31; John 21:12). But then something spectacular happened.

> **"Jesus said to her, 'Mary.' She turned toward him and cried out in Aramaic, 'Rabboni!' (which means 'Teacher')" (John 20:16)**

Jesus only had to pronounce the name of Mary, and immediately she recognized him. There was no doubt that Mary was a sheep of

Christ, for she was able to hear the true voice of Lord calling to her. Mary was a blessed woman; she had the privilege of being the first to be an eyewitness to the risen Christ. It was then that she immediately said, "Raboni!" which means supreme teacher, magistrate, or teacher of great esteem. The term Raboni is a higher way of saying Rabbi (which means teacher).

> **"Jesus said, 'Do not hold on to me, for I have not yet ascended to the Father. Go instead to my brothers and tell them, "I am ascending to my Father and your Father, to my God and your God ""' (John 20:17).**

It is impossible to understand how emotional Mary Magdalene must have felt at this moment. It sure was an unbelievable experience what she was witnessing. Just thinking about this makes my heart jump with hope and joy, imagining that one day I, too, will be able to say: "Raboni! My God! My Jesus! My savior!". I hope that I will also have the privilege of hugging my Jesus, falling before him, worshiping Him with all my heart and express my deep gratitude, when I can finally be close to Him, see Him face to face and express with great joy the love that I have for Him —because He fills every corner of my thoughts— and I hope that when I hug Him, it will be so strong and so long, that the Lord will have to tell me to release him. As in another version of the Bible says:

> **"'Don't cling to me,' Jesus said, 'for I haven't yet ascended to the Father...'" (John 20:17, NLT).**

I love my life, my wife, my daughters; my parents, my in-laws, my brothers and friends; I also love my brothers and sisters in my church. I do not have a desire to die or leave this life; Despite this, I am well aware that my heart's greatest yearning and ultimate wish is to be with my Lord. This will be the happiest day of my life! The day when I'm finally in his presence and see with my eyes the One who created me, the One who gave me life when I was dead in my sin (Romans 5:8); the only One worthy of praise, power, glory and majesty (Revelation 5:12); the One who first loved me, even when I rejected Him and persisted in my sin (1 John 4:19).

Brothers and sisters, let us have the love that Mary had for Christ. He must be what we love most in this world. Let us give our life for Him; and let it be Him whom we constantly seek. May Christ be the one we think about day by day, from the moment we wake up until the moment we lay our heads down to rest at night. If Christ is not your first love, then go to his feet and ask for his forgiveness. Turn from your spiritual coldness and do not let that indifference to God end up separating you from his blessings; blessings that He has for everyone who humbles themselves before Him. Eventually the lack of love for God not only becomes love for the world but ends up corrupting even the most faithful church (Revelation 2:1-7).

This was the first time anyone had been resurrected with a glorified body. Mary Magdalene, in this case, had a unique experience: Christ Jesus was in front of her just as He had prophesied of himself; he was God himself in the person of Christ Jesus, but in a new glorified body. The Giver of life was in front of her, and in an instant, all her pain and despair, all her crying and suffering (what she had lived through for the last three days of her life), all of this pain disappeared in a second with the presence of the Lord. It doesn't surprise me that Jesus had to ask her to let Him go (or not cling to him). She tried to hold onto him so tightly that she didn't want to let Him go ever again.

This event reminds me of the passage from Psalm 30:11: "You have turned for me my mourning into dancing; you have loosed my sackcloth and clothed me with gladness". This verse perfectly describes what Mary Magdalene was experiencing: her heart —in an instant— was changed from being plunged in lamentation, to a grateful and joyful heart.

Christ now clearly confirms that salvation has come to the world, and that, by his death and resurrection, the wages of sin have been paid. The divorce or separation between God and man ended with Christ, and He not only reconciled us to God, but now we can call God our Father! Christ said to Mary: "I am ascending to my Father and your Father, to my God and your God" Our sins were officially blotted out forever. Another way of saying what Jesus is said to Mary could be something like this: "Mary, you are now my sister, and also, you are a daughter of God, you have been adopted, now my Father is also your Father." What an incredible statement by Jesus! What good news of salvation! What an unprecedented gift our Lord Jesus gave us! Christ gave us, through his death and resurrection, something that no one will ever be able to understand: our adoption as children of God (John 1:12)

Mary obeyed Jesus and went to tell the other disciples what had happened. There are two possibilities, one is that Mary Magdalene met the other women on the road while she was going to where her other disciples were; or that Jesus appeared separately to the other women (after they had seen the angels). This was the second appearance of Jesus after his resurrection.

> **"And behold, Jesus met them and said, 'Greetings!' And they came up and took hold of his feet and worshiped him" (Matthew 28:9).**

What a great privilege these women had; that they were chosen by Christ to be the first to bring the good news, and to be the first spokespersons of Jesus to speak of the good news of his resurrection to all his disciples. Why did Christ choose these women to appear for the first time? We will study this topic in more depth later (when we scrutinize the disciples' response to the testimony of the women), and we will learn how Christ restored the powerful testimony of a woman who decided to give herself to Jesus.

Before I end this chapter, I want to leave you with a few thoughts: Are you ready today to see the risen Jesus, bow down before Him, and give Him the adoration He deserves? Is your heart preparing for that moment when you meet Jesus after death? What would Christ say to you if He came for his church today? Do you think he would come for you? Will you have part in the first resurrection to life, or will it be rather in the second resurrection (to death and judgement)? (Revelation 20:5-6). Do you think Jesus would say to you, "I never knew you; depart from me, you workers of lawlessness" (Matthew 7:23)? Or will he say to you: "Well done, good and faithful servant. You have been faithful over a little; I will set you over much. Enter into the joy of your master" (Matthew 25:21).

Brothers and sisters, if you are reading this book, it is most likely because you love Jesus; but it may also be that your walk with Christ is struggling due to continual practice of sin in your life, and you have things that are being an obstacle in your relationship with Christ.

If the latter is the case, do not wait another day more to humble your heart before God. Christ came to this earth to be sacrificed for us; and He died and defeated death so that —through His blood— all who believe in him may have free entry to the throne of God, and live lives that glorify Him. Let us stop fixing our eyes on the vanities and empty things of this world and let us fix our eyes on Jesus "the founder and perfecter of our faith" (Hebrews 12:2

Chapter

V

THE GUARD'S REPORT

So far, we have studied how Joseph of Arimathea and Nicodemus anointed the body of Jesus and buried it in a new tomb near Golgotha. We also learned about how this tomb was sealed by the Romans and a guard was placed in front of it so that no one could enter. We discussed how an angel removed the stone from the entrance of the tomb, and that the soldiers fainted when they saw this angel; then they fled from that place when they saw that the body of Jesus was no longer there.

We have seen how the first to arrive at the tomb was Mary Magdalene, who, while seeing the tomb stone removed, went to look for Peter and John. And then, during this time, the other women arrived who saw the angel sitting on the stone and two angels inside the tomb. Then they went in search of the disciples; and when they left, John and Peter arrived and found the tomb empty; from there they returned to their homes and Mary Magdalene was left alone, broken, and without hope. It was at this time —while she was longing to see Christ— that she saw the Lord in His first appearance after He was resurrected. Jesus then appeared to the other female disciples, who went to tell the good news to the other disciples.

In this chapter we will learn about what happened to the Roman guards who fled, and about the testimony they gave to the priests who ordered the tomb to be secured. But before going into the explanation of those verses, it is important to understand how ingrained unbelief is in the human heart; so that both those who had never believed in Christ and the disciples themselves, both groups did not believe in the resurrection of the Lord.

Such is the depth of our incredulity, that even if in our days Christ came in his glory to install Himself as King in the world, many, deceived by the devil and for the love of sin, would not honor Him. The world would rebel against Christ and seek to remove Him from the throne, given the world hates the light of Christ.

The heart of man has become so insensitive to God, that seeing he does not see, and hearing he does not understand, although the manifestations of God are clear before his eyes. If man had just a little faith in his heart, even if it was faith the size of a mustard seed (I speak of faith in the true God), he could see, and understand in his heart the truth of the Gospel, and this faith would lead to repentance and forgiveness of sins. I dare say that the percentage of true faith in God in the human heart [without Christ] is zero percent without the Holy Spirit.

"For this people's heart has grown dull, and with their ears they can barely hear, and their eyes they have closed, lest they should see with their eyes and hear with their ears and understand with their heart and turn, and I would heal them" (Matthew 13:15).

Faith is a gift from God that only He can give (Philippians 1:29). This faith that God gives us must be continually exercised in our dependence on Him. It is impossible for a human being to please God without having true faith (Hebrews 11:6). We ourselves as believers, those of us who profess to be Christians, on many occasions and circumstances are deaf, we do not listen, we do not understand the message that God is sending us. We become deaf to the Word of God, and our trust in it fades away. We begin to trust what we see, what we have, above the God we do not see, and we want to have complete control and dominance of our lives.

When we let fear take over our hearts, in that moment we forget that God has promised to be with us. Isaiah 41:13 says: "For I, the Lord your God, hold your right hand; it is I who say to you, 'Fear not, I am the one who helps you.'" When we are easily filled with anger, either because we are attacked or accused, then we show a hardened heart, conceited, haughty and not compassionate; but Matthew 5:44 says, "But I say to you, love your enemies and pray for those who persecute you." We do not follow the example of Christ, who on the same cross asked the Father to forgive those who were crucifying Him (Luke 23:34). Many times, when a problem arises, the last person we turn to is God, and we do this when we see that we alone cannot solve it; and this is because we want to maintain as much control as possible over our lives.

Many believers accuse God when things don't turn out the way they think. And when we suffer for some reason, we forget that God is forging his image in us; We also forget that He is a Father who only knows how to give love to his children. The Bible says: "And we know that for those who love God all things work together for good, for those who are called according to his purpose"

(Romans 8:28).

What then should be the attitude of a true believer in the midst of difficulties, when he is going through a trial that God sends into his life to transform him into the image of Jesus? Look at what the book of James says regarding the attitude that the Christian should show.

"Count it all joy, my brothers, when you meet trials of various kinds, for you know that the testing of your faith produces steadfastness" (James 1:2-3).

This does not mean that it would be easy, nor does it mean that there will be no suffering. Rarely does God reveal to His children the purpose behind their trials or the timing of their deliverance. My brothers and sisters, we do not belong to ourselves. We should not question God because of our trials or difficulties; rather, we must praise Him in the midst of them, and raise our hands in thankfulness to Him always.

Do not allow the Word of God to become fruitless due to tribulation or be let astray from our walk with God; the tribulation just shows where your faith truly is. Do not let the Word of God fall on stony ground, which symbolizes affliction, persecution and lack of understanding (not knowledge) (Matthew 13:20-21); rather, allow the Word of God to fall on fertile ground, that is, he who understands the Word (and knows it), and bears fruit at his time (Matthew 13:23).

Trials are meant to help us come to God, and to produce in us a greater dependence on Him. Trials change our character, they help us to be more patient, humble, to pray more for those who make us suffer. The trials must produce in us patience and hope, and in that wait, we learn to trust God.

"Not only so, but we also glory in our sufferings, because we know that suffering produces perseverance; perseverance, character; and character, hope" (Romans 5:3-4).

We must understand something very important: God does not need us; and when we give God the throne in our heart, we are giving Him only what corresponds to him, that is all; and the beneficiaries of this are ourselves. The God we have doesn't get bigger when we praise Him, He doesn't get more powerful when we follow Him; He does not become more perfect or more holy when we obey Him. God is God, and He does not change. Hebrews 13:8 says, "Jesus Christ is the same yesterday, today, and forever."

God does not need anyone, but we all depend on Him. Everyone, believers and non-believers, and everything that inhabits the universe, everything is sustained by the Word of God (Hebrews 1:3). It is convenient for all of us to be with Him, because God is the source of life, and apart from Him we can do nothing fruitful (John 15:5). We need Him every minute of our lives, but more so in times of trials.

For this reason, the love that I have for God must be above everything else in this world; and if this is not the case, then I am living in sin, and separated from Him. If my heart is not totally given to the Lord, then I will be deceived, believing that I am someone important, and that while others go through afflictions, I will not go through them because I'm someone special. However, Christ himself went through great trials and told us that in this world we would have affliction (John 16:33).

It is best to trust in the One who has overcome the world. One thing is certain: that we all deserved to go to eternal fire, and that, thanks to Christ, all of us who have believed in Him have been delivered from that terrible place; therefore, any affliction we have in this world does not compare at all with the glory that awaits us when we are one day in His presence.

Take your eyes off yourself, from your affliction, from your needs, from your problems, from your hardened heart, and go to Him alone. Cry out to God when you're alone in your room; Cry out to Him for mercy, ask Him for forgiveness and tell Him to give you grace, to give you a clean heart before Him, and restore to you the joy of His salvation (Psalms 51:12). And your God, who sees you in secret, will reward you in public (Matthew 6:6).

If at this moment you are in a prison from which you do not see any escape, praise God even being in that condition; and others who are there with you will hear your voice. They will hear the love that is in your heart even in the midst of the trial, and how your faith remains firm. In this way, they may experience your faith in God, and possibly they may repent, and be saved (Acts 16:25-26). Nothing should take the place of Christ in our life, He, and only He, must take first place; therefore, anything that is above Christ becomes an idol, and becomes our worship. It is time to give our lives to the Lord! The Bible says:

"Whoever loves father or mother more than me is not worthy of me, and whoever loves son or daughter more than me is not worthy of me" (Matthew 10:37).

When a person believes in Him, believes His Word, and follows it, then their life will be transformed and renewed, and God brings about a life change in them that is evident to others. This is how we begin to live in the Spirit and reflect the image of Jesus.

"But the fruit of the Spirit is love, joy, peace, patience, kindness, goodness, faithfulness, gentleness, self-control; against such things there is no law" (Galatians 5:22-23).

But for those who have not believed in the Gospel, and live a false faith, an empty faith; for those who possess a ritualistic spirituality and believe that they will earn God's favor by "keeping up with Him", they have never really believed in and followed Christ; for them, the consequences of living apart from the Word of God will also be evident to the world.

> **"Now the works of the flesh are evident: sexual immorality, impurity, sensuality, idolatry, sorcery, enmity, strife, jealousy, fits of anger, rivalries, dissensions, divisions, envy, drunkenness, orgies, and things like these. I warn you, as I warned you before, that those who do such things will not inherit the kingdom of God" (Galatians 5:19-21).**

The works of the flesh are not necessarily external and physical since these are first conceived in the heart of man. God is going to judge even our thoughts, because even these bad thoughts are sin before God. For example, Jesus said, "But I say to you that everyone who looks at a woman with lustful intent has already committed adultery with her in his heart" (Matthew 5:28). Therefore, the root of the problem is not in the change of behavior, but the change of heart, or of the mind, so that the person thinks according to the Word.

Many think that if God is Almighty, why not just manifest himself to the world? In this way we could all believe and there would be no doubt that He exists and that His Word is true. Why doesn't God give us a sign that He exists in a tangible way? If we could only see the glory of Him, surely the whole world would worship the true God, right? However, the reality is that thousands and thousands of people saw the miracles of Christ, and still did not believe. This question was asked by the scribes and Pharisees and Christ's answer was clear about it.

> **"Then some of the scribes and Pharisees answered him, saying, 'Teacher, we wish to see a sign from you.' But he answered them, 'An evil and adulterous generation seeks for a sign, but no sign will be given to it except the sign of the prophet Jonah. For just as Jonah was three days and three**

nights in the belly of the great fish, so will the Son of Man be three days and three nights in the heart of the earth'" (Matthew 12:38-40).

Christ told them that this would be the sign he would give to the world: His resurrection. If we demand a sign from God, that proves to us His power over life and death, let us only contemplate His empty tomb. This was the sign that Christ left us to show us that we can have faith and trust in Him. If we do not believe this sign, even if Christ Himself descended from heaven, we would not believe in Him. We would see that it is true, and He exists, but, even so, we would not believe in Him in the sense of loving and following Him. Even seeing with our eyes, we would remain haughty and in sin, just like the Pharisees.

The unbelieving heart always asks for signs, but even seeing the signs, it does not believe, because it is a heart that has not yet been transformed and has not surrendered to God. They believe that witnessing a heavenly sign or a dead man coming back to life would be sufficient for them to believe. Christ left us a parable that explains this clearly to us.

In Luke 16:19-31 we read the parable of Lazarus and the rich man. In this parable the rich man celebrated parties in his house every day, and at his door was a man named Lazarus, who was poor and sought to fill himself with what was left over from the parties. Lazarus died, and then the rich man died. Lazarus went to a place of rest and abundance, a place without sickness or pain.

On the other hand, the rich man went to Hades, and being in torment, asked Lazarus to dip the tip of his finger in water and cool his tongue. Between the two there was a great abyss that separated them; however, we see that —somehow— the rich man had a conversation with Abraham, the man called the "Father of faith". Faced with this request, Abraham replied that when Lazarus was alive, he suffered, and now he was being comforted; while the rich man lived comforted and is now suffering. So, the rich man made another request to Abraham; He asked him to send Lazarus back to earth so that he could preach to his five brothers, so that they would not end up in that place as well. To this new request, Abraham replied:

> "But Abraham said, 'They have Moses and the Prophets; let them hear them.' And he said, 'No, father Abraham, but if someone goes to them from the dead, they will repent.' He said to him, 'If they do not hear Moses and the Prophets, neither will they be convinced if someone should rise from the dead'"
> (Luke 16:29-31).

In other words, Abraham replied that miracles are not those that convert the heart, but faith in the word of God, in what has already been revealed. For me to believe in the resurrection of Christ, I must first have faith in what is revealed about Him.

By the way, what is faith? Faith is the total conviction that a person has regarding something that has not yet happened or has not been seen; something that he/she is fully convinced that he/she will see and that will happen; therefore, he/she faithfully expects such an event to occur or such a thing to appear.

> "Now faith is the assurance of things hoped for, the conviction of things not seen" (Hebrews 11:1).

We have never seen the risen Christ, nor have we contemplated God in His glory (like Isaiah). We did not have the experience of seeing Lazarus come out of the tomb, nor Jesus' healing thousands of sick people. We were not present when the Lord was crucified; we didn't see the Red Sea parting in two, nor the plagues of Egypt. However, we believe by faith what God has revealed in his Word. That is why faith comes by hearing and hearing the Word of God (not by seeing miracles).

> "So, faith comes from hearing, and hearing through the word of Christ" (Romans 10:17).

Even the miraculous resurrection of Christ cannot change the minds of those who choose not to believe; although the resurrection of the Lord is the most important evidence of the veracity of the ministry of Christ, and it is also the sign given to the unbelievers.

Why are we discussing so much now about the subject of unbelief in the heart of man? Because this was exactly the case with the Roman guards guarding the tomb of Jesus: they, having seen such a portentous miracle, were still more interested in receiving the bribe money than giving their lives to the one true God.

> **"While they were going, behold, some of the guard went into the city and told the chief priests all that had taken place. And when they had assembled with the elders and taken counsel, they gave a sufficient sum of money to the soldiers and said, 'Tell people, "His disciples came by night and stole him away while we were asleep." And if this comes to the governor's ears, we will satisfy him and keep you out of trouble.' So they took the money and did as they were directed. And this story has been spread among the Jews to this day" (Matthew 28:11-15).**

Given the situation, the soldiers went directly to the main Jewish priests (since they had been the ones who had assigned them the protection of the tomb), and they went to give the report of what had happened. Then, even with the testimony of these soldiers, the chief priests continued to harden their hearts; and even having the evidence before them, they planned a conspiracy and bribed the witnesses to deny the undeniable. For their part, these soldiers, having seen with their own eyes the angel of God who rolled away the stone, decided to take the bribe. They preferred to follow the path of lies and greed, rather than repent and give their lives to God.

According to the facts, these Roman soldiers had not faithfully fulfilled their work, for the Roman seal had been violated, and the stone rolled away; therefore, they had reason to fear the consequences of their failure to guard the tomb. But it certainly was not that they had failed, —for these soldiers were strong men, ruthless killers, trained for war, and very brave— nevertheless, they could do nothing in the face of such a mighty event, and were terrified when they saw the angel of God.

We do not know exactly how many soldiers were watching the tomb, but we can imagine it was a bunch of them. These soldiers guarding the tomb witnessed that supernatural vision: they saw when the angel descended and powerfully removed the stone. Thus, with this it was verified that it had not been just the case of an isolated testimony, but of the experience of all these soldiers, who, by the way, were all incredulous gentiles.

The appearance of this angel must have been impressive. And this is a common denominator in angelic appearances throughout the Bible (Genesis 26:24; Luke 1:13, 30; 2:9-10, etc.). The appearance of angels almost always brings fear, so they have to say to those who they appear to (before saying their message), "do not fear." Angels are beautiful beings; however, they are powerful, strong, and fast. They have the ability to kill, bring diseases, or simply serve as God's messengers.

The expected response would be that, having witnessed such an event, those soldiers would have continued investigating to fully understand what had happened, in order to find out about the plan of salvation and believe it. Anyone would think that seeing such an act would bring anyone to the knowledge of who Christ is, and would make them cry out in repentance before Him; however, instead, these guards fled. They traded the truth for lies, sold God's truth for a few pieces of silver, and preferred dishonor and corruption to honoring the Creator and testifying to the truth of the Lord's resurrection.

Such was the case with Judas, who betrayed Jesus for 30 pieces of silver (the equivalent today of about $400); in the same way, these soldiers were bribed (perhaps for much more money) but whatever the amount, the fact is this: they sold the truth. How many of us, knowing the truth, have lied (knowing full well what we are doing)? How many of us have said something that we know is not true, and have thus defended our position so as not to look more foolish before men, to hide something that is shameful? How many of us have ever told what we call "white lies"?

If a person does not have a true commitment to the truth, lies will easily emerge from their heart. That is, the further they live from the truth, the closer they will live to the lie. Consequently, the more a person lives in the lie, the more they will identify with the father of lies, that is, the devil. When a person lies, they show that they are not a child of God, or currently not behaving as such, given they are living in sinful practice.

"You are of your father the devil, and your will is to do your father's desires. He was a murderer from the beginning, and does not stand in the truth, because there is no truth in him.

When he lies, he speaks out of his own character, for he is a liar and the father of lies" (John 8:44).

These chief priests professed to follow God; However, upon learning the truth from the testimony of these Roman guards, they decided to hide it and made the soldiers lie. In this way, these false teachers gave these gentile soldiers a terrible witness of what it means to follow God, and they shamed the Israelite nation, leading them to lie and act dishonestly.

In the Gospels we can see —from the narration of the birth of Jesus— that the priests showed a total lack of interest in truly serving God. Always their attitude was a selfish and hypocritical attitude; they pretended to love God, but their hearts were totally turned away from the truth. Despite their knowledge of the Word, they merely pretended to follow it strictly and even taught it, but in reality, they were spiritually lifeless, sightless, and deaf.

In the narration of the birth of Christ some wise men came from the east (Matthew 2:1). We do not have much information about them, but we can infer that they were important and well-known men in their time, who possibly dedicated themselves to crowning kings. They perhaps, upon the revelation of the birth of the "King of the Jews", thought that he would be born in a palace; possibly they thought that he would be born in King Herod's palace; but when they went to talk to him, Herod did not know what they were talking about. It was then that he consulted with the chief priests and scribes.

"When Herod the king heard this, he was troubled, and all Jerusalem with him; and assembling all the chief priests and scribes of the people, he inquired of them where the Christ was to be born. They told him, 'In Bethlehem of Judea...'" (Matthew 2:3-5a).

These priests knew perfectly well that these great men of the time —who were possibly crowning kings— had come looking for a king to honor him; and they also knew that these wise men were looking for the Messiah expected and promised by God. These wise men knew exactly where this Messiah would be born, but none of the religious of that time went to Bethlehem to find out if He had been born there.

None of the priest were interested. They knew the Word, but they were not interested in anything other than religiousness and social prestige.

The birth of Jesus did not matter to them, nor His ministry, nor His preaching, nor His miracles, nor His resurrection. The Gospel was presented to them in every possible way, but they did not repent; rather, they persisted in their sin and unbelief.

There is no single work outside of the saving work of Christ on the cross that can cleanse our sins (Ephesians 2:8-9). If my sin has not led me to cry out to God for His forgiveness, it means that I have not yet understood the terrible gravity of my it, nor the work Christ has done for me on the Cross.

If God is the truth, I must live in the truth. Therefore, the lie should never leave my lips, regardless if the truth seems to be against me. And if I do lie, then I must repent of it and change my ways, to live as Christ lived. If I lie, I dishonor the name of God. No matter how innocent the lie is, we must tell the truth and live in the truth always.

"Jesus said to him: I am the way, and the truth, and the life; no one comes to the Father except through me" (John 14:6).

Just as the truth is presented as a Person, the lie is also presented as a person. When I speak the truth I identify with Christ, when I lie, I identify with Satan. Some of us could still teach our children that it is okay to lie in some circumstances. When we teach that Santa Claus is real, and he comes to leave toys for well-behaved children at Christmas, as beautiful as this may seem, this is not true, and we are thus exchanging the truth for a lie. The point is not necessarily to get Santa Claus out of the house, but that we always speak the truth to our children and explain to them what this really is.

When I lie, whoever listens to me may not even know that I lied. My heart is known by God, and my immense love and reverence for Him will always guide me to live in honesty and righteousness. One thing is totally true: We cannot hide anything from God.

"You know when I sit down and when I rise up; you discern my thoughts from afar" (Psalms 139:2).

The soldiers could face severe consequences if they publicly admit they failed in their mission and this information reaches Governor Pilate. It was for this reason that, in addition to the amount given as bribe, these leaders offered to give them protection: "And if this comes to the governor's ears, we will satisfy him and keep you out of trouble." (Matthew 28:14).

This lie was widely disseminated by them, and they did this job so well, that even after 30 years —when the book of Matthew was written— the prevailing belief among the people (among the unbelievers of the resurrection of Jesus) was that the disciples had stolen the body of Christ (Matthew 28:15).

This was the lie that these soldiers spread: the disciples of that deceiver (as they called Jesus) stole the body of their Master. But what did this mean? These soldiers were talking about men (the disciples) who didn't believe that Jesus would rise again; who fled in fear while Jesus was crucified, they were not present to lower his body or when they buried Him; they did not even believe the testimony of the women (who told them of the resurrection of the Lord); and then, the story was that these men went and outwitted the soldiers (these expert and trained assassins, who guarded the tomb in turns), broke the seal, moved the huge rock at the entrance, and took the body of Jesus. However, before, they took away the canvases, folded them, they put them on the bed of the sepulcher; and finally, as time passed, these same disciples died for the lie that they themselves had created.

I ask you: how much is the truth worth? For how much would you sell or trade the truth for? For what amount of wealth would you sell Christ for? Now, I'll ask you something else: Why would you do it? Because of group pressure? For the love of money? Would you sell your sanctification in Christ for an hour-long movie with sexual content? For lust? For a party? for alcohol? For a woman or for a man? For a relationship outside of marriage?

How serious is this matter of lying to God? Let's read this story from the Bible in the book of Acts.

"But a man named Ananias, with his wife Sapphira, sold a piece of property, and with his wife's knowledge he kept back for himself some of the proceeds and brought only a part of it and laid it at the apostles' feet. But Peter said, 'Ananias, why has

Satan filled your heart to lie to the Holy Spirit and to keep back for yourself part of the proceeds of the land?'" (Acts 5:1-3).

Who are we really lying to when we tell falsehoods within our hearts? It is to the Holy Spirit of God, who knows all our thoughts. The consequence of the sin of Ananias and Sapphira was sudden death, and this was the way in which God showed us what is the consequence of living a life of sin, and of lying to the Spirit of God. The one who lives a life of falsehood and lying, deceiving, shows who he/she really serves. They were left for us as an example of the consequences of sin even in the New Testament.

None of us, even being believers, will enjoy the fruits of the Spirit while practicing any type of sin. Whoever practices sin —while calling himself a Christian— is rather a religious man who lives in hypocrisy before God. I don't want to pretend to live in the presence of God (who is the truth), while living in a lie. Christ alluded to this false religiosity when he told the Pharisees the following:

"Woe to you, scribes and Pharisees, hypocrites! For you are like whitewashed tombs, which outwardly appear beautiful, but within are full of dead people's bones and all uncleanness" (Matthew 23:27).

A life built on falsehoods reveals a heart disconnected from God. God asked Cain where his brother was (right after Cain had killed him), and he lied to God (Genesis 4:9). Abraham lied that his wife Sarah was only his sister because she was afraid of death (Genesis 20:2). She was his half-sister; therefore, he did not tell the whole truth, and he willingly and knowingly lied. Jacob lied to his father by posing as his twin brother Esau (Genesis 27). King David slept with Uriah's wife, Bathsheba, who became pregnant; Because of this, He lied to her husband and then had him killed. This sin cost David the life of his son (2 Samuel 11).

This matter goes deeper still. If I say that I love God and believe in Him, but I do not live according to His Word, this makes me a liar and the truth is not in me. My own conduct is what condemns me, and what I say I believe is precisely what testifies against me.

> "And by this we know that we have come to know him: if we keep his commandments. Whoever says 'I know him' but does not keep his commandments is a liar, and the truth is not in him; but whoever keeps his word, in him truly the love of God has been perfected. By this we know that we are in Him" (1 John 2:3-5).

Someone might say: Why is God so demanding of us? Why is His Word so harsh? However, there is no wisdom in questioning God, because those of us who don't understand the seriousness of sin in our own lives, will still not be able to understand his spiritual blindness we are living in and will not be able to surrender to the Lord. Sin is what makes us unworthy of Him. All kinds of sin: lying, pride, lust, jealousy, contention, etc. It's a reflection of a life apart from God. Therefore, God calls us to repentance, to change our lives, to be transformed by his Word. God knows everything, He knows how empty, dirty, and foolish our hearts are and knows every thought that goes through our minds. We have a Holy God (Revelation 4:8), so we have been called to be holy before Him.

> "Even as he chose us in him before the foundation of the world, that we should be holy and blameless before him" (Ephesians 1:4).

Given this, the question arises: how can I be holy? How can my heart become clean from my sin? We have the answer in the word of God.

> "The sacrifices of God are a broken spirit; a broken and contrite heart, O God, you will not despise" (Psalms 51:17).

> "But that is not the way you learned Christ! —assuming that you have heard about him and were taught in him, as the truth is in Jesus, to put off your old self, which belongs to your former manner of life and is corrupt through deceitful desires, and to be renewed in the spirit of your minds, and to put on the new self, created after the likeness of God in true righteousness and holiness" (Ephesians 4:20-24).

Brothers and sisters, let us continually cleanse our hearts before God through His Word. Let us recognize the seriousness of our sin and learn each day to love and obey our God. Holiness produces joy in the Lord; that is the truth and freedom we have in Christ. So, each one is free to say no to sin and yes to the Lord Jesus. If we have sinned, and our hearts have turned away from God, then let us say like David: "Restore to me the joy of your salvation…" (Psalms 51:12a).

I invite you to live in the truth, set apart for God, loving and obeying His Word all the days of our lives. Let's not be like these priests and these soldiers, who, still confronted by the truth, decided to ignore it, and followed a path that only led them to perdition.

Chapter

VI

THE TESTIMONY OF WOMEN

Bearing witness to Jesus is extremely important. We have all received the mandate to take the Word of God to our homes, to our neighbors and to all people. It is with the preaching of the Word of God that our eyes will be opened, and those who have not yet believed in the Gospel will one day become part of the family of faith if the Word of God reaches their hearts. However, it is also a fact that, even fulfilling the mandate to preach the Word of God, there will be those who will not believe our message. Even many people who attend church, and who constantly listen to the Gospel have a clouded mind, and do not believe it, therefore, they do not put it into practice.

Let us now return where we are in our study and situate ourselves in the time of the events circumscribed to the resurrection of Jesus. The year of these events is not fully defined, but it is located between the year 30 and 33 AD. Jesus died on the 14th of the month of Nisan (a Friday) around 3:00 pm (the ninth hour, Mark 15:33). The resurrection occurred on the 16th (on the third day, Sunday), and must have occurred around 6 am, before the sun rose.

We have already seen how the guards fled after fainting at the sight of the angel. Then Mary Magdalene arrived, while it was still dark, and she ran out in search of Peter and John. Meanwhile, the other women arrived, saw the angels who testified that Jesus had risen, and went to tell the others.

I also commented on how John and Peter arrived at the tomb, and they did not see the body (with them Mary Magdalene arrived). Then they returned to their homes; Mary was left alone, and she had the impressive experience of seeing the risen Jesus for the first time. After this, Jesus appeared to the other women, while they were on their way in search of the disciples, for Christ had commanded them to go and tell others that He had risen. They were the first witnesses of the resurrection of the Lord. All this happened early in the morning, on Easter Sunday.

The news spread throughout Jerusalem. Everyone was talking about the prophet who was killed on the cross; everyone talked about the empty tomb and wondered if Jesus had really risen or if His body had been stolen. The disciples were in hiding and frightened because the soldiers spread a false rumor that they had stolen the body of Jesus, and this could mean that they could also be persecuted and martyred like Jesus was. It was not a small thing to have broken the Roman seal of the tomb, and to have supposably outwitted the Roman guards.

The one they were going to crown as King when he entered Jerusalem riding on a donkey, was crowned with thorns. The one who should be dressed in royal clothes was stripped naked, spit on and humiliated in front of men. Those who should have loved him, hated Him. Those who should have received Him, rejected Him, and crucified Him.

There was no doubt about one thing: the tomb was empty; and of the body there was so much uncertainty. However, there were some women (Jesus' disciples) who had been witnesses of the resurrection, who were telling everyone what they had seen and heard, and their testimony was shared first with most Jesus' disciples.

What follows in the story never fails to impress us all. Perhaps we could say that the message that these women gave the disciples regarding the resurrection of the Lord would be enough for them to believe and give glory to God that Jesus lived; that they would prostrate themselves and praise fervently, rejoice and immediately go out to preach that Jesus had risen; however, it was not so, the truth was that the disciples did not believe the testimony of these women.

"Now when he rose early on the first day of the week, he appeared first to Mary Magdalene, from whom he had cast out seven demons. She went and told those who had been with him, as they mourned and wept. But when they heard that he was alive and had been seen by her, they would not believe it" (Mark 16:9-11).

"While they were perplexed about this, behold, two men stood by them in dazzling apparel. And as they were frightened and bowed their faces to the ground, the men said to them, 'Why do you seek the living among the dead? He is not here but has risen. Remember how he told you, while he was still in Galilee, that the Son of Man must be delivered into the hands of sinful men and be crucified and on the third day rise.' And they remembered his words, and returning from the tomb they told all these things to the eleven and to all the rest. Now it was Mary Magdalene and Joanna and Mary the mother of James and the other women with them who told these things to the apostles, but these words seemed to them an idle tale, and they did not believe them" (Luke 24:4-11).

Here we can observe how these women, Mary Magdalene, Joanna, Mary (the mother of James), and others, went where the disciples of Jesus were, and possibly gave the testimony, not only to the eleven, but likely also other disciples. At that time there could be perhaps as many as 120 faithful followers of Jesus (Acts 1:15); however, none of them believed the testimony of these women.

They were sad, distressed and in suffering; therefore, they did not believe them (Mark 16:10-11). The pain due to the death of Jesus was so strong that there was not a shred of hope in their hearts that Jesus would rise again. But the surprising thing about this was that not only did they not believe them, but they thought that the testimony of the women was foolishness, nonsense (Luke 24:11). However, if we think about it carefully, it was the testimony of at least six women! If it had been the testimony of only one, there would be reason to doubt; but here it was at least six people who claimed that they had seen the risen Christ.

How can this be possible? The Sanhedrin received the testimony of the Roman guards and believed their testimony of a divine intervention (although they had voluntarily decided to lie and bribe these soldiers, in order not to submit to the truth or ask for forgiveness for the horrendous murder they had just committed). They were always thinking about their personal prestige, and that was the only thing that mattered to them, (Matthew 28:11-15). It is incredible that the Pharisees did believe the testimony of the guards, while the disciples did not believe the testimony of fellow believers. Rather, they believe that the testimony of the women was nonsense, and they did not believe them.

Why was the heart of these disciples so incredulous? Why couldn't they believe the women after Christ had already said several times that he was going to die and rise again? Didn't they remember that Christ raised three people from the dead? The number of people who believed that Jesus was going to rise after death was zero. Why didn't they believe?

> **"'And after flogging him, they will kill him, and on the third day he will rise.' But they understood none of these things. This saying was hidden from them, and they did not grasp what was said" (Luke 18:33-34).**

Their understanding was veiled, and until then they did not understand these things. Additionally, the disciples of Jesus were not only in the dark about the resurrection, but they also struggled to comprehend many of his teachings. On numerous occasions, Christ spoke to them in parables, but they often failed to comprehend and required further explanation from Him. (Matthew 13:10-17).

The disciples, like the Pharisees, craved personal prestige. They wanted to have the first places in the kingdom of Jesus; sit next to Him in His heavenly realm and they even fought over this. We see on one occasion that John and James spoke with their mother so that she would intercede for them before Jesus so that one would sit on the right and the other on the left in His kingdom (Matthew 20:20). They saw Jesus do many miracles; however, they still did not fully understand who it was that they were truly following, nor what the kingdom that He came to establish was about.

This incredulity and blindness were due to the fact that God had not wanted to reveal the fullness of the truth to them yet, perhaps so that the impact of seeing the risen Son of God with their own eyes would be even greater; so, unbelief alone, in this case, supports the reality of His resurrection.

Paul is an example of what happens when a person is confronted by the truth itself. Paul was a Pharisee of Pharisees, an expert in the law, proud to be a Jew and a Roman, and a persecutor of the Church. Paul was all of that; but what happened to his unbelief when he saw Christ? His unbelief faded away completely.

Paul had two options: surrender his heart totally to Christ, or do the same as his fellow Pharisees did, continue in rebellion. He could have seen Jesus alive and still not follow Him. He too could have followed the Lord for a while and then turned away from Him and returned to his evil ways. But when he saw the risen Jesus, his life was transformed.

Paul's conversion is one of the greatest pieces of evidence of the resurrection of the Lord Jesus. Paul was the one who wrote almost a third of the New Testament; and he was the one who likely worked the hardest for the advancement of the Gospel of all the apostles. He left behind all his titles, and had them as garbage, for Christ's sake. He wrote:

"Indeed, I count everything as loss because of the surpassing worth of knowing Christ Jesus my Lord. For his sake I have suffered the loss of all things and count them as rubbish, in order that I may gain Christ" (Philippians 3:8).

The disciples received the Holy Spirit in John 20:22. When Christ appeared alive to them, He breathed on them and said: "Receive the Holy Spirit." This Holy Spirit, the same one who gave the breath of life to Adam and who guides us unto truth, is the one who would give life to these men blinded to the truth of the Lord's resurrection. For to believe the truth, the Spirit of God must intervene. In John 16:13 Jesus says that the Holy Spirit will guide us into all truth, but can I have the Holy Spirit and not believe the Word of God?

The answer to this question is yes. This is what sin does in our lives. Even if we are believers, the practice of sin will lead us away from the truth, blind our eyes, and dull our conscience. And before this, another question arises: how can someone say that he believes in Christ and persist in a path apart from God? The truth is that a person shows that he does not really believe Christ if, knowing the Word, there has not been a real change in his/her lives. I may have the knowledge, but if I am not living as a believer, it is because I am not really believing God. It is knowledge without understanding. It is an empty knowledge, which does not produce true faith; so, a person in such circumstances, when trials come, will turn away from God.

In the book of Hosea, we see how the lack of knowledge of God, and true faith in Him, led to the destruction of a nation.

> **"Hear the word of the Lord, O children of Israel, for the Lord has a controversy with the inhabitants of the land. There is no faithfulness or steadfast love, and no knowledge of God in the land; there is swearing, lying, murder, stealing, and committing adultery; they break all bounds, and bloodshed follows bloodshed. Therefore, the land mourns, and all who dwell in it languish, and also the beasts of the field and the birds of the heavens, and even the fish of the sea are taken away. Yet let no one contend, and let none accuse, for with you is my contention, O priest. You shall stumble by day; the prophet also shall stumble with you by night; and I will destroy your mother. My people are destroyed for lack of knowledge; because you have rejected knowledge, I reject you from being a priest to me. And since you have forgotten the law of your God, I also will forget your children. The more they increased, the more they sinned against me; I will change their glory into shame. They feed on the sin of my people; they are greedy for their iniquity. And it shall be like people, like priest; I will punish them for their ways and repay them for their deed"** (Hosea 4:1-9).

Through these verses, we see that those who are not fed by the Truth of God's Word and reject His knowledge, ultimately turn to sin as their source of sustenance, their essential nourishment for survival. The lack of knowledge of God and fear of Him results in infidelity to the commandments and spiritual coldness towards God; therefore, sin flourishes in such a person and wickedness multiplies, until it reaches the point where theft, adultery, and murder become commonplace in the nation.

One key factor behind the disbelief of Christ's disciples in the resurrection message was the limited credibility that women held as messengers back then. Most likely, if at that moment it had been Peter, for example, who proclaimed the good news of the Lord's resurrection, many would have believed immediately (Luke 24:34). The guards brought the message to the priests, and they believed them; But they did not believe the women, who were the first to announce the resurrection to the disciples. The credibility of the guards' message was greater, since it came from men; but since the message of the resurrection came from women, although it was the same message, it did not have the same credibility.

Women were not highly esteemed or trusted during that time in history. Therefore, they were easily despised and mistreated, and their testimony was not considered as reliable. After the Fall, women suffered greatly because of sin; and since Eve was deceived in the garden, the word of women from then on was underestimated; women were not valued or taken into account for many centuries, just like it occurs in many countries still today; and this is the reason: instead of following God's guidance, Eve chose to follow Satan's words.

Likewise, the man sinned when he heard the voice of his wife, when she had already sinned and what she offered him at that moment was not from God. Instead of restoring his wife, crying out to the Creator for her so that He would forgive her; instead of offering his life for her, the man ate and sinned too. Therefore, man was to blame for the fall and not Eve (although she was the instrument).

> **"Therefore, just as sin came into the world through one man, and death through sin, and so death spread to all men because all sinned" (Romans 5:12).**

When Eve sinned and led her husband to sin, it brought condemnation upon her. Instead of having a husband clothed in holiness, she would now have a husband clothed in wickedness and sin. That tender love of her husband (who should treat her as the weaker vessel, 1 Peter 3:7) was turned—due to sin—into adultery, into verbal and physical abuse, into mistreatment, and contempt. Instead of treating her as a more fragile vessel, man, throughout history, has treated women as an iron vessel.

After the fall, men stopped treating their wives as their friends, their confidants, and their suitable help. They, instead of delighting in being with them, instead of giving them their complete trust to enjoy together as a couple, turned marriage into a fight, a war, a relationship of constant fighting between two selfish people, who fights to establish their own will.

We should not be surprised by the high divorce rate in the United States (about 50%), for this has been the condition of man and woman since their downfall: they have been divorced from God, and that is just a reflection of that. The divorce statistics in the world are an x-ray of the human heart before God. And of those who remain married, very few are those who together seek to do the will of God, and who, as a couple, truly desire to reflect the love of Christ.

From the Old Testament we see that the love between a man and a woman was to be cultivated, nurtured, and fostered so that both could learn to love and make each other happy. For example, the Bible says:

"When a man is newly married, he shall not go out with the army or be liable for any other public duty. He shall be free at home one year to be happy with his wife whom he has taken."
(Deuteronomy 24:5).

The verse above indicates that Jewish men were to be granted a year of leave after marriage to ensure the happiness of their wives. In the New Testament we see God's command in this regard: that the man must love the woman as Christ loved the Church (Ephesians 5:25). And how did Christ love his church? He gave his life for her!

"And being found in human form, he humbled himself by becoming obedient to the point of death, even death on a cross."
(Philippians 2:8).

Throughout his ministry, Christ sought to restore women from sin and return her to her original position, the one she had at the beginning. Here we can see some examples:

1. God chose a woman — who also needed to be saved from her sin — to be the earthly mother of Jesus; a God-fearing young woman, who throughout her life would carry a stigma of contempt, since everyone thought that she had been unfaithful to her husband (John 8:41). Mary was the chosen vessel by the Lord for the arrival of the Messiah; however, she recognized her own need for salvation and said, "My spirit rejoices in God my Savior" (Luke 1:47).

2. When Christ had his public ministry, He went to Samaria, a region that the Jews avoided. The Samaritans were the result of intermarriage between Israelites and Gentiles, and they practiced a type of religious syncretism (the blending of a pagan's worship and the true God's worship). The Samaritans have a history that begins with Jeroboam, when Israel was divided into two nations: the North (Israel) and the South (Judah). After the return of the Jews from the Babylonian Captivity and the Median-Persian empire, about 500 years before Jesus, the Samaritans were already consolidated as part of the apostate Israel.

It was then that Christ went to Jacob's well to meet a Samaritan woman (John 4:1-39). She was a promiscuous woman who had had five husbands. She was also an adulterer, because the man with whom she was living at that time was not her husband. When reading the story, one can realize that this woman had been rejected by her own people, because she went alone to get water at noon (sixth hour) (and not early in the morning, when the sun was not so strong, hour of the day when the other women used to come to draw water from the well).

It is to this woman that Jesus presents himself as the Messiah (and she may have been the first individual to whom Jesus publicly showed himself as such). He decided to go through Samaria and share with the Samaritans the Gospel of salvation (beginning specifically with this ungodly woman). At the end of His conversation with her, Christ restored her: she repented, and God transformed her heart. Then her testimony helped many others to believe in Christ.

3. Another notable woman in the Gospel accounts is a woman who was considered unclean for twelve years (Luke 8:43-48). She was the one who touched the hem of Jesus' robe and received healing from Him. In the case of a woman in this condition, anyone she touched became unclean according to the law, and she was strictly prohibited from doing so. She knew that Christ could heal her, but she was afraid that someone would know about her illness because it was shameful and a reason for contempt. However, Christ's holiness and power were greater than her sin and her illness, and He healed and saved her because of her great faith.

4. Mary Magdalene, who was freed from demonic possession by the Lord (as she was afflicted by seven demons, Luke 8:2), was the chosen one to be the first to witness Jesus Christ alive after His resurrection.

Christ himself restored the testimony of faith-believing, God-fearing women. He restored her fallen nature and made the women the first to carry the message of His resurrection to the other disciples.

Eve's sin brought death and corruption to herself; and when she caused her husband to sin, she caused the sin to be passed on to future generations. However, with Christ, we see that women are now instruments, not to bring judgment and death (as in the case of Eve), but to bring the message of salvation to humanity, that is, the testimony of the resurrection of Jesus.

How then does a woman who has truly been restored by God live? A woman who has been saved by Christ, and who now truly loves Him, presents certain evidence of her new life. Such evidence is at least the following:

1. She loves God above all things, and her neighbor as herself (Matthew 22:37-39).

2. If she is single, she dedicates her life to God, consecrates her heart to Him, and voluntarily sets herself apart to serve Him (1 Corinthians 7:32).

3. If she is married, she is a suitable help for her husband; She helps him to do the will of God. The Christian woman is key to helping her husband make good decisions, that is, decisions that please God. Even if her husband is not a believer, she, through

her testimony, behavior, and love, sanctifies him (1 Corinthians 7:13)

This means that the Christian woman who lives faithful to the Word of God brings blessing to her home. She must encourage even the unbeliever husband by her pious character to do good, and if God so permits, her husband and her children will come to the feet of Christ.

This means that the Christian woman, by her testimony, may help her unconverted husband to live a life that is not consumed by sin, and to live a more moral life (in other words, he would sin less as long as he remains married to her).

4. She knows and uses the Word of God to teach other younger women to walk in the way of Christ, and to love their husbands and children (Titus 2:4).

5. Christian women guide their children to Christ (Titus 2:4).

6. She is not given to wine, nor does she slander anyone, but is prudent (Titus 2:3,5).

7. The woman who truly loves Christ takes care of her house and strengthens her home (Titus 2:5; Proverbs 14:1).

8. She is content to submit to her husband counsel (Titus 2:5).

9. The woman transformed by God dresses modestly, not with ostentatious hairstyles, nor with gold, or pearls, or expensive clothing, but with good works (1 Timothy 2:9-10). This is equivalent, in a culture like ours, to those sensual clothing and attire that invite men to sexual or immoral enjoyment.

Sensual women, that is, those who strive to show the world how beautiful they are in an immoral and provocative way, end up doing things that God hates; and these actions bring condemnation upon themselves, as this causes men to commit adultery in their hearts, and turn away from God. Consequently, a man separated from God's will not be a blessing to his family, nor to his environment or nation.

But if women would clothe themselves with good works, with love for others, with consecration, and their bearing is decent, they will not contribute to being agents of perdition for men, but rather they will help them to restore their hearts before God, being examples of how one should live for the glory of God.

Regarding the roles or functions of men and women, it is evident that after the Fall, women have endeavored to dominate men and reverse the functions instituted by God regarding marriage and the family. Men, for their part, have historically fought to keep women in an inferior position. And all this is a consequence of the lack of understanding of God's will for each one.

The best way to think of a biblical marriage is this: that the man must dearly loves his wife, and should be her guide and strength; He needs to be totally faithful to her (even in the realm of thoughts), and should aid in her sanctification before God; He should be a strong support for her and someone she can fully trust. For her part, the wise and prudent woman will be subject to her husband, she will love him dearly, respect him, trust his direction, and feel safe under his care. This is God's design, and it is precisely the relationship that exists between Jesus and his Church (the bride of Jesus).

> **"But I want you to understand that the head of every man is Christ, the head of a wife is her husband, and the head of Christ is God" (1 Corinthians 11:3).**

The man represents Christ, and the woman the Church. Christ is the one who sanctifies us, loves us, cares for us, protects us; He provides for us, guides us, helps us and sustains us. The Church, for its part, depends on Christ, she is subject to His will; she trusts in Him, honors Him; she is faithful to Him, serves Him and seeks Him with all her heart. Christ came to restore the positions and responsibilities of men and women in marriage. However, there are still believers who do not want to adhere to the perfect will of God, and they stubbornly continue living in the same fallen system of the past.

Man and woman are equal before God in terms of spiritual dignity, intelligence, etc., and they have the same value before God: a woman is as important to God as a man. However, their roles are different. And if I, as a man, delegate my role as spiritual guide to my wife, and she must do what it is my responsibility to do; or if my wife delegates her role to me, and I have to do what she is supposed to do, then we are both not honoring God in the marriage.

The value of women in the time of Christ was not the same as that of men, and their testimony was not very credible. This was something that Christ came to restore. The women disciples had a good testimony since their conversion; they dared to remain at the foot of the cross until Jesus's death; they had shown love in many ways (for example, by going to the grave early on Sunday); nevertheless, even all this, their testimony was not powerful enough. The male disciples should not have despised these women's testimonies, but there is something even more important: they should have trusted the words of Jesus. Eve, being a saint, trusted the word of Satan, but these women, being sinners, trusted the command of the angels and Jesus, and faithfully carried out His command.

The same thing we are commanded to do today: to preach the Gospel, whether people believe or not. When Christians share the Gospel, not everyone will listen; however, they are responsible for preaching the Gospel, and the Holy Spirit will always make His work in peoples' hearts to believe in Christ.

One thing was certain: although the disciples did not believe the women's good news regarding the resurrection of the Lord (and even found their testimonies foolish), they still spent the entire day discussing what had really happened to the body of Jesus. Quickly, the news that Jesus' body was not in the tomb spread throughout the city, and everyone was wondering the same thing as the disciples: where would be the body of Jesus? Regarding this, we can assume that some believed the untrue version of the Roman guards: that the disciples had stolen the body. That was the news of the moment in Jerusalem. Meanwhile, in the midst of all this confusion, there were two disciples who decided to leave the group and return to their old life. We will be reviewing this in the next chapter in which we will learn about the disciples of Emmaus.

Chapter

VII

THE DISCIPLES OF EMMAUS

In this chapter, we will discuss the encounter that Jesus had with two disciples who had heard the testimonies of the women about the resurrection. These disciples, of whom we have not yet studied, had an important interaction with the risen Christ. These two men were with all the other followers of Jesus when the women arrived to deliver the message of the resurrection; however, they didn't believe their testimony either and decided to leave the ministry that Christ had entrusted to them and return to their old lives.

In this chapter, we will study a long portion of Scripture, which I have divided into several parts. I firmly believe that this account of Jesus with the disciples of Emmaus has great teachings, especially for those of us who are already believers.

While reading and studying this narrative, we may find similarities between ourselves and these two individuals. The entire portion of Scripture that I will be discussing in this chapter is found in Luke 24:13-35.

The reason I have to divide this portion into several sections is because I see in each of these topics an important teaching, and these topics will help us better understand the entire passage since they are aspects that have to do with the interaction that Jesus had with these two disciples. I urge you to read these verses in your own Bible before continuing to read this book so that you can better understand the message that we will be studying. The themes I see in each of these sections clearly show a progression. It is a progression with a specific purpose: Christ wanted to put into practice his love and his grace toward these two unbelieving disciples. Let's outline of the topics that we will see in this chapter.

- Luke 24:13-16 — The Meeting.
- Luke 24:17-24 — The Test.
- Luke 24:25 — The Rebuke.
- Luke 24:26-27 — The Instruction.
- Luke 24:28-30 — The Invitation.
- Luke 24:31-32 — The Conviction.
- Luke 24:33-35 — The Call.

Something we can meditate on before continuing with our analysis is: how many disciples did Jesus have? These two disciples were surely not from the twelve apostles, but part of the group of disciples who followed Christ (a group of which we know very little, although Christ did know them well since they were his sheep). We do not know how many disciples truly followed Christ, but perhaps we could get an idea.

Christ had a multitude of disciples, and of all those who followed Him, He chose twelve (Luke 6:6-19). He chose Simon Peter and Andrew his brother; James and his brother John (the beloved disciple); Philip, Bartholomew (also called Nathanael in John 1:45-49), Matthew (also called Levi); Thomas, James the son of Alphaeus, Simon the Zealot, Judas the son of James; and Judas Iscariot. Jesus chose these twelve to be his apostles and leaders. He handpicked them for closer connections and a more personalized teaching approach.

However, the truth is that Jesus had many disciples. On one occasion he sent 70 of them to preach in pairs of two (Luke 10:1). We can also see that at Pentecost, 120 disciples were present. Paul says that 500 people at a time saw the risen Jesus (1 Corinthians 15:6). By the way, it is possible to think that some of these disciples had walked with Jesus from the beginning and were very devout. We see it in the example of Matthias, who was chosen to replace Judas Iscariot as an apostle.

The requirement that Matthias had to meet to replace Judas was to have accompanied Jesus throughout His ministry, from the time John the Baptist baptized Him in the Jordan until the day He was received up into heaven so that he might be witness with the other apostles of His resurrection (Acts 1:12-26). Let's now look at the interaction that occurs when Jesus initially meets these two disciples on their way to Emmaus.

The Meeting

> "That very day two of them were going to a village named Emmaus, about seven miles from Jerusalem, and they were talking with each other about all these things that had happened. While they were talking and discussing together, Jesus himself drew near and went with them. But their eyes were kept from recognizing him" (Luke 24:13-16).

These two disciples had already heard the news of the resurrection; however, like the others, they did not believe the testimonies of the women and decided to return to their old lives. They stopped following Christ since they did not believe in the possibility that a person could survive a crucifixion, much less rise again three days later.

These disciples came from Jerusalem and were probably going to their homes in Emmaus, about 11 km from Jerusalem. Thus, given this distance, it should take them two to three hours of walking to reach their destination. That was a Sunday afternoon, maybe around 4 or 5 pm They had spent all that Sunday arguing about what happened to the body of Jesus with the other disciples, and after this, they decided to return to their hometown, Emmaus. But even on the road, they kept discussing the same topic; it was the current news.

Emmaus means "hot springs", although its location is not known today. Hot springs are a kind of water that normally comes from the underground layers of the earth and springs to the outside with about four or five degrees Celsius more than any other water on the surface. It is possible that there were natural spas in the area, and perhaps this city was a recreational site in the area.

"While they were talking and discussing together, Jesus himself drew near and went with them." (Luke 23:15).

We do not have much data regarding these disciples; however, we might suppose that they kept Jesus company in His ministry long enough, say, perhaps at least two years; however, despite this, it took them a while to recognize Him. Christ veiled their eyes so they would not know who He was, or perhaps changed His appearance. It took hours for them to identify Christ, they couldn't understand that it was Him, the risen Christ. The disciples on the road to Emmaus had followed Jesus in His ministry; they had heard His voice; they knew they loved and believed in Him; yet they had not truly understood Christ's message, while He was with them in his earthly ministry.

I have already commented on how Mary Magdalene, upon hearing her name from the resurrected Jesus, recognized him immediately, practically moments after meeting him. But these two disciples, after walking with Christ for two to three hours on the road from Jerusalem to Emmaus, did not recognize Him.

Let us now try to dive a little deeper into what this meeting means for us (those of us who are disciples of Jesus), and what it means for those who are still not convinced of who He is. It is important to emphasize that these men had been disciples of Christ for probably several years but walking with Him (on the road from Jerusalem to Emmaus) they could not immediately recognize Him; In the same way, it takes a long time for many of us who have started to walk the path of the Gospel to understand who Jesus truly is.

When we really know Christ, when the Word of God comes true in our lives, and we understand who the Lord is, there is a definitive change in us, and that change is so strong that our lives will never be able to continue being the same. Many hear of Christ; many know the story of Jesus and His miracles (since His life is known to almost the entire world). Many who know about Jesus and have some knowledge of Him; yet at the same time, they continue to walk through life spiritually blind.

The truth is that most of us don't know Christ. We have not seen Him as he really is, because if we knew Him indeed, our life would be consumed by our love for him daily. If we knew who Jesus is in all his splendor, and our hearts understood His greatness and what He represents, I'll tell you again, our lives could not continue to be the same. I can't turn away from Christ once he reveals himself by lifting the veil from my eyes. It is practically impossible for my heart not to be confronted every day with my sin if I truly meditate on God's Word every day with a humble heart, and there would be a desire that would lead me to obey him even if I sin.

In this way, many have belonged to a church for years, but God's Word has not yet become true in their hearts. Many live fulfilling what the Word of God mandates but do not truly love it, they are not passionate about it. If this is your case, I'll tell you this: the longing for the Word of God must far exceed any other desire for the things of this world. The Word of God must be your water; your food; your sustenance; your joy; your peace; your light; your guide, and much more because the Word of God leads and guides us to know Christ. The Bible is the Mind of God for us plastered before our eyes to know our Heavenly Father, our Savior Jesus, and the work of the Holy Spirit in us.

Regarding this, the psalmist said: "How sweet are your words to my taste, sweeter than honey to my mouth!" (Psalms 119:103).

The Word of God is sweeter than honey. She should not be a burden to anyone, nor a yoke; if this is the case for someone, it means that they have not yet understood the general message of Scripture, nor have a good relationship with God through the Holy Spirit. The same thing happened to these disciples as to Job. Job knew of God, lived for God, and followed Him; he complied with Him but he did not understand who God was indeed. When the Lord appeared to Job and asked him the 77 questions, he did not know what to say: he was speechless for the first time since his affliction started. It was then that the presence of the Almighty so impressed this man of God that he finally exclaimed: "I had heard of you by the hearing of the ear, but now my eye sees you" (Job 42:5). Hearing God didn't return his deceased children, make his wife more loving of God, but helped Job understand who God is.

The veil was taken from him; and this man, although he was perfect before God (Job 1:8), after his trial, realized how little he knew Him. These disciples had heard of Christ, walked with Him, heard His voice, and obeyed Him; however, their eyes were veiled, and they could not truly see Him and know Him.

Did any of us come to Jesus alone, without being drawn by the Holy Spirit? None of us have come to Christ by our own account. None of us has a genuine desire from our hearts and on our own initiative to seek God, because of this, the intervention of the Holy Spirit is indispensable. Everything that concerns salvation is a gift from the Almighty. Salvation is a priceless gift.

"They have all fallen away; together they have become corrupt; there is none who does good, not even one" (Psalms 53:3).

If none of us have come to God on his/her own, God had to come to us first. God is the one who opens our eyes; He opens our minds to believe His Word. He is the one who gives us the faith to believe. If you understand who Jesus is, it is because He removed the veil from your eyes.

A question arises here: How do I know if I have that veil? This is a difficult question, and it is difficult because you cannot realize how blind you are by yourself. However, we could look at some insights. If your life does not give glory and honor to God; if it is not totally surrendered to Christ; if your constant desire from the moment you wake up until you go to bed is not to do His will with love (before yours); if you are not willing to give your life for Christ and do not enjoy serving Him with all your heart; if reading the Word of God does not bring you great delight; then that veil is still on your eyes. You are still blind to the glory God offers you in His presence; it means that you are still loving more the vanities of this world than God's spiritual fullness.

However, the good news is this: Christ will remove that veil from you if you listen to His voice and follow Him. We have to listen to the voice of Christ and follow Him, otherwise, even as believers, we will live in darkness; worried more about the things of this world; for day to day, for what we need to eat, drink and dress; for the chores and worries of earthly and temporary things; rather than pay our due attention to the eternal things of God.

What is the joy of your heart? Is it thinking about the weekend, the next vacation, your birthday, or a party? Shouldn't it be when night arrives, or early morning, to have your private time with God? Shouldn't it be presenting yourself before God to talk to Him, and learn from Him?

The most fulfilling moments in our lives are those in which we demonstrate our love for our eternal Father and our love for our neighbor. When we demonstrate our love for our neighbor without seeking recognition for our acts of service. It is not about fulfilling a devotional, but about truly loving. When one truly loves God, there is no more special place than being before His altar, breaking our hearts in private, only before Him, before the God who came to seek and save us.

Who am I to receive such love? Do I think I am worthy of such great love from God? Definitely not. It's amazing to think that He sought us out, not the other way around.

"You did not choose me, but I chose you and appointed you that you should go and bear fruit and that your fruit should abide, so that whatever you ask the Father in my name, he may give it to you" (John 15:16).

When Jesus first comes to us, we still do not know Him as He really is, because knowing Him takes time. Christ spent years with His disciples, teaching them, guiding them, speaking to them, and correcting them. In the same way we: spend years attending church and listening to His Word; and we rejoice in it without yet understanding who Jesus really is. However, even if we do not see Him clearly yet, although we may think we do, He does see us, just as we are; He knows us perfectly.

What about a person who believes in Christ, but still curses, has bad thoughts, an unbelieving heart, etc.? If a person lives like this, it means that he has heard of Christ, but his eyes have not yet seen Him. If an individual walks in sin, without bearing spiritual fruits, and it doesn't hurt them in their hearts to live like this, it means that they have heard of Christ, but still can't see Him. I ask now, who are those who follow Christ? Is it possible for anyone to follow Christ? The truth is that the invitation is open to all, but only His sheep can hear His voice and follow Him.

"My sheep hear my voice, and I know them, and they follow me. I give them eternal life, and they will never perish, and no one will snatch them out of my hand" (John 10:27-28).

This is our Christ, our Good Shepherd, who loves us, cares for us; and from whose hand no one, absolutely no one, can snatch us away. Even if I don't see Him in all His splendor, even if I don't clearly understand who He really is, he does see me and knows me. Even if I feel lost along the way, my Good Shepherd knows exactly where I am. I am completely secure in Him if I am truly His. I may not fully understand who He is yet, but He does know who I am.

Do you know what we are? We are a gift from God the Father to his Son Jesus Christ, we are His Church, the bride of Christ. We are a part humanity that is to be rescued from sin and restored through the precious blood of Christ. Jesus came to sanctify humanity through His blood when He died for us. Adam allowed himself to be corrupted by his wife, but Jesus forgave and sanctified His wife, who had been corrupted by sin just like Eve was.

"I am the good shepherd. The good shepherd lays down his life for the sheep. My Father, who has given them to me, is greater than all, and no one is able to snatch them out of the Father's hand" (John 10:11, 29).

That is why Luke 24:32 says that the hearts of the disciples of Emmaus burned when they heard His voice, since they were of His flock: hearing the voice of their Shepherd — the voice of Jesus Christ. It gave them great joy, although they could not recognize Him immediately.

During His three years of ministry, Jesus spoke constantly to the crowds and performed many miracles before their eyes; however, even so, they did not believe Him. Why didn't these disciples believe Jesus when He predicted His resurrection? They had already seen with their own eyes such great wonders of God. There was so much evidence to confirm that Jesus was living the fulfillment of God's as the Messiah.

- *The time was right.* We see how John the Baptist giving testimony of Him, and John was the prophet who came to prepare the way for the Messiah (Malachi 4:5-6).
- *His lineage was correct.* Christ was descended from King David, both through the line of Mary and Joseph, and

the prophecy said that the Messiah would be a descendant of David (2 Samuel 7:1-17).

- *His deeds were correct.* He performed many miracles, freed many from demon possession, and healed all kinds of diseases (Matthew 8:16-18).
- *His life was perfect.* Jesus Christ never sinned (Hebrews 4:15).
- *His message was correct.* Christ was zealous for the Word, forgiving, full of love and grace, always showing mercy to the repentant in heart, and rebuking the haughty (Luke 4:18).
- *His death was announced.* He was the Lamb who laid down his life for us (Isaiah 53).
- *His prophetic word was the right one.* Christ himself predicted His death and resurrection (Luke 18:33).

The Lord Jesus lived such a holy life that His enemies had to lie and condemn Him at night so that no one would find out that they were condemning Him unjustly, because they could not find a real reason to accuse Him.

Why then did the people of Israel not believe? Christ said, "But you do not believe because you are not among my sheep" (John 10:26). If you are not interested in hearing the voice of God, if this is not your deepest desire and most precious yearning, then you must ask yourself: Am I a sheep of Christ? Why don't I long to hear his voice? Why doesn't my heart burn when I hear or read his Word?

If Christ is calling you to come to Him; if you have not yet been born again; or if you have believed in Christ, but still persist in living in sin, apart from God and His Word, what are you waiting for to give yourself, once and for all, in totally surrender to Jesus Christ?

In this passage, the disciples of Emmaus are sought out by Christ himself. This means that, even if we stray from the path, if we are truly part of His church, children of God, then we will listen to His voice, we will be sensitive to His Word, and finally, we will turn to Him. Christ came to look for his lost sheep (The Emmaus Disciples), to bring them back to the fold.

The Exam

Jesus is currently revealing the disciples' hearts to expose the extent of their distorted views and misconceptions about the Messiah. We observe how Christ came to them to share His interpretation of the events that transpired a few days prior. But before, He desired to know if they grasped the wonderful truth that his death and resurrection had bought their lives and that their sins were already pardoned.

> "That very day two of them were going to a village named Emmaus, about seven miles from Jerusalem, and they were talking with each other about all these things that had happened. While they were talking and discussing together, Jesus himself drew near and went with them. But their eyes were kept from recognizing him. And he said to them, "What is this conversation that you are holding with each other as you walk?" And they stood still, looking sad. Then one of them, named Cleopas, answered him, 'Are you the only visitor to Jerusalem who does not know the things that have happened there in these days?'" (Luke 24:13-18).

In Luke 14:17 we notice first, that when Jesus asked them what they were talking about, their countenance changed. It is possible that, at that moment, the disciples stopped walking or stood still, paralyzed from the question, and thinking about how to answer this. The pain in their hearts was so great, they were so broken by what they were experiencing, that they could not but express their sadness; and that attitude alone was a demonstration of the sincere love they truly had for Jesus.

Nevertheless, their faith was not placed on the truth of who Jesus was, why? Because of their perception of what they understood to be true, was false; they believed *sincerely* that Jesus was the king who would free them from the bond of Rome; the leader who would restore the earthly kingdom of Israel during that time. Their faith was placed in the right person, but given they had their own idolatrous and false idea of who Jesus was to be, they missed who He truly was.

Cleopas could not believe Jesus' question (v.18). It would seem unlikely that some did not know of the injustice committed towards the God made Man just three days back. By the way, Cleopas is the only one of the two disciples who is mentioned by name here.

Who was this man? Cleopas was a faithful disciple of Jesus Christ, one who loved Him and who followed Him during His ministry; he was part of a family devoted to the service of Christ.

Perhaps the reason he is mentioned by name is that he was most likely married to Mary, the mother of James, son of Alphaeus. It is believed that Cleopas and Alphaeus are actually the same person, since the Hebrew etymology of these two names is very similar. Epiphanius (315-403) wrote that Joseph (Jesus' adoptive father) and Cleopas were brothers, and that both were sons of Jacob; if this is so, Cleopas was technically the uncle of Jesus of Nazareth, but this is not verified in Scripture. Also, we see mentioned to be present at the crucifixion: Jesus' mother, His aunt (His mother's sister), and Mary Magdalene (John 19:25). Would there then be next to the cross a blood aunt and an aunt by marriage, in addition to His mother and Mary Magdalene?

In Matthew 27:56 three women are mentioned. Two of them are mentioned by name (Mary), but in reality, all three were called Mary. One of these Marys mentioned was the wife of Cleopas, who also had a son named James (who was part of the twelve) and another son named Joseph.

At least four James are mentioned in the NT: two of them were part of the twelve apostles of Christ; a third James, the brother of Jesus; and a fourth James, the father of Judas Thaddeus (not the Iscariot). Of these, two James were apostles: one was the son of Zebedee (John's brother), and the other James was the son of Alphaeus (or Cleopas) and Mary, who incidentally was the younger of the two James apostles and because of this was called James the Less.

Mary, the wife of Cleopas, was one of those who saw the risen Jesus and one of those who brought the good news of the resurrection to the apostles (Luke 24:10). This was the message that the disciples judged as nonsense and madness. And if Cleopas was married to Mary (the mother of James, the apostle, and Joseph), then we deduce something surprising: he had not believed the testimony of his wife; that is, he thought that his wife was talking nonsense, and he did not believe anything she had said.

Perhaps, in those moments, Cleopas could be thinking: "What is going on here? Jesus, our hope of the restoration of Israel has died, my son has already lost the opportunity to be a great man in Israel, and now my wife has lost her head and is saying crazy things. I can't put up with this situation anymore, I will return home, I will return to Emmaus."

Cleopas was confused, and possibly he wanted to go back to Emmaus to continue doing what he used to do before following Jesus. Cleopas was a sheep straying from the fold, one returning to his old life, leaving the ministry Christ had commanded him. His heart began to stray from the truth, even since he closed his heart to his wife's testimony. However, the Lord, in His patience, does not allow him to stray too far, He goes himself to meet him where he is, to open his understanding of knowing the true Christ.

You can be confident that as one of Jesus' sheep, you are under the care of a Good Shepherd. When you're lost, he will come for you. I only ask you to be attentive and to listen to his voice when He speaks to you through His Word. Brethren, Christ came to look for us, the King of glory, majesty and power, the Creator of heaven, earth and everything that exists. The most important Being in eternity will focus especially on you, to find you and bring you back to His fold. What humility and meekness of our God! He has no need of me, but He knows my need and dependence on Him.

Cleopas answered Jesus and said: "Are you the only visitor in Jerusalem who does not know what has happened these days?" In other words, where were you during Easter? Are you the only foreigner who doesn't know about this? It cannot be that you ignore what has happened these days! Cleopas then gives Him a brief account of what he understood regarding everything that had happened.

"And he said to them, 'What things?' And they said to him, 'Concerning Jesus of Nazareth, a man who was a prophet mighty in deed and word before God and all the people, and how our chief priests and rulers delivered him up to be condemned to death, and crucified him. But we had hoped that he was the one to redeem Israel. Yes, and besides all this, it is now the third day since these things happened. Moreover, some women of our company amazed us. They were at the tomb early in the morning, and when they did not find his body, they came back

saying that they had even seen a vision of angels, who said that he was alive. Some of those who were with us went to the tomb and found it just as the women had said, but him they did not see." (Luke 24:19-24).

When Christ asked them, "What things?" (v. 19), he was wanting them to explain what they thought or believed they knew to be true regarding what just had occurred in Israel. In other words, Jesus was asking them: "What is it that you think that just happened in Israel? What do you understand about these events?" Christ wanted to show them their great ignorance regarding the biblical message of the Messiah; and that the interpretation they had of what happened to Him in those days was totally wrong. The reality was this: these disciples did not know who Jesus was yet.

They viewed Jesus of Nazareth as a powerful prophet, but they did not recognize His divinity. They thought He was like Elijah, Isaiah, or Moses: a great and powerful prophet of God; perhaps like no other, very powerful in deed and word, like none of His predecessors, but nothing beyond. They were convinced that Jesus had unequaled understanding and that He handled and understood the Scripture as if He had written them himself. But their mind failed to comprehend that Jesus was, really was: the Son of the living God, and God incarnated.

Likewise, they accepted that the works of Jesus could only come from God and that no other prophet beforehand did as many works as Christ; yet, they had not truly seen Jesus for who He was. The truth is that these men sincerely loved and followed Jesus. They witnessed His ministry and could speak of His works firsthand (things they saw with their own eyes); they had the authority to tell this stranger what they knew of Jesus: the power, miracles, and great things that Christ had done (v. 19); they could bear witness to His crucifixion and death (v. 20); likewise, they also testified to the empty tomb (v. 22-24); however, these disciples were missing the most important, essential and crucial part: believing and bearing witness to the resurrected Christ. In Luke 24:21 we can see here what they understood regarding Christ:

"But we had hoped that he was the one to redeem Israel." (Luke 24:21).

These two disciples expected Jesus to be the long-awaited Redeemer of Israel. The Jewish people —even today— have the same longing and understanding of the Messiah. They had been expecting one who would finally rule the land through a theocratic kingdom in the nation, and with whom they were to lead in high positions in the government. They thought they would be freed from Roman oppression. By the way, you must understand that the Jews had been subjugated under other nations during Jesus' time for over 600 years now, and they were hungry for political freedom and independence.

Since 583 BC (which was the year Judah was taken captive to Babylon), the Jews had been in subjugation. After the Babylonians, the Medo-Persian Empire came, followed by the Greeks, and now —from 63 BC—, the Romans were ruling Israel. By then, they were already in the year 30-33 AD and the Jews were tired, they had been waiting for God to bring them a liberator (as in the time of the judges) or a king like David, and thus again be an independent kingdom, one that would recover the earthly glory they had during the time of king David and king Solomon. God had already done it dozens of times with the judges, kings, and prophets before Christ and they expected the Messiah to do the same.

The disciples of Christ had in mind to be free from that government's oppression; they had an earthly in mind, a political and temporary salvation. They didn't understand the message of Christ or the meaning of His kingdom. However, Christ had made it clear that His kingdom was not of this world (John 18:36). The Lord consistently communicated in spiritual language, focusing on freeing people from sin. He spoke of eternal life and death; from heavenly abodes and hell. Jesus never got involved in politics, and even spoke ill of the Roman government. He said: "Give to Caesar what is Caesar's..." (Matthew 22:21).

This resembles the life of many today. People constantly complain about the government, work, what they lack at home; they hope that things will change through a better government. Their hope is placed in a political leader who will fix all their problems. They think a brighter economic future and of more and better opportunities for material growth, etc. However, as life goes by, they do not realize that all these things are temporary. Even that having a great government that cares for people is great, it is very foolish to place our faith in political leadership and not in the God that gives all authority.

We must realize that believers are the ones who transform the world by depending on God. This transformation impacts everyone around us, starting with our family, our friends, and workspace. In this way, if every person in the nation would love and fear God, most of the social problems would disappear. God has placed the Church in the world to be the salt of the earth and the light of the world.

Like these disciples, many of us have our eyes veiled, despite being believers in Christ. Our hearts are set on earthly things rather than on Jesus, the Author of our faith. We can hear about Jesus, go to church, and say we are His disciples and still not really know the One we say we believe in.

Let's ask God for wisdom so that this veil would be removed from our eyes to see our glorious Christ and understand who He truly is. Let us imagine Jesus standing before us, speaking to us through His Word. We still may remain blind to Him, unable to recognize Him, but the Lord is constantly speaking into our lives, through friends, family, preachers, church brothers, books, etc. Therefore, we can't have an excuse to seek Him truly.

The Rebuke

The verses we will be studying now are related to what the Word of God produces when we truly listen to it, and how it confronts us. God's Word can be misinterpreted or misunderstood; therefore, we must always have a humble heart to recognize the truth (even if I may currently differ from what is being shown clearly to me). The Holy Spirit rebukes us and corrects us through his Word.

We see an example in these two disciples, who had lived their entire lives misinterpreting the Word of God. They had in mind a political Messiah who would free them from their current condition, but their faith was in the wrong place; they had twisted the Word of God in order to make it fit their cultural and social condition and fulfill their desires. However, the Bible —the Word of God— transcends and goes beyond all ages; therefore, it cannot be interpreted in the light of my own situation, nor can it be molded to my desires or my thoughts. Rather, I must look for its original meaning, that is, what God intended us to know about in the Bible, and this understanding is what must be applied to my life.

Those of us who have had children or currently are raising children know that we must constantly correct them so that they learn to live righteously. We understand that teaching a child to do evil is unnecessary as evil is already inherent in our nature. If parents fail to consistently guide their children to do what is right, there is a high likelihood that these children will grow up to be disobedient and arrogant, lacking respect for authority, including their own parents. For this reason, since Jesus is our Good Shepherd, He went out to meet these men —who were His sheep—, so that, after listening to their misconceptions, He would rebuke these interpretations with the Word of God and instruct them on the actual true revelation.

What happens when we have a wrong concept of God? Why is it so important that we interpret the Bible correctly? The Word of God must be understood and applied correctly, otherwise, we will have our faith placed on false hope, which, when tested, will crumble very easily. This was what happened with these men. If they believed in Jesus as a political liberator (according to their Bible-based beliefs), when this did not happen, their lives fell apart, and their faith in God plummeted to unbelief and despair.

We can believe that we serve God, that we follow and obey Him, but if what we think and do is not based on God's truth, our idea of God will not be true either. If our expectations of His behavior and thoughts do not match His Word, we will live a life filled with frustration, lacking true understanding, and holding onto a faith that is misplaced and misguided, ultimately causing us to doubt God. We could then say; why does God do this to me? Why doesn't God answer my prayer? Why did God allow all this to happen to me? etc.

If faith is set on a certain belief, and this belief is not correct or true, then my faith cannot be a true faith either, and my trust in God will be shaken during trials and afflictions. Therefore, to have a strong and tenacious faith, my belief should always be based on the true interpretation of Scripture, and I must conform my thinking to what God has revealed to us there. On the other hand, let us be clear what Jesus pursues with His rebuke: it is not to destroy, insult, harm or humiliate us, rather, what He wants is to take us to His feet to contemplate Him for who He truly is.

Some points that we are going to touch now are:

- Without understanding, there is no true faith.
- Faith needs to be based on a correct knowledge of the Bible.
- True faith withstands tests.
- True faith is lived daily.
- Faith is a Gift of God to us.

"And he said to them, 'O foolish ones, and slow of heart to believe all that the prophets have spoken! (Luke 24:25).

WITHOUT UNDERSTANDING, THERE IS NO TRUE FAITH

In this passage, Jesus rebuked the disciples on the road to Emmaus for not believing His Words, nor the testimonies of the women. Jesus faithfully spent years teaching them the truth, but they did not believe, understand, or accept it. They ended up with a completely mistaken understanding of why Christ came. They believed in Christ as the Messiah, but their lack of understanding prevented them from having enough faith to continue following Him in the midst of His affliction.

Some may believe they know a lot about a subject, but it may not be so. Proof of this could be the number of people who participate in forums giving their opinion and posing as experts, but who do not master the subject, nor do they have enough authority. However, the listeners will not realize this until they are confronted by another (an expert) who exposes the superficial misconceptions that those presumptuous have. In this way, the true expert in a certain topic will have the opportunity to correct, clarify things and align them with the correct instruction.

This happened with these Jewish disciples, faithful followers of Christ, who truly loved Him, but their understanding of the Word was lacking. Their faith was not based on a true understanding of Christ; for if it were, they would have never decided to abandon the other disciples; yet their faith was somewhat superficial, and they could not have greater faith because they lacked understanding.

Faith can only be sustained if it is based on the truth that the Bible clearly reveals. Otherwise, it is not faith in God, but a superstition. A person can have faith in what is revealed by God if they understand it, otherwise their faith will be baseless. A new convert can have a lot a faith but will lack spiritual maturity given of the lack of comprehension of the Bible. A person who has identified as a Christian for an extended period without dedicating time to spiritual growth through regular study of the Bible and active faith practice may exhibit a lack of spiritual maturity, resembling a new believer in many aspects.

This is why a new convert should try to limit (not avoid) his service to God to the local church first, to mature enough in faith, so that later, in God's time, he/she can serve in a personal ministry. Otherwise, due to this lack of knowledge, and understanding of the Word, it will be easy for he/she to be deceived, and fall into temptations. The faith of a new convert is not yet mature enough or equipped to withstand the temptations and trials that might come in the ministry. Regarding this, and speaking of those who wish to be bishops or deacons, Paul writes to Timothy:

"He must not be a recent convert, or he may become puffed up with conceit and fall into the condemnation of the devil."
(1 Timothy 3:6).

When a person puts his faith in something besides biblical truth, that faith will be unfruitful, lasting, or will it help him/her to resist problems when they come. If I believe something that is not supported by the Scriptures, then that faith is not in God, but a false perception of what I believe to be truth.

When we ask for something in prayer before the Lord, are we basing our prayer on the Word of God? Are we praying according to God's will? If we pray this way, we can expect God to listen and act through our prayers, which He promised to do: "Therefore I tell you, whatever you ask in prayer, believe that you have received it, and it will be yours" (Mark 11:24). God acts when we believe in his Word; He knows the best for each of us, He desires to be the best for each of His children,

On the other hand, the devil's job is to make us doubt the Word of God, everything that God has said in favor of humanity. And when this enemy of God manages to make us doubt God, then faith vanishes, there can be no faith, and "And without faith it is impossible to please him..." (Hebrews 11:6).

Jesus called us to have faith in God, that is, in what He has said and promised. It is wonderful to trust in the Word of God and expect great things from Him. The psalmist said: "I believe that I shall look upon the goodness of the Lord in the land of the living" (Psalms 27:13). Therefore, every Christian must place their faith in Christ, that He will show us His love and kindness, that He will be our help in all the tribulations that arise in life. The Bible says that… "God is our refuge and strength, a very present help in trouble" (Psalms 46:1). So, we can all place our faith and trust in the promises of the Lord.

But when you pray to God, do not come haughty, nor ask anything for your selfish benefit, for God has been merciful to us (1 Timothy 1:13). We always must recognize that the only thing we deserve is to be condemned for our sins. However, due to His everlasting love and grace, God has let us come into His presence through the blood of Jesus, and He lends an ear to our prayers. So, when you come before your Heavenly Father, before the King of kings, before the Lord of lords, before the Holy of Holies, whom no one has seen, nor will ever be able to see, before the one who is full of glory and majesty, whose throne we are not worthy to look at, let us come before Him as David came, humble, humiliated, broken, and bowed.

In the Bible, we can see that God loved David very much, and after reading what he did in a certain episode of his life, this fact might seem very surprising to us. If we only read what happened to him in 2 Samuel 11, we would have the image of a terrible man, a man who did not keep his heart from committing adultery with the wife of one of his most faithful soldiers, and later he murdered him; these are the actions of a terrible man! One of whom we could never say he was "after God's own heart" (Acts 13:22). However, by reading the Psalms we can understand why God loved him so much. He understood who he was before God, and he always prayed humbling himself before Him, with a sincere heart, searching for intimacy with God, without hiding anything from Him, and being aware of the condition of his heart.

In Daniel 3 we read of Sadrac, Mesac and Abednego. They showed faith in God by refusing to worship the statue of Nebuchadnezzar, agreeing to die, if necessary, rather than bow their knees before it. They knew that God had the power to deliver them from death, but even if He would not deliver them, their faith would not change. This is a faith truly placed in God. If I trust that my faith can manipulate

God's will, then my faith is misplaced, as God cannot be controlled. If I pray demanding that God would do my will, then it means that I have put myself in His place, I am not accepting His authority over me. Satan is an example of what I am saying. Satan, the angel of light, became what he is now due to his sin of rebellion (Ezekiel 28:2), because he wanted to sit on the throne of God, pretending the Almighty to obey him or at least be equal to him.

The story of the three young Hebrews in Daniel 3 ends when God saves them from death, leaving us all a great lesson: the faith of Sadrac, Mesac and Abednego was placed in God, and they remained firm in Him no matter what, come what may. They were not worried about what would happen to them, but just placed their faith in God. Christ, our Lord, said, "Have faith in God" (Mark 11:22). First-century Christians had great faith in God; also, Paul had great faith in God. However, the Lord allowed His church to suffer persecution, pain, suffering, and death, and this happened precisely because they had faith in God and were willing to suffer anything for Him.

In the parable of the Sower in Mark 4:3-20 we find four types of people:

1. Those who do not understand the Word (those along the road) (v.4): These are the ones who hear the Word, but Satan immediately removes it from their hearts; they prefer to listen to the voice of their father (the devil) rather than to hear the voice of our heavenly Father. In other words, they have no interest in what has been preached, and it is as if they have never heard anything. This could be the case of a believer who walks in sin at that moment in his life, therefore, the Word of God has no effect on them.

2. The joyful (those on the stony ground) (vv. 5-6): These are the ones who receive the Word of God with joy, but have no deep root; thus, their faith is not lasting but temporary: when affliction or persecution comes because of their belief they stumble and fall. Many times, these are the ones that focus on purely emotional things. They do not worry about filtering their emotions through the teachings of the Bible, nor do they dedicate time to their spiritual growth, therefore their biblical foundations are not strong enough. Joy leaves because they have not matured in their faith.

3. The worried (those with thorns) (v. 7): These are the ones who listen to the Word of God, but the worries and problems of this life, the deceitfulness of riches and the desires for the things of the world drown out their faith. These may also be believers who get involved in many chores, worry with great distress for their needs, and are overwhelmed by day-to-day problems. This happens because they haven't completely placed their trust in God. They listen to the Word of God, but they don't understand it, they haven't learned to place their worries unto God. They may study it, they may preach it and may teach it to others, but when the test comes, their hearts crumble, they see no way out of their situation and don't understand God is the one that brings trials to our lives to teach us to depend on Him.

4. Those who bear fruit (Mk. 4:8): These are the ones who hear the Word of God, accept it, believe it, understand it, and bear fruit. These listen to the Word of God, receive it with joy, and they do not let the problems of this life —however difficult they may be— take away their confidence in the One who gave them life, but rather, amid of all the trials, difficulties and persecutions, continue to bear fruit and show clear evidence that they love God above all else. It doesn't mean the trials won't be difficult, but their knowledge or understanding of God shows them God has them there for a reason. These believers have their faith in the right place.

When I truly believe in the Word of God then, as a Christian, I must bear fruit. If I don't bear fruit, it's because I haven't truly believed yet. Believing always involves action. I can say that I believe in Jesus, that He rose from the dead, but if my belief is distorted, thinking that He only rose in spirit, or that this is something symbolic, my belief automatically becomes false, therefore, it will not bring true fruit, nor salvation. Also, I may believe Jesus was resurrected, but my life reflects that I'm not a believer, then I know the truth, but I don't understand what this means, and therefore have not truly believed given there has been no change in my life.

Faith Needs to be Based on a Correct Knowledge of the Word

In this section, we will see what the Bible says about the importance of having a correct and true understanding of the Word of

God. Likewise, we will see the consequences of not having that understanding.

> **"And he gave the apostles, the prophets, the evangelists, the shepherds and teachers, to equip the saints for the work of ministry, for building up the body of Christ, until we all attain to the unity of the faith and of the knowledge of the Son of God, to mature manhood, to the measure of the stature of the fullness of Christ, so that we may no longer be children, tossed to and fro by the waves and carried about by every wind of doctrine, by human cunning, by craftiness in deceitful schemes" (Ephesians 4:11-14).**

God has placed believers around us, elders, deacons, and other knowledgeable people, and has left us His Word with the purpose that together we can be edified through its preaching. God's purpose is that we may grow in Him and become spiritually mature, with a full and true knowledge of Christ. The reason for this knowledge —says the passage from Ephesians— is that we reach spiritual maturity, so we may be like Christ. Well, how could I mature if there is no desire in me to study and learn the Word of God, and grow in the knowledge of Him? We scrutinize the Word not to flaunt our knowledge, but because we really love our heavenly Father, because we want to know Him and be more like Him.

What happens if we do not mature in faith? We will be like a spiritual child, and thus, the lack of maturity will lead us to be moved by any wind of doctrine (Ephesians 4:14), to believe what any pastor or preacher says from a pulpit (even if what he says is not biblical, or they made an erroneous interpretation), we will not be able to distinguish between true and false bible teaching.

One of the signs of true spiritual maturity is discernment. Those with insight are able to make accurate judgments, differentiate between right and wrong, and discern between good and evil. Spiritual discernment makes the Christian recognize when a doctrine, teaching or preaching is <u>well-founded</u> in the Word of God; and if the person is not sure, as a mature Christian they would search the Holy Scripture, would seek the guidance of others, and the Holy Spirit, to be sure that what has been taught is true. A developed Christian would be able to admit their errors when faced with the truth.

The disciples of Emmaus were shaken because their knowledge and understanding of the person of Christ and His mission was wrong. Although they had seen Jesus, heard, and touched Him. Although they had walked with Him for a long time, they still did not understand the purpose of His coming. Since they had a wrong concept of the person of Jesus, their hope was placed on a false foundation, on something that God had not promised. They were true believers, but their faith was not well-founded. Their hopes were placed on something visible, earthly, and temporary, in liberation from political oppression; while Christ came to give them a spiritual liberation, to free them from sin.

Truly knowing Christ leads us to believe:

- In what He has revealed of Himself.
- In how He has revealed it.
- In the correct biblical context.
- Within the historical context of Jesus time; and,
- In putting faith into action before the world (showing our true love for Christ).

It wouldn't be correct that I would erroneously transport the Bible to the 21st century mentality, but rather, it is I who must transport myself to the historical time in which it was written, to understand its context to the best of my ability. If what I teach is a mere personal interpretation of the Word, looking for passages that support my ideology, altering it to support what I believe, and ignoring what I disagree with, then the knowledge I will have it is no more than an idolatry, a false god that I have created to serve my own benefit and enjoyment, by adulterating the Word of God for my benefit. This is why, if my understanding of Christ is wrong, I will have a false Christ before me, like the one these disciples of Emmaus expected. They wanted or expected another Jesus, not the Jesus who died on the cross.

Christ told Thomas in John 20:29 "Jesus said to him, 'Have you believed because you have seen me? Blessed are those who have not seen and yet have believed.'" When Thomas saw Christ physically, he finally became truly convinced that Jesus had risen. When he saw Him in person, he was finally convinced that he was to surrender all his heart, his sin, his desires, his longings, all at the feet of Jesus, because he saw Him, and he believed.

We shouldn't judge Thomas on this, because before seeing the risen Christ not one of the disciples believed that Christ would rise again because their faith was not in the right place, and because of this it couldn't be a true reliable faith. They did not understand what Jesus had taught them, so they could not bear fruit. Again, they were true believers with an immature faith. By the way, at that time, before the resurrection, these disciples of Jesus could have never given their lives for Him, because they really did not know Him yet, nor did they understand His Words.

True Faith Withstands Tests

I can have faith in Christ without yet fully understanding who He really is. And of course, for as long as we are not in God's glory yet in heaven, we will never know Christ on the spiritual level in comparison with those who are already with Him. However, we can know, understand, believe, and live what has been revealed about Him in the Word of God. If I don't know Christ, as He has been revealed in the Bible, then, in the midst of trials, the faith that I say I have will not endure, and that trial will not fulfill its purpose in me, it will not help me to mature. In such a case, the tests may cause a person to succumb and desist from continuing to follow Jesus; and the Word that has been planted in him/her will be like the one that fell on rocky ground (Mark 4:5-6).

If you are a new believer, or even if you have been attending a church for many years but have not yet dedicated yourself to studying the Word of God, I urge you to take the necessary time to know Jesus through the pages of Scripture, the One who has revealed himself to humanity in the Bible. The conviction that comes from the constant study of His Word, praying to our God, and humbling yourself before Him, will help you mature, and then you will be prepared when trials and afflictions come: you will have your heart in the right place.

If you do not have a correct understanding of the Word of God, then you will have no defense against the temptations and trials that will come into your life. I can tell you, without me being a prophet, that trials will come into your life. If you do not have the shield of faith (Ephesians 6:16), then these trials, and attacks that you receive will have no defense. You will see yourself fighting against the fiery arrows of the enemy without a sword and without a shield.

Only the correct understanding of the Word of God can transform our hearts, placing our faith in a true spiritual reality. If a person is convinced of a lie, this lie will not transform for the good his/her life (even if he/she is very sincere in what they believe). It is possible to be sincerely wrong.

> **"Count it all joy, my brothers, when you meet trials of various kinds, for you know that the testing of your faith produces steadfastness. And let steadfastness have its full effect, that you may be perfect and complete, lacking in nothing." (James 1:2-4).**

We must see trials as a gift from God, not as mere afflictions; however, it is not easy to see them when we are in the middle of them. We must receive trials with joy, that is, accepting His will, knowing that our heavenly Father knows what is best for us every day of our lives, and He has sent this trial into my life. Trials should make us seek God for His provision and deliverance. They encourage us to bend our knees towards Him and be patient, trusting in our Father. They should keep us close to our heavenly father in constant prayers. These are meant to help us realize how dependent we are on God, and how fragile and weak we are without Him.

If you see a car online for sale and decide to buy it (because it looks like new, and the seller says it's in excellent condition) how will you know it works if you've never started or driven it? Also, how will you know if your faith is true if it is never tested? How will you know your level of dependence on God without going through the trials in your life?

Trials are meant to draw us closer to Christ so that we recognize that we are completely dependent on Jesus for everything so that by spending enough time with Christ, we become more like Him. Therefore, let us receive the trials with joy, by praising God and honoring Him in the middle of them, just like Christ did, who came to this world knowing He would be afflicted for us, and for the joy before Him gave His life for our rescue. We can see how the faith of the Emmaus' disciples was tested to forge them into the image of God, so that they would understand who Jesus really was and what was the purpose of His death on the cross.

When we hear and believe the Word of God, it will reach the depths of our being and God will bring about the change we need.

"For the word of God is living and active, sharper than any two-edged sword, piercing to the division of soul and of spirit, of joints and of marrow, and discerning the thoughts and intentions of the heart." (Hebrews 4:12).

A key question would be: is the Word of God penetrating our thoughts and hearts? If it's not, it is perhaps because we don't have true faith yet. I can know about the Bible, but perhaps I am not convinced that this is the truth, since with my mouth I say I believe, but when affliction comes, my faith fades. If I put my faith in the things of this world, in temporary things, when these things are removed from my life, my world will be broken, and the ruin will be great. Nevertheless, if I choose to trust in God, I will always turn to Him and give Him praise when temporary things are taken away from me. My praise should be just as Job said, "And he said, 'Naked I came from my mother's womb, and naked shall I return. The Lord gave, and the Lord has taken away; blessed be the name of the Lord.'" (Job 1:21).

What if my knowledge of the Word is not correct? Then I will not be able to discern between good and evil; between what is false and true; I will not be able to see how dirty and dark my thoughts are. So, if this does not happen, there will be no confrontation with my sin, and there will be no repentance, nor will there be true transformation in me.

The trend today is to preach attractive sermons that encourage the clowns. Some of these messages even applaud worldliness. Those who preach these things promise people that their teachings will make them live better, happier, and freer; however, how can this be possible without facing their sin? Ponder this: what good is it for people to attend a church whose preaching makes them feel good, but since sin is not confronted, there is no root change in their lives? Everything in their lives continues the same. Then, when the trial comes, the faith they think they have will immediately evaporate.

False teachings will lead us to have an incorrect idea of God, Jesus, and the Spirit of God; consequently, your faith in God, and in Christ will be founded on a false idea of who they are. Due to this, your faith will be bound to fail when the trials come to test it.

The faith the Emmaus' disciples had in Christ was in the wrong place, in the wrong understanding of Christ, therefore, their belief in what He came to do did not correspond to reality; therefore, Christ rebuked them, saying, "O foolish ones, and slow of heart to believe all that the prophets have spoken!" (Luke 24:25).

The Greek word that Luke used (translated into English as *fools*, is "Anoetos") is a compound word: "A" (without) and "Noieo" (to think) or "without understanding." What Christ was saying to these disciples was this: "You are not thinking," you are not analyzing with proper logic the words I have taught you.

The profound richness of Christ's truth will remain beyond complete comprehension for anyone, but at the same time, He revealed Himself in His blessed Word so that we may meditate on it daily. The truth is that, like the disciples of Emmaus, any of us could be sincerely wrong, and worship Jesus incorrectly due to a lack of knowledge. However, one thing is clear: the Lord will direct His sheep and lead them into His presence because His sheep listen to His voice (John 10:27). Just as the Lord Jesus went looking for these disciples of Emmaus, He will also reveal himself to us as long as we seek him with all our hearts. He will guide us to the truth.

True Faith is Lived Daily

The Christian faith is lived minute by minute, day by day, week by week, year by year. It is a continuous and daily search, with all our heart, with the presence of the Spirit of God in our lives, who always sanctifies and helps us. Although our fight against sin continues, we have God's guarantee of victory through His Spirit. He gives us the understanding to do His will and live as His beloved children, His children will seek to be like their heavenly Father. However, all those who continue to practice sin lack spiritual understanding and are slow of heart to believe in Jesus and His word. Let's look at the following verse:

> "But be doers of the word, and not hearers only, deceiving yourselves. For if anyone is a hearer of the word and not a doer, he is like a man who looks intently at his natural face in a mirror. For he looks at himself and goes away and at once forgets what he was like. But the one who looks into the perfect law, the law of liberty, and perseveres, being no hearer who forgets but a doer who acts, he will be blessed in his doing."
> (James 1:22-25).

If a person listens to the word of God, reads it, studies it, and is continually exposed to it, but there has not yet been a change in their life, and he/she persists in the same sins and bad habits; he/she persists in their lust, lies, cheating, adultery, in their sexual immorality; or continues to covet what belongs to others, then a true salvation has not likely taken place in he/she. This person deceives himself/herself thinking that he/she has believed the Word.

This passage shows us a person who exposes themselves to the Word of God, and when they see their condition, then recognizes that they must change their way of living, thinking, speaking, and acting; however, once the exposure to the Word ends, that person does not make any decisions or make any changes in their life. Rather, they leave, forget about it, and persist in their sin. This means that if we receive the Word of God with joy, or are confronted when we hear it, but there is no change in our way of living, we are only hearers of the Word.

As we examine the Word of God closely and with love, studying and practicing it diligently, we show that we have been transformed by the Gospel. We have then become doers of the Word.

God needs to be the first person on my mind when I rise out of bed, who leads me to sleep as I lay in bed every night. If God doesn't consume my heart this way daily, this is a sign that I have not yet understood the love I should have for God. God does not demand 10%, 20%, 30%, or 90% from us, he wants 100% of us to be His because He bought us completely for Himself with the precious blood of Jesus (1 Peter 1:19).

If I am a forgetful listener, then I will not be able to persevere in the Word of God; and the blessedness mentioned by James is for those who persevere in faith. How can a person give evidence that they persevere in faith? By constantly bearing fruit for God. That is why James also says:

> **"So also faith by itself, if it does not have works, is dead" (James 2:17).**

The disciples on the road to Emmaus had not yet understood the Word of God. They never came to truly understand what Christ had instructed them. Their faith was tested, and it turned out to be a weak, vain, and dead faith, and as a result, they reverted to their former lives and neglected their calling. Their faith had plummeted because they did not comprehend the Word of God.

Faith is Forged by God in Us

Another important aspect of the passage is the rebuke of Christ to the disciples on the road to Emmaus as a sign of His intention to correct them. He not only rebukes them for their lack of faith and understanding but speaks to them to bring attention to what they currently believe (actually, this is one of the powerful effects of the Word of God). The Bible must be used to instruct and correct; to confront the lie with the truth, this is why the apostle Paul says:

> **"All Scripture is breathed out by God and profitable for teaching, for reproof, for correction, and for training in righteousness, that the man of God may be complete, equipped for every good work" (2 Timothy 3:16-17).**

Do you want to be a man or a woman with a heart according to God's word? Do you want to walk in truth? Do you want to do His will? Do you want to fulfill your calling? Then, you must let yourself be taught, rebuked, corrected, and instructed by the Word of God. If your heart is not humble enough for this, you must first repent of your sin, and ask God to give you a new heart, a heart of a servant or slave, completely submissive to Him, so that you may be like Christ, who did everything the Father wanted. Then you will be able to receive His Word with humility.

One of the beatitudes that Christ mentions in Matthew 5 speaks about peacemakers: "Blessed are the peacemakers, for they shall be called sons of God" (Matthew 5:9). There Jesus says that a characteristic of the children of God is their constant desire to bring peace to others. Let's now go into a little more detail on the definition of a peacemaker.

Is a peacemaker one who avoids all conflict? Is it someone with a submissive spirit in all circumstances? Or is it someone who remains silent to prevent others from being offended? In this world, our governments, in theory, should bring peace and order to societies, but instead, they cause a temporary truce from the next war, just a temporary peace that prepares them for the next conflict.

Christ is the peacemaker par excellence. A biblical peacemaker raises the truth above all else even if this means conflict to raise the name of God. He is the one who corrects the lie and confronts sin. A true biblical peacemaker knows that true peace comes from understanding the importance of the sinner's need to be reconciled to God.

This leads the peacemaker to preach the Word at any time, and he is always willing to tell others about Christ; to correct the lie with the truth, with love and grace (1 Peter 3:15). The only way for humanity to achieve peace with God is this: to confront their sin with the truth of the Gospel. It will always be necessary to rebuke and combat sin; not with guns or insults, but grace and love. Therefore, we never preach to win an argument but preach with grace so that people hear our love and can be reconciled with God, just like we were.

The Apostle Paul —while on his missionary journeys— worked hard to bring peace with God in peoples' hearts, confronting their sins and always preaching the Word of God boldly. What was the result of that? Conflict. In Lystra, for example, Paul was stoned (Acts 14:19), but that was not the only time he suffered serious persecution. In 2 Corinthians 11:24-25 we can read about what he suffered as a result of his mission to bring peace with God: he was whipped five times with thirty-nine lashes, three times whipped with rods, etc., many times his enemies wanted to kill him, until in Rome they finally succeeded in doing so. Paul died as a martyr for the Gospel, beheaded (according to tradition) for his faith, likely in the year 64 AC.

The first martyr of the church, Stephen, was stoned to death for preaching the truth of the Gospel (Acts 7:59-60), but after him —and through the centuries— thousands of others have been persecuted and even killed for their faith in Christ. In the 16th century, in a well-known incident, Martin Luther was persecuted by the Catholic Church and had to go into hiding for two years. Persecution for the sake of the Gospel has never completely stopped and persists in many countries around the world to this day. For this reason, the last beatitude (which comes after that of the peacemakers), says: "Blessed are those who are persecuted for righteousness' sake, for theirs is the kingdom of heaven" (Matthew 5:10).

The faithful proclamation of the Word, confronting sin, and teaching the Gospel can result in persecution and conflict, as many people are not open to receiving God's truth. There are even those who hate the truth of God because they love darkness more than light (John 3:19). However, observe Paul's heart regarding all that he suffered, how he viewed his own experience of persecution, and the difficulties he went through because of the preaching of the Word and for following God. He writes:

"Not only that, but we rejoice in our sufferings, knowing that suffering produces endurance, and endurance produces character, and character produces hope" (Romans 5:3-4).

Paul had true faith in Christ and was willing to suffer persecution; everything that happened on this earth and all his sacrifices were made solely to do the will of God. He left his old life and counted it as rubbish (Philippians 3:7-9) to live for Christ, and when he suffered for Him, he knew that the trial of his faith would bring him closer to God, not further away.

God has already given us the faith to believe, now is the time to exercise that faith and believe our Christ. True faith is founded only in the truth, not on a lie or incorrect assumption of the Bible; only true faith (one that is placed in the Word of God, and on the true interpretation of it) will help us be ready for our spiritual battle. This is the reason why God allows trials to come into our lives.

Up to now, we have seen in the first part of our analysis, the encounter of the disciples of Emmaus with Christ, and we have seen of the examination that Christ does to them, and then his rebuke. Now we will see how the Lord instructs them in love for several hours so that they understand the Scriptures correctly. Christ takes his time to correctly guide and instruct them in the truth and give them the correct meaning of the Word of God so that they understand who Christ really is and what his mission was when He came into the world. This is a great demonstration of our Lord's patience with His beloved sheep.

The Instruction

"Was it not necessary that the Christ should suffer these things and enter into his glory?" And beginning with Moses and all the Prophets, he interpreted to them in all the Scriptures the things concerning himself." (Luke 24:26-27).

In this topic we will discuss several important ideas. We saw how Christ rebukes these disciples for having a wrong understanding of the Scriptures, and a misconception of who He is. Such a lack of knowledge and misunderstanding led these disciples to have a faith rooted on a false belief, which, in the midst of afflictions, collapsed and could not prevent them from returning to their old life. Now, in this subtopic, we will see three important points.

- The importance of understanding the Word of God.
- The necessity of Christ's death and resurrection; and,
- Christ in the Old Testament.

THE IMPORTANCE OF UNDERSTANDING THE WORD OF GOD

Understanding why a Savior is necessary is essential to the Gospel. Failing to recognize the bad news means I won't be able to experience the joy of the Good News or the Gospel. If I am not aware of the weight of my sin, I will not be able to appreciate the value of my salvation either. If I do not value my salvation, then I will despise it, and in turn will take my spiritual life lightly, living without a sense of urgency to be sanctified by the Word of God. If I do not value my salvation, I will cherish it and not guard it with fear and trembling, as the apostle Paul says (Philippians 2:12).

Understanding the truth is fundamental. And when I refer to understanding or knowing, I mean in the sense of relationship, rather than just knowing something. Biblical understanding revealed by the Holy Spirit leads a person to action, which in turn is evidence that they have come to understand what God is teaching in His Word, this is evidence of a spiritually renewed or reborn person. True biblical understanding results in fruits of faith or works of faith, love, and fear of God. Therefore, knowing the Bible and its stories does not necessarily mean knowing the Word of God, or understanding it.

Christ said in John 8:32: "and you will know the truth, and the truth will set you free". Likewise, Christ himself said that He is the truth in John 14:6. Christ is the truth that makes us free from every chain of sin. This understanding of the truth that Jesus speaks is impossible to comprehend without the Holy Spirit. God's truth revives our spirit, and not merely in our intellect; it is a spiritual understanding that goes far beyond the knowledge of a story or a biblical passage, it is a truth that brings back to life a dead soul, and in turn, transforms human hearts for the glory of God. The truth of Christ frees believers from ties that bind us to sin and the ways of the world and directs us to the love of God. Sin no longer reigns in the mortal body of those who follow Christ (Romans 6:12). We are no longer slaves to sin; we are now slaves to Christ.

THE FEAR OF GOD

A very important principle needs to be understood: the meaning of fear of God. The fear of God has to do with great respect and reverence before the great King of the universe, the King of kings, and the Lord of lords.

> **"The fear of the Lord is the beginning of knowledge; fools despise wisdom and instruction" (Proverbs 1:7).**

This is similar to children who fear the consequences of their actions and the punishment they may receive from their parents. When parents discipline their children to help them lead a disciplined life in the future, the child learns to fear them. They tend to be more careful not to do wrong things because they know their parents will discipline or punish them; their parents show their children love, but they also teach them to understand that actions have consequences. Disobedience will bear its fruit, that is the message that parents should convey to their children when they are young, and they should always discipline with love and grace, explaining the reason to their child's level of comprehension, is an important part of children's education.

This is the kind of fear that God's children should show toward their heavenly Father. They have complete trust in Him and know that their heavenly Father loves them, but they also know that God is holy and jealous and will not overlook the disobedience of His children. Good children seek to honor their earthly parents and to bring them respect. Similarly, the children of God should seek to bring glory to their heavenly Father with their lives. But as for a child of God who strays from the way, the heavenly Father, in His love and patience, will correct them so that they may turn from their sins, and this correction is a sign of His love.

"For the Lord disciplines the one he loves and chastises every son whom he receives. It is for discipline that you have to endure. God is treating you as sons. For what son is there whom his father does not discipline?" (Hebrews 12:6-7).

For us who are adoptive children of God through Christ (John 1:12), and saved by His grace, will be disciplined by God when we are living in sin, because we need that discipline to be partakers of His holiness (Hebrews 12:10).

The connection between parents and children is the foundation for the love and fear a child feels towards them. Thus, children who feel that their parents care and love them, may develop a good respect for the authorities in their lives. The opposite will happen if a father does not correct his children. The most certain thing is that these children may become spoiled, insolent, arrogant, and will not respect the authorities; they will always do what they want without any restraints. These children do not mind hurting others or doing physical or emotional harm to their peers or family as long as they get what they want. What do such children look like? Like God or Satan?

The absence of proper parental correction is not a sign of love for your child, quite the contrary. A Father who does not correct his children is not showing them love, rather he is causing great damage in their formation and character and steering them away from God. If a child does not learn to respect the authority of their parents, then they will not learn respect to God's authority as their Lord.

The punishment I'm talking about is not the one where the child is whipped with a leash in a fit of rage. Rather, the correction must be rational: the child must understand the reason for the correction, and the parents must take the opportunity to instruct their child in the path of truth. Love and grace should always be shown towards children, and discipline is one of the ways we show love for them.

I have three daughters, and believe me, I don't like correcting them, I don't enjoy it, I don't take pleasure in it, and I feel pain when I see them crying when I have to correct them for their inappropriate behavior. But one thing I always try to do is show them —in light of the Word of God— why I have to. One must never be a tyrant towards their children, but as God is a God of grace, patience and love, so we must also be; but yes, parents should not be negligent in applying discipline, when necessary, because this is not only a duty, but also a manifestation of the love we have for them.

The punishment must also be the consequence of the violation of a norm, or of a rule imposed in the home, which is known to them. It is not something that should be practiced without warning, since the child should already be aware of the consequences derived from the transgression of a rule established at home; Thus, the child, before committing the offense, already knows the consequences that will come. The same happens to us, because the consequences of our disobedience are clearly established in the Word of God.

Correction includes admonition, rebuke, and as I also mentioned, instruction. Therefore, if I am not a child of God, I would have no reason to fear God's correction, because God is not my Father. So, the people who are not believers have no fear of God, they don't love Him. But if I am His child, then I should fear God and I should love Him greatly. The lack of this fear of God, and of love for Him, leads us to persist in evil ways.

"The fear of the Lord is the beginning of knowledge; fools despise wisdom and instruction" (Proverbs 1:7).

Fools are not interested in receiving the teaching and instruction of our heavenly Father because they are not His children, and they despise His teachings and instructions. This happened to me before I became a believer. Unbelievers, unfortunately, do not see God as the authority of their lives. Let's look at another passage:

"The fear of the Lord is the beginning of wisdom; all those who practice it have a good understanding. His praise endures forever" (Psalms 111:10).

Good understanding or wisdom is demonstrated by practicing the divine commandments, that is, when the believer maintains a life of obedience to the Word of God. There are who love to talk about spiritual things and show their deep knowledge of things. They like to speak in public and be seen by men when they do charitable works, and in public, they are good people; however, in private they live a sinful life.

When this is the case, we are dealing with a fool, one who has no understanding of the Word of God. It is one of the whitewashed tombs that Jesus spoke of when describing the religionists of His time, (Matthew 23:27). These people were clean and beautiful on the outside, but dead on the inside. I can say that even being a believer and a child of God, many times I have been in this spiritual condition, giving the external appearance of faithfulness, but inside dead, cold and dry, separated from God, living in sin, as a fool, without understanding, and all for not wanting to follow the voice of my Father, but rather that of my own desires.

That is why a true knowledge of the Word is evidenced by a life of obedience (John 14:15). The obedience that is practiced, not as an obligation and grudging, but the one that produces delight, and that is surrendered with love and joy.

The disciples of Emmaus still did not know who their Master was, they lacked understanding, and their lack of understanding prevented them from doing God's will; it was then that Christ's rebuke came. The beauty of Jesus' approach is that He rebukes them, but also instructs them. Christ guides His sheep, teaches them, and loves them. The Word of God not only rebukes you, but also helps you get up and turn away from sin (2 Timothy 3:16). The Word teaches you the consequences of disobedience, and how serious it is to live apart from God.

In summary, the knowledge of God is demonstrated in our lives, not by what we know of the Word of God only, but by its fruits in our hearts, and by the works that denote faith. These works are a burning lamp in a fallen world, and its light represents the glory of the One who gave his life for us.

The Necessity of Christ's Death and Resurrection

"Did not the Messiah have to suffer these things and then enter his glory? (Luke 24:26).

In Luke 24:26 we read a fundamental question that Jesus asks them. A question for which they had no answer. For at least two hours, these disciples were listening to what this stranger (given it was unknown to them it was Christ) had to tell them on the subject. A subject that these disciples were totally ignorant of. They did not know why the death of Jesus was necessary.

Matthew Henry's commentary says that Christ, before wearing His crown of glory, wore a crown of thorns. We know that the Word of God teaches that man's sin broke His relationship with God, since then a sinful humanity could not have true fellowship with a Holy God.

The angels, intelligent creatures, also rebelled against God, and were driven from His presence without the possibility of redemption. These are now led by Satan (Rev. 12:4). On the other hand, we —and this by grace alone— were the object of God's love and while we were still sinners, Christ died for us (Romans 5:8). Why did Jesus have to die? Why was it necessary for Christ to die nailed to a cross? This was an extremely unfair type of death for a man like Jesus, given He was absolutely innocent. Why did He have to die in such a bloody, shameful way? Why did it have to occur with so much pain and suffering?

Christ was condemned with the worst and most humiliating sentence that a man could receive at that time. Today, a prisoner on death row is treated with much more dignity than Christ was treated; such a person can enjoy their favorite meal the night before the death sentence is completed. The most common way today to end the life of one who is sentenced to death is by lethal injection. On the day that the sentence will be carried out, he is given a drug that anesthetizes the person, after which a muscle paralyzer is given, and finally a drug to stop the beating of the heart. Normally, this process does not take more than five minutes.

During the time of Jesus, the intention was that the death of those criminals (who were considered the worst criminals of the time) to be extremely cruel. The Roman government wanted such people to serve as an example to those who resided in their territories, and that they were thus warned that breaking roman law would bring serious consequences: a slow and shameful death full of suffering. Therefore, these criminals were raised on a cross for people to see and fear the consequences of breaking Roman law.

When we think about the crucifixion of Jesus, we rarely stop to think that many other Jews, and from many other nations, also suffered this painful crucifixion. Thousands received the punishment for their actions, suffering with this cruel and harsh death. This served as an earthly example to us of how the condemnation of sinners who have rejected Jesus Christ will be; only that suffering will not be for a few hours or days but for all eternity.

The practice of crucifixion as a method of torture was first introduced by the Syrians and Babylonians around the sixth century BC. Initially, the prisoners were tied by the hands —they were not nailed—, and their feet were left free. In its beginnings, the prisoners of death were hung on a tree, not on a cross. Later, Alexander the Great continued this practice after invading Persia, after the battle of Cartagena, in the 3rd century BC. By that time the Romans adopted and practiced this way of torture for the next five hundred years. It was the Romans who modified this practice so that it was the cruelest form of torture at the time and feared by all.

Rome normally did not crucify its citizens —due to the shameful nature of this death—, but it did crucify slaves and foreigners, those who were seditious, thieves, murderers, etc., and this practice was common in those days. For example, the Roman general Publius Quinctilius Varus alone, who ruled in the first century AD, crucified around two thousand Jews. Finally, the crucifixion was abolished by Constantine in the fourth century.

The crucifixion represents eternal punishment, the consequences of sin, and everlasting hell. If we could visualize thousands of people suffering this public shame, and this cruel condemnation, this would give us an idea of the sufferings of hell. Many times, the soldiers gouged out the eyes of the prisoners, cut out their tongues, or other parts of their bodies before crucifying them, so that they would suffer more. Some would display extreme cruelty by strangling the son of the condemned man and then hanging the lifeless child around their neck while they were on the cross.

This was something extremely horrifying, terrible, disgusting, dirty, vile; and exercised without any kind of mercy or grace. It was a vision of hell on earth. From this condemnation it is that Christ has sought to save us; for this is our eternal destiny without Him.

"And throw them into the fiery furnace. In that place there will be weeping and gnashing of teeth" (Matthew 13:42).

Why was Christ's death then necessary? All those who have physically died up to now have received the fair price of the wages because of their sin. This body is corrupted by sin and must die. No one will be spared from this death, except those believers who will be alive when Christ returns.

Christ came to fulfill what God had promised, and He was the Lamb who redeemed us from sin. Just as the sacrifice of an animal was unjust (for that little animal in the Old Testament paid for the sin of others and had done nothing to deserve that death), Christ died for the sin of all of us; His death was unfair to Him, because He was totally innocent.

"For the wages of sin is death, but the free gift of God is eternal life in Christ Jesus our Lord" (Romans 6:23).

If the wages of sin were death, then my damnation was certain, and I had to pay for my sin, but God allowed another to die in my place, to bring me to Him. Without the death of Christ, I would have never been forgiven.

> **"For Christ also suffered once for sins, the righteous for the unrighteous, that he might bring us to God, being put to death in the flesh but made alive in the spirit" (1 Peter 3:18).**

It was necessary for Christ to die to bring us sinners to God. The just (Christ) paid for the unjust (us). So, everyone who persists in a life of sin, who is not interested in the Word of God, who has no desire to come to Him, and no desire to honor His Name, this person will be belittling the sacrifice of Christ.

In the Gospels we can see that next to Christ were two thieves, both were condemned to death (Matthew 27:38). One despised Jesus and the other honored and showed love towards Him. One of the thieves was condemned, and the other went to paradise. All of us condemned are to die due to our transgressions against God, and we are like those hung on a cross, unable to save ourselves. Then my question to you is, with which of the thieves do you identify with?

Will we belittle what God has given us? His thoughts, His Word, love, grace, patience, and His Holy Spirit. Our relationship with God should never depend on a church, or a pastor; our relationship with God must be maintained by each and every one of us, with an intimate and personal communion with Him. Each one of us must be part of a local congregation of true believers or a faithful church, and must fellowship with one another, which is an essential part of following Christ, for we know our Lord Jesus instituted His beloved Church (Matthew 16:18). However, within the children of God who walk in obedience, there should always be a fervent desire to know and honor Him, and this desire should become a constant seeking of God in private, where no one sees us.

Just as it was necessary for Christ to suffer and be killed, so it is necessary for me also to die, and for Christ to grow in me.

> **"We know that Christ, being raised from the dead, will never die again; death no longer has dominion over him. For the death he died he died to sin, once for all, but the life he lives he lives to God. So you also must consider yourselves dead to sin and alive to God in Christ Jesus." (Romans 6:9-11).**

These disciples did not understand they needed to be saved from their sins. Perhaps they were used to seeing other people crucified all their lives, and did not understand, regarding the crucifixion of Jesus, that God was showing them the harsh condemnation that comes for those who do not believe, and how Christ was carrying in His body that condemnation for the benefit of all of those who would believe. Despite having listened to Christ and His message for three years, they had not understood that they needed to be delivered from death through the death of another and that the resurrection was the evidence that Christ had defeated death.

Christ in the Old Testament

> **"And beginning with Moses and all the Prophets, he interpreted to them in all the Scriptures the things concerning himself" (Luke 24:27).**

Here we see how Christ gave these disciples an overview and a walk through the Old T*estament*, showing them the passages about Him. Virtually all of Jesus' life, including His death and resurrection, and most of His life and ministry are reflected in the Old Testament. Christ spoke to them from Moses and through all the prophets, since they all spoke of Him or pointed to Him in one way or another. Let's see then some passages in Moses' writings and the prophets that speak of Christ.

Moses spoke of the coming Redeemer in the Pentateuch (the first five books of the Bible), in multiple occasions. Moses wrote Genesis, Exodus, Leviticus, Numbers, and Deuteronomy. In these books, we find many symbolisms pointing to Jesus. Now, I will present some examples of what Moses wrote about the coming Messiah.

The redemption promise

In Genesis chapter 3 God promised a Redeemer for the lost world (v.15). After the fall, God condemned all the sinners: Adam, Eve, and the serpent. However, the condemnation God gave to the serpent was not only about her, but, at the same time, a promise of restoration for humanity.

> "I will put enmity between you and the woman, and between your offspring and her offspring; he shall bruise your head, and you shall bruise his heel."
> (Genesis 3:15).

Here we see how Satan would hurt the seed promised to Eve in the heel, that is, he would hurt him slightly and briefly, but this would not be fatal or permanent. Instead, Eve's seed was going to hurt the serpent on its head, that is, He was going to destroy Satan with a death blow. This promise was fulfilled on the cross, where Jesus was wounded for us, but He rose again in glory. The final fulfillment of this promise about Satan will come when He is condemned to the lake of fire for eternity (Revelation 20:10); however, Paul has revealed to us by the Spirit that the death of Christ and His resurrection made Him the rightful owner of all, and He —and His kingdom— was publicly exhibited as defeated. Jesus Christ triumphed over the devil on the cross. The Bible says:

> "And you, who were dead in your trespasses and the uncircumcision of your flesh, God made alive together with him, having forgiven us all our trespasses, by canceling the record of debt that stood against us with its legal demands. This he set aside, nailing it to the cross. He disarmed the rulers and authorities and put them to open shame, by triumphing over them in him." (Colossians 2:13-15).

Therefore, it is our privilege and our responsibility to make this victory achieved by Christ on the Cross over Satan and his kingdom a living and powerful reality.

The substitutionary payment of sin

In Genesis 22 we can see a representation of what Christ did for us. We see this during God's test of Abraham's faith in relation to his son Isaac's.

> "After these things God tested Abraham and said to him, 'Abraham!' And he said, 'Here I am.' He said, 'Take your son,

> your only son Isaac, whom you love, and go to the land of Moriah, and offer him there as a burnt offering on one of the mountains of which I shall tell you." (Genesis 22:1-2).

In this passage, God asked Abraham to sacrifice his son Isaac as a burnt offering. This was the son of the promise God had given him, the one he had waited so long for. However, Abraham's faith is evidenced here, since he put his love and faithfulness to God before the love he had for his son Isaac.

> "Then Abraham reached out his hand and took the knife to slaughter his son. But the angel of the Lord called to him from heaven and said, 'Abraham, Abraham!' And he said, 'Here I am.' He said, 'Do not lay your hand on the boy or do anything to him, for now I know that you fear God, seeing you have not withheld your son, your only son, from me.' And Abraham lifted up his eyes and looked, and behold, behind him was a ram, caught in a thicket by his horns. And Abraham went and took the ram and offered it up as a burnt offering instead of his son. So Abraham called the name of that place, 'The Lord will provide'; as it is said to this day, 'On the mount of the Lord it shall be provided." (Genesis 22:10-14).

This event in Genesis clearly shows us an analogy to Jesus' substitutionary and atoning sacrifice. Abraham, a picture of God, who stands with his knife in hand, ready to sacrifice (or pass judgment) his son Isaac, who represents believers, those who are saved by faith in Jesus, for whom God provided a lamb (Jesus Christ).

In the case of Abraham, the lamb that had its horns caught between thorns (this likely represents the crown of thorns placed on the head of Christ) was sacrificed instead of Isaac; thus, Christ died for us, showing Himself as our substitute by dying on the Cross. He is the Lamb of God who takes away the sin of the world (John 1:29).

The priest without beginning or end

Another passage in Genesis that is a prelude to the person of Christ is in chapter 14. I this passage Abraham had an encounter with

Melchizedek. Melchizedek was the king of Salem and a priest of God. We see in the passage how Abraham gave him a tithe of the loot he brought, after the battle with the kings who had taken his nephew Lot captive. This act was a symbol of honor to God, a prelude to Christ as High Priest.

"And Melchizedek king of Salem brought out bread and wine. (He was priest of God Most High.) And he blessed him and said, 'Blessed be Abram by God Most High, Possessor of heaven and earth; and blessed be God Most High, who has delivered your enemies into your hand!'" (Genesis 14:18-20).

Melchizedek was king of Salem (which means King of peace), and He was also a priest of the Most High God. So, He was both a King and a Priest, just like Christ is our High Priest and King. No descendants or genealogy of this man are mentioned, symbolizing that He has no beginning or end. This man, Melchizedek, represented the priesthood of Christ as our high priest, without beginning or end, a holy and immutable priesthood, of a different order from that of the Levites, since this priest of God appeared before the Jewish people existed. He was also the King of peace, and Christ is our King, the King who died for us and brought us peace with God through His own sacrifice (Romans 5:1).

"So also Christ did not exalt himself to be made a high priest, but was appointed by him who said to him, "You are my Son, today I have begotten you"; as he says also in another place, "You are a priest forever, after the order of Melchizedek." (Hebrews 5:5-6).

The institution of Passover

In Exodus, we have the description of the ten plagues God sent to destroy Egypt because Pharaoh refused to free the Jews from slavery. In the last one, the angel of death passed through Egypt to kill the firstborn. However, for the Jews whose homes were marked with the blood of the lamb on the door lintels, the angel of death passed over and caused no harm. That event pointed to the sacrifice of Jesus, symbolizing that all who were covered by the precious blood of Christ would be protected from the coming judgment of God.

> "The blood shall be a sign for you, on the houses where you are. And when I see the blood, I will pass over you, and no plague will befall you to destroy you, when I strike the land of Egypt" (Exodus 12:13).

Christ is the Lamb that takes away the sin of the world (John 1:29), and it is through the sacrifice of this Lamb —of which the Jewish Passover is a type— that we can find forgiveness for our sins.

The Great I AM

God first introduced Himself to Moses and identified with Him by a name that the patriarchs had never heard. He introduced Himself as the great I AM (YHWH, Jehovah, YAHWEH).

> "God said to Moses, 'I am who I am.' And he said, 'Say this to the people of Israel: "I am has sent me to you".'" (Exodus 3:14).

Christ revealed Himself with this name —Making Himself equal to God— seven times during His ministry. In the Gospel of John, which presents Christ as God, we find Jesus showing Himself by this name before the Jewish people.

1. I AM the true vine (John 15:1-5).
2. I AM the way, the truth, and the life (John 14:6).
3. I AM the resurrection and the life (John 11:25).
4. I AM the good shepherd (John 10:11-14).
5. I AM the door (John 10:7).
6. I AM the light of the world (John 8:12).
7. I AM the bread of life (John 6:35).

One of the reasons the Pharisees hated Jesus was because He made Himself equal to God, and they sought to kill Him.

> "This was why the Jews were seeking all the more to kill him, because not only was he breaking the Sabbath, but he was

even calling God his own Father, making himself equal with God" (John 5:18).

The Passover Lamb

In Numbers 9 we read regarding the establishment of the Jewish Passover (celebrated in the month of Nisan, on the 14th day of the month). This was the same day that Christ died on the cross. We also read there something interesting: that the Jews could not break a single bone of the lamb that they would eat for the Passover.

"They shall leave none of it until the morning, nor break any of its bones; according to all the statute for the Passover they shall keep it" (Numbers 9:12).

This same prophecy is also mentioned in Psalm 34:20 where it says: "He keeps all his bones; not one of them is broken." Roman soldiers used to break the crucified legs to hasten their death in some circumstances, because when they did this, they quickly suffocated as their legs couldn't push the muscles up, preventing the diaphragm muscle from relaxing and breathing. This they did with the thieves who were on the sides of Jesus so that they would die faster (since the Jewish Passover was celebrated that night); but with Christ, it was not necessary because He was already dead.

"The Jews then, since it was the day of preparation for the Passover, so that the bodies would not remain on the cross on the Sabbath (because that Sabbath was very solemn), asked Pilate to break their legs. and they will take them away. So the soldiers came and broke the legs of the first, and also those of the other who had been crucified with Jesus; but when they came to Jesus, as they saw that he was already dead, they did not break his legs" (John 19.31-33).

The bronze serpent

In Numbers 21:4-9 we read the bronze serpent's story. The people of Israel had sinned against God. They had stopped trusting in God's provision and were complaining against God and Moses. Therefore, as punishment for their sin, God sent venomous snakes that caused death to those who bitten. This deadly venomous poison from the snakes represents the sin's bite.

> **"Then the Lord sent fiery serpents among the people, and they bit the people, so that many people of Israel died. And the Lord said to Moses, 'Make a fiery serpent and set it on a pole, and everyone who is bitten, when he sees it, shall live.'"**
> **(Numbers 21:6,8).**

Just as Eve did not trust the Word of God, and was bitten by the sin proposed by the serpent, these people were also bitten by sin and did not trust the Word of God. The people then repented, and God instructed Moses to make a bronze serpent.

This represented the sacrifice of Christ on the cross, which was necessary to pay for our sins. Christ (represented by the serpent) bore our sins and was lifted on a cross (like the serpent on the pole). When Jesus spoke to Nicodemus, He associated the bronze serpent's event with His atoning death.

> **"And as Moses lifted up the serpent in the wilderness, so must the Son of Man be lifted up" (John 3:14).**

Likewise, another way of understanding this is that the serpent represents Jesus Christ, who took up our sins, so that every time a sinner lifts his/her eyes to Him, he/she would be healed from the venomous bite of sin. Those who didn't up their eyes to see the serpent on the pole were not healed and died.

Some Examples of Biblical Prophecies of Christ Among the Prophets

1. The eternal kingdom that would come from the descendants of King David:

> **"When your days are fulfilled and you lie down with your fathers, I will raise up your offspring after you, who shall**

come from your body, and I will establish his kingdom. He shall build a house for my name, and I will establish the throne of his kingdom forever" (2 Samuel 7:12-13).

2. His resurrection was predicted:

"For I know that my Redeemer lives, and at the last he will stand upon the earth." (Job 19:25).

3. He would be raised from the dead:

"For you will not abandon my soul in Sheol, nor will you allow your Holy One to see corruption" (Psalm 16:10).

4. He would be thirsty, His hands and feet would be nailed, His nakedness would be revealed, and His clothes would be divided: Psalm 22:9-31.

5. He would be betrayed by a friend:

"Even my close friend in whom I trusted, who ate my bread, has lifted his heel against me" (Psalms 41:9).

6. He would have a virgin birth, and this child that would be born would be God with us.

"Therefore, the Lord himself will give you a sign. Behold, the virgin shall conceive and bear a son, and shall call his name Immanuel." (Isaiah 7:14).

7. He would be from Galilee:

"... But there will be no gloom for her who was in anguish. In the former time he brought into contempt the land of Zebulun and the land of Naphtali, but in the latter time he has made glorious the way of the sea, the land beyond the Jordan, Galilee of the nations. The people who walked in darkness have seen a great light; those who dwelt in a land of deep darkness, on them has light shone" (Isaiah 9:1-2).

8. A child would be born who would be God made flesh:

"For to us a child is born, to us a son is given; and the government shall be upon his shoulder and his name shall be called Wonderful Counselor, Mighty God, Everlasting Father, Prince of Peace." (Isaiah 9:6).

9. His Name was prophesied. The name of Jesus (Yeshua in Hebrew), is translated in our English version as salvation:

"Behold, God is my salvation (Yehsua); I will trust, and will not be afraid; for the Lord God is my strength and my song and he has become my salvation (Yeshua)." (Isaiah 12:2).

10. They would not believe in him, and He would be rejected:

"He was despised and rejected by men, a man of sorrows and acquainted with grief; and as one from whom men hide their faces he was despised, and we esteemed him not." (Isaiah 53:3).

11. He would bear the sin of humanity:

"All we like sheep have gone astray; we have turned —every one—to his own way; and the Lord has laid on him the iniquity of us all." (Isaiah 53:6).

12. Jeremiah predicted that He would be both God and man:

"Behold, the days are coming, declares the Lord, when I will raise up for David a righteous Branch, and he shall reign as king and deal wisely, and shall execute justice and righteousness in the land. In his days Judah will be saved, and Israel will dwell securely. And this is the name by which he will be called: 'The Lord is our righteousnes.'" (Jeremiah 23:5-6).

13. Daniel predicted the exact time at which Jesus would come to earth:

"Seventy weeks are decreed about your people and your holy city, to finish the transgression, to put an end to sin, and to atone for iniquity, to bring in everlasting righteousness, to seal both vision and prophet, and to anoint a most holy place. Know therefore and understand that from the going out of the word to restore and build Jerusalem to the coming of an anointed one, a prince, there shall be seven weeks. Then for sixty-two weeks it shall be built again with squares and moat, but in a troubled time. And after the sixty-two weeks, an anointed one shall be cut off and shall have nothing. And the people of the prince who is to come shall destroy the city and the sanctuary. Its end shall come with a flood, and to the end there shall be war. Desolations are decreed." (Daniel 9:24-26).

14. The Messiah would live in Egypt:

"When Israel was a child, I loved him, and out of Egypt I called my son." (Hosea 11:1).

15. He would defeat death:

"I shall ransom them from the power of Sheol; I shall redeem them from Death. O Death, where are your plagues? O Sheol, where is your sting? Compassion is hidden from my eyes. (Hosea 13:14).

In the Old Testament, we have hundreds of prophecies detailing who Christ would be and when He would come. There are more than 350 fulfilled prophecies regarding the Messiah, not counting theophanies, that is, the appearances of the Son of God in the Old Testament. Christ was the cloud that shaded the Israelites, and the fire that guided them by night when they left Egypt. He was that Rock that gave the Israelites water in the desert, and who spoke with Moses face to face (Exodus 33:11). It was also the Son of God who spoke to Abraham in Genesis 18:2-3, and who appeared to Joshua with a drawn sword in His hand (Joshua 5:13-15).

Christ is the visible image of the invisible God (Colossians 1:15). He was the one who made everything that exists:

"For by him all things were created, in heaven and on earth, visible and invisible, whether thrones or dominions or rulers or authorities—all things were created through him and for him. And he is before all things, and in him all things hold together." (Colossians 1:16-17).

It is possible that Jesus recited many of these Old Testament passages and many others to them. He wanted these disciples fully understand what the Scriptures say about Him; He fervently wanted His disciples to understand the Scriptures and have strong faith in the Word of God; a true and firm faith. So, after the explanations of the risen Christ, surely the faith of these disciples was placed only in Him and all the mistaken concepts they had of Him were demolished and thrown out.

The Invitation

Let us continue now with another aspect of the passage. I have previously commented on how we have seen Christ examine the hearts of the disciples of Emmaus and reveal their true heart's desire, that is: that Christ would reign on earth as a military leader, an earthly king, and that He would free them from the Roman oppression (from an external oppression). They had not understood that Christ did not come for this reason, but to free them from the oppression of sin (internal oppression).

I have already commented on how Christ rebuked these men, making them see how far they were from the truth. For about two hours (if not more), Christ was teaching them what Moses and the prophets wrote about Him so that they would understand His purpose in coming to the world: to sacrifice Himself for our sins. Now let's see what happened next.

> **"So they drew near to the village to which they were going. He acted as if he were going farther, but they urged him strongly, saying, "Stay with us, for it is toward evening and the day is now far spent." So, he went in to stay with them. When he was at table with them, he took the bread and blessed and broke it and gave it to them" (Luke 24:28-30).**

Let's visualize these verses and admire their beauty: what a moment! What a privilege these two disciples had! This is the point where both, the will of God and humans, meet. This is the decisive moment. They were at a crossroads, with the road to heaven on one side, and the road to hell on the other. A stairway that led to heaven was laid out for them, but continuing the same path would lead to eternal damnation. Christ now had preached to them and taught them the truth, the instruction came from the risen Jesus Himself, and such an explanation could never have been given in a better way by anyone else; therefore, there couldn't come a better time than this for them to hear the truth.

The Author of the Word of God had explained it to them; they were presented with the kingdom of God and the plan of salvation. Their sins were exposed, and their wrong ideas had been dismantled. The Word of God had been sown in their hearts, and now what? Christ had taken the initiative at first, but now the turning point had come from them. Then Christ appeared as He was going to continue His journey by himself, and they were faced with a decision: either invite Him to stay with them or let Him go to continue His journey. They had the choice of letting this "stranger" go or inviting Him to dwell with them.

What can this mean? What difference would have made that Christ continued his way, or that He would stay to dwell with these men as a special guest? Why did God want this to write in the Word of God in this way?

In Revelation 3:19-20, Jesus spoke to the Laodicean church, addressing them —one of the seven churches Jesus Christ addresses in Revelation—. He called this church a lukewarm church in which God no longer dwelled. This church was neither cold nor hot: They didn't want to surrender to God, nor completely give in to this world. A church that, believing itself self-sufficient, thought it was serving God, but really served itself. This church was on the verge of collapse, and so far from God, that Christ was not even amid the church at that moment, rather, knocking on the door from the outside, rebuking their ways, and waiting for them to repent from their sins. It is then that Christ, in His love and patience, knocked on the door showing this church their error and their sin, knocking so they can open back their hearts to Him and to have a relationship with this church again. Laodicea was a church where Christ no longer dwelt; yet He called out to them, waiting for them to open the door.

Christ rebuked them and commanded them through the Apostle John's letter to change their ways and repent of their sins. This is the invitation and warning that Christ gave to these Laodicean believers:

"Those whom I love, I reprove and discipline, so be zealous and repent. Behold, I stand at the door and knock. If anyone hears my voice and opens the door, I will come into him and eat with him, and he with me" (Revelation 3:19-20).

This verse is widely used as the basis for evangelistic messages, to preach to non-believers on the topic of salvation. "You just have to open the door of your heart to Christ and he will dwell with you!", they are told; However, when looking at the context, these words are not addressed to unbelievers, but to the Lord's church, to an apostate church who He loved and was rebuking, to people who had been washed with the blood of Jesus and integrated into the body of Christ and a congregation falling astray. They were people who had been walking with Christ, but who had turned away from His love, His Word, and at that time the church was living in grave sin; therefore, they were about to be judged by God and be vomited out (separated) completely from the body (v. 15-16), unless they repented.

The rebuke was for them, and it was to them that Christ said: "Behold, I stand at the door and knock. If anyone hears my voice and opens the door, I will come into him and eat with him, and he with me." So, this rebuke was not for the ungodly or unbelievers, but for the members of the Laodicean church. Jesus told them that if they repented and invited him in, He would come, forgive them, and dwell among them.

Some believers think that, although they have already been saved, they will still always be sinners; and therefore, they become lax and practice sins in their daily lives. Then they get used to living like this, they learn to live for themselves, to satisfy their desires, and they deceive themselves into thinking that they please God because they think that God accepts them anyway, even if they are Christians following God "In their own way".

These men and women are stagnant and content with their current situation, and abandon even the desire to truly serve and surrender to the Lord. They stop contemplating the greatness and majesty of God; and then their love for the Lord wanes and dies; They become lukewarm, they are neither cold nor hot. They become religious and self-sufficient; they pretend to be believers in front of others, but internally they are very far from Christ, they leave him outside. They know they are living in sin, but because they are so engulfed in their sin, they don't see a way out, they are defeated and broken and their love for their sin outgrows their love for God.

"I know your works: you are neither cold nor hot. Would that you were either cold or hot! So, because you are lukewarm, and neither hot nor cold, I will spit you out of my mouth. For you say, I am rich, I have prospered, and I need nothing, not realizing that you are wretched, pitiable, poor, blind, and naked." (Revelation 3:15-17).

This is the condition of many believers today. We might think that believers could never turn away from God if they are true believers, but many of us have turned away from God for periods in our lives. Some even end up falling into serious sins including rape, fornication, theft, assault, and other serious sinful conditions. Perhaps many of these were never true believers, but others were. However, they gave way to sin, and their heart was hardened. For these believers who have fallen away, Christ has compassion and seeks them; This is the compassion that God has for His children.

The sinful state of the Laodiceans resulted from their love of the world; their lack of humility; their lack of meekness and knowledge of

God; for their lack of a true decision to stand up and honor the name of God (and remain that way every second of their lives). This church desired to be served rather than to serve, seeking status in the church over each other. Such churches aim to draw in new members using human and earthly tactics, trusting in their own abilities, eloquence, or intellect to convince people to embrace the Gospel. In this way, some manage to fill the buildings with sympathizers attracted by what is offered, but not with true disciples of Christ, and so end up with a worldly sick church.

Some people praise themselves when others come to the feet of Christ, but the glory belongs only to God. Likewise, when praised for what we do, our hearts may become proud. When this happens, we are to be pitied; we become miserable before an Almighty God, a thrice Holy God, who is the One who does His work in us, and through us.

The case of the Laodiceans is the same as that of the disciples on the road to Emmaus. Numerous people have professed faith in Christ, yet do not authentically walk in His ways, as evident from their desires and aspirations. If my greatest desire each day is not to honor God and remain surrendered to His mercy, then I need to realize I have a serious sin problem and need genuine repentance. Christ is at the door and knocks, and He does so through messengers, preachers, friends, books, etc. God is the one who rebukes those who have fallen astray from Him and knocks at the door of their hearts in different ways to make them return to His eternal grace.

We have to invite Jesus to dwell with us; open the door and have communion with Him. We must stop removing Christ from our thoughts, actions, decisions, and work life. Some think that it is enough to have communion with Christ only on Sunday in church, but those who think this way, in reality, they do not have any communion with Him at all, He is outside, calling to them.

This condition of spiritual lukewarmness that the Laodiceans experienced translated into spiritual blindness (v. 17), that is, they did not realize their condition and needed to be harshly rebuked by Christ before they could repent. He will knock on the door of their lives to enter to live among them and have communion with them. Therefore, it is necessary —first of all— to value our communion with Christ, because if we do not appreciate the enormous value of our time with the Lord, how will we be interested in inviting Jesus to dwell in us?

This was also what happened with the disciples on the road to Emmaus, which is why the Lord harshly rebuked them and taught them while they were on the road, so that, when the time came, they would be prepared and ready to invite Him to dwell with them. If Christ had not rebuked them as harshly as He did, nor taught them for more than two hours, they would never have invited Him to dwell with them.

Most of those who open their hearts to the Gospel and believe in the Lord do not achieve a level of total surrender on the same day. Nevertheless, if they have the desire to please Christ within them (when they submit to Him), they will be able to echo Paul's words: "I have been crucified with Christ. It is no longer I who live, but Christ who lives in me. And the life I now live in the flesh I live by faith in the Son of God, who loved me and gave himself for me." (Galatians 2:20). Would you be able, with all your heart, to say what Paul said in this passage?

We must invite Christ to be the Leader of our life, that only He would be the one who has complete control of our lives, so that His desires, wants, will, mind, heart, eyes, and thoughts become ours. He is our Lord; we are His slaves. He is the Father; we are the children. He is the Husband; we are the wife. So, let us leave behind our thoughts, weaknesses, insecurities, pride, and evil desires. Let us stop desiring personal recognition and praise from others to heartily long for His glory to be praised. This is the true invitation: Jesus wants to reign and rule in our lives.

I am convinced that the objective of Christ's saving and redemptive work is to embody Galatians 2:20, because there is still much of ourselves in them, and very little of Christ. Not all believers have given themselves to the service of God. And I'm not just talking about giving everything to serve the local church, but rather, being stripped of ourselves to serve Christ wherever and under the conditions He wants.

I hold the view that Galatians 2:20 represents the end goal of Christ's saving and redemptive endeavors, and the victory of the work of the Holy Spirit in us here on earth. It is the peak of our conversion, the moment when we truly see Christ and our true condition. It is the moment when, after having known Christ for years (without understanding who He truly is), a new panorama unfolds before our eyes. This is the moment when everything clicks, and the perspective of our life changes: your desires change, your treasure becomes heaven, and the earth becomes nothing more than a temporary dwelling where you wait for the time to return to the home you have never seen.

We came to the Lord; believed, heard the Word of God regularly, and called ourselves Christians. However, we still found ourselves struggling with sin every day, with our passions, with a mind rooted on earthly and mundane things, and not set in heaven, still living in a time in which our desires and love for the things of this world were above the desire for God. Our thoughts were constantly earthly and not heavenly. Our delight in the things of this world seemed better than the times we spent meditating on the Word of God and worshiping the name of God. But once we open our eyes to Christ, everything shifts. We find ourselves able to reject our sin, with our utmost wish being to honor our Lord Jesus and walk in His footsteps regardless of the sacrifice.

At this peak moment of the encounter, the believers on the road to Emmaus became fervent disciples; the fire of their hearts was ignited, and the flame of love would now remain burning. Now they were fully determined to surrender their lives to Him. This was what Moses, Job, Mary, Peter, Paul, Stephen, and many others experienced: they welcomed Christ into their hearts and started loving Him wholeheartedly, above all else. Their unwavering aim was to honor God in all they did, driving them forward.

This is where lukewarm believers transform into passionate followers, fully committing to serving God. Their lives are transformed, and they become a light amid darkness.

The will of man and the will of God

We know that salvation is by grace (Ephesians 2:8-9), that there is nothing we can do to earn it, and that before the foundation of the world God wanted us to be His children (Ephesians 1:4-5). However, it is our responsibility to decide whether or not to embrace the preached Word, as one cannot become a child of God without being exposed to the Gospel message.

> "Because, if you confess with your mouth that Jesus is Lord and believe in your heart that God raised him from the dead, you will be saved" (Romans 10:9).

"Come to me, all who labor and are heavy laden, and I will give you rest" (Matthew 11:28).

We are the ones who must repent, humble ourselves, pray, study, and grow for the glory of God. God will not do this for us. It is evident that there is a human responsibility, something that each person has to do, and all actions of obedience to the preached Word are evidence of salvation, since He who is saved bears fruit for God. Likewise, the man and woman who have come to Christ Jesus to give Him their lives must grow every day in wisdom and knowledge of God.

After experiencing a spiritual rebirth and committing to God, one is blessed with a burning passion to seek a deeper relationship with Jesus. When we invite Christ to reign in our hearts, the things of the world no longer have the same value, because all our love is concentrated in Him. Our ultimate love should be for Christ alone, and we should be ready to do and endure anything for Him. When we have surrendered to the Lord, we no longer run from suffering or pain. We are willing to go through trials and difficulties, if necessary, to gain Christ. We know that whatever we suffer in this world is nothing compared to our gift: to dwell with our Lord for eternity. Regarding this, the apostle Paul said by the Spirit: "For I consider that the sufferings of this present time are not worth comparing with the glory that is to be revealed to us" (Romans 8:18).

Our love for Christ becomes the most important thing in our lives. This is what the apostle Paul is thinking when he writes: "But whatever gain I had, I counted as loss for the sake of Christ." (Philippians 3:7). When you decide to renounce the way of the world to gain Christ, you no longer care about losing, leaving, and abandon everything you do to honor the Name of God, whatever the cost, without fear, knowing that the greatest gain we have is Christ.

We all have a different walk with Christ. We come to Him in different times, circumstances, and moments. Christ presented himself to Mary, and she recognized Him within minutes. The same thing happened with the other women; it was almost immediate. However, this was not the case with these disciples; it took them several hours to recognize the resurrected Christ. This illustrates that some need more time to see the living Christ, while others recognize Him immediately; but, regardless of the circumstances, encountering Jesus will always result in life transformation.

LISTEN TO THE MESSAGE, NOT THE MESSENGER

It is crucial for the messenger to uphold integrity and honor to prevent the Gospel from being blasphemed by our poor example. The leader chosen by God to spread the Gospel must maintain their integrity in the eyes of others, as succumbing to public sin could tarnish God's name. That is why leaders are called to be blameless in the church, they are to be held to a higher standard than the sheep before God (1 Tim 3:1-7), and to give an account for their ministry and works. However, we must all keep our eyes fixed on Christ, not on the servants of God. The focus of the Lord's sheep should not be the shepherd or Pastor of a congregation, and the shepherd of the congregation should have the goal of leading or pointing the sheep to Jesus, not to themselves.

We all have received God's mandate to spread His Word to the world. The people to whom we preach don't realize it, but it is not we who bring the Word, but God himself in His grace and goodness through us. When a person hears the Gospel through us, who do they see? Who do they hear? They see the messenger, the person of flesh and blood before them.

Many of us find ourselves idolizing pastors, evangelists, and men or women of God for this very reason: they cannot see God but only the messenger. Many of these messengers have a natural talent for communication, and some worship them to the point of seeing them as if they were Christian celebrities. The Word of God comes from God, not from man. When we carry the message of the Gospel, we express the words that come from God, and it does not belong to us (as long as it is preached faithfully, of course).

> **"And when they had prayed, the place in which they were gathered together was shaken, and they were all filled with the Holy Spirit and continued to speak the word of God with boldness" (Acts 4:31).**

When we preach the Word of God, it is not up to us whether a person believes or not, that depends on the work of the Holy Spirit in their hearts. Our job is to share the Gospel. If the listener wants to listen more, it will be up to them to continue listening or not.

> "And if the house is worthy, let your peace come upon it, but if it is not worthy, let your peace return to you. And if anyone will not receive you or listen to your words, shake off the dust from your feet when you leave that house or town" (Matthew 10:13-14).

We can present the Gospel in love and grace, and then keep walking. This is what Christ did, He preached to these disciples, and then He passed on; He knew that if these disciples were starving to hear the Word, they would invite Him to dwell with them to hear more from God. Despite the listener's lack of full comprehension of the Word, they will feel a strong desire in their hearts to keep on listening. Believers have an unsatiating curiosity to know more about God.

The disciples of Emmaus had the option of letting Christ continue His way; however, the consequence of this (if they let Jesus go) would have been that their eyes might have never been opened: they would continue with their worldly lives, and eventually they would completely turn away from God. Fortunately, it happened differently: these disciples of Emmaus were willing to host this "stranger" to continue learning from Him. That is why the Bible says that some have hosted angels without realizing it (Hebrews 13:2), and in this case, it was no one else than the King of kings and Lord of lords.

I am surprised by the reaction of these men. What would be the natural reaction of someone rebuked the way Jesus did? He had told them that they were foolish, and slow to understand! The natural reaction to an offense like this would be anger, resistance, denial, aversion, etc. They had been harshly reprimanded by a stranger, who still makes them pay attention and listen —for more than two hours— to an Old Testament class about the Messiah. All they had done was express their opinion of the latest events in Jerusalem, and in response, they had received a scolding and hours of teaching from a stranger.

Therefore, something we can admire in these disciples is their humility. Although they had initially dismissed the women's testimony, they were now open to listening to the voice of God. So, after listening to Christ, they invited Him to stay with them and He agreed and entered their house. When Christ accepted, something happened to these men: their eyes were opened, allowing them to finally understand the message of the Lord. What exactly caused these men to receive this blessing?

> **"When he was at table with them, he took the bread and blessed and broke it and gave it to them."** (Luke 24:30).

These men finally understood the importance of Jesus' resurrection. What was the decisive point for this to happen? The dinner with Christ. Perhaps these disciples had eaten together with the Lord several times during his earthly ministry, and they had permanent memories of it. This certainly has a close relationship with the Holy Communion, the Communion that Christ had instituted when He ate the last time with his apostles. These disciples had not been there (for the Bible says that Jesus ate alone with His apostles), but they most likely knew what had happened there, given the powerful events contained in that event.

> **"And he took bread, and when he had given thanks, he broke it and gave it to them, saying, 'This is my body, which is given for you. Do this in remembrance of me.'"** (Luke 22:19).

This was the moment when these men were finally convinced that the person standing before them was Jesus. They also understood — through the Lord's explanations— what was the true mission of Jesus by coming to this earth: to live a life without sin and die on the cross in our place and thus save humanity from the consequences of sin. It was during this event that they finally understood what Christ meant when He said He is the bread of life, the manna that came down from heaven.

In John 6 we see the miracle of the multiplication of the loaves; and the crowd after this followed Jesus to Capernaum. They sought Him out because they wanted a free meal, not because they really believed in Him. In this case, people followed Jesus as a politician who gives away food baskets. In response, Jesus told them to believe in Him. However, the response of the crowd -even after having seen with their own eyes the wonderful miracle of multiplication of the bread and fish- was this: "Our fathers ate the manna that he gave them in the desert, what sign do you do?". Then Christ said to them:

> **"For the bread of God is he who comes down from heaven and gives life to the world"** (John 6:33).

And also:

> "Jesus said to them, 'I am the bread of life; whoever comes to me shall not hunger, and whoever believes in me shall never thirst.'" (John 6:35).

The manna that God gave to the Israelites in the desert daily was nothing more than a message to them: a bread would come from heaven that would be sent by God for the eternal sustenance of their lives, and this manna represented Christ Himself. All who ate the manna in the wilderness died, so all who eat Christ must now die to be resurrected (1 Cor. 15:42). But the purpose of this manna, of this Bread that came down from heaven, which is representative of Christ, is that we would have eternal life with Him, and He will resurrect us on the last day.

> "And this is the will of him who sent me, that I should lose nothing of all that he has given me, but raise it up on the last day" (John 6:39).

Now some other questions arise: When did these men decide to leave their worldly thoughts (for they were slaves to sin), and become servants of Christ? When did they understand the message of Christ's death and resurrection? When did they understand that the body of Christ had to be broken and buried for us so that we could be saved? Let's look at it in more detail.

The Conviction

> "And their eyes were opened, and they recognized him. And he vanished from their sight. They said to each other, 'Did not our hearts burn within us while he talked to us on the road, while he opened to us the Scriptures?'" (Luke 24:31-32)

After spending years in His company, these disciples finally beheld Christ in His true light for the first time. They had walked with Him for many days, but at precisely that hour, they finally realized the identity of the One standing before them. The disciples on the road to

Emmaus were believers (as are many of us), but they did not understand who Jesus truly was.

They really did love Him, they were also true believers, therefore, their hearts burned when they heard his words. God had salvation plans for them, and showed them compassion, so He went to meet them where they were. Now, after exposing the Word of God and entering to pose with them, the test had passed. God had helped them overcome all sin; their ignorance and their wrong and poor concept of Christ, the image of their expected messiah had been demolished, therefore everything was ready to see Him. Then the miracle happened: they were able to recognize Him. The Holy Spirit opened their eyes, and they could see the Son of God. At last, they beheld with their own eyes the manifestation of the Word in human form, dwelling among us. They could see the glory of God in front of them.

Once they had truly seen Jesus, He disappeared before their eyes. They no longer needed more proof, guidance, or instruction, now they were ready to fulfill their purpose and wait for the coming of the Holy Spirit. Because their faith had been solidified, they were ready to continue their walk with the Lord, and with the Holy Spirit's help, they would remain firm to the end. The disciples who were heading to Emmaus to start afresh were ready to abandon everything once more for Christ, and dedicate their lives to Him unto death.

If I do not invite Jesus to dwell in me—as we have already seen—if I do not invite Him to be the King of my life and guide my path, then I will not be able to do what is coming next (in the next section), which is what these disciples did after recognizing who was before them. The only way to effectively fulfill their call is for me to obey Him and follow Him wherever He calls.

The Call

> "And they rose that same hour and returned to Jerusalem. And they found the eleven and those who were with them gathered together, saying, 'The Lord has risen indeed, and has appeared to Simon!' Then they told what had happened on the road, and how he was known to them in the breaking of the bread." (Luke 24:33-35).

These disciples did not wait a minute to share the resurrection's message. They stayed awake and immediately shared the news of the resurrected Christ with others, without waiting until the next day. It was already night; however, they decided to return to their original calling, and thus continue the work of Christ on earth. They couldn't wait, they couldn't contain the reality of what they had just seen; Therefore, they immediately went to testify to others that Christ had risen, and they were witnesses of this.

Brethren, the joy of preaching the Word of God and speaking of Jesus only occurs when our eyes are opened to the reality of the majesty of the Lord. The desire to serve Christ at any time and any moment; and bring the Cross message and resurrection to every place was what moved these disciples to walk for two to four more hours, at night, to tell the other disciples what had happened, that they had seen Christ resurrected. What it had previously seemed a crazy thought to them was now the greatest thought in their hearts.

Christ Left Us a Great Commission

"Go therefore and make disciples of all nations, baptizing them in the name of the Father and of the Son and of the Holy Spirit, teaching them to observe all that I have commanded you. And behold, I am with you always, to the end of the age."
(Matthew 28:19-20).

This is our calling, and this is what the disciples of Emmaus did after facing the reality of the resurrection. Just as the women, who saw the resurrected Jesus and immediately carried the message to others, the disciples of Emmaus rushed to do the same. Similarly, the Lord was seen by Peter at one time (even though this event is not described in the Gospels but is only referenced in Luke 24:33). Consequently, by the time these disciples showed up, Peter had already persuaded the other apostles with his testimony about Jesus' resurrection. However, the testimony of the disciples on the road to Emmaus reinforced all the previous testimonies: that of the women and that of Peter. Although initially the apostles had not believed the women's testimony, Peter's testimony was sufficient for them.

Our duty is to spread the message of the resurrection and the good news of salvation to anyone willing to listen. If you listen and believe, your eyes will be opened, and you will receive the gift of salvation.

> **"For 'everyone who calls on the name of the Lord will be saved." How then will they call on him in whom they have not believed? And how are they to believe in him of whom they have never heard? And how are they to hear without someone preaching? And how are they to preach unless they are sent? As it is written, "How beautiful are the feet of those who preach the good news!" (Romans 10:13-15).**

Jesus took these men, who, although they truly loved Him, had a misplaced faith; likewise, when Jesus approached them they were doubters, lost, separated, of little faith, without any type of merit, and amid all this hopelessness, He made them witnesses of His resurrection. And thanks to the fruit of these men, and that of the apostles, you and I are here to continue being spokespersons for the glory of God to a world that lives in darkness. It was the encounter with the resurrected Christ that transformed the hearts of these disciples.

What does all this mean to you? Has Christ changed your heart like He did with these disciples? It is my prayer that our eyes also may be opened so that we may see Christ as He truly is, and the burning fire of the Holy Spirit may be awakened in us, for then we may live by Him and for Him, today and forever. Amen.

Chapter

VIII

THE FIRST APPEARANCE TO HIS DISCIPLES

Before continuing, I recommend you to read Luke 24:36-42, where this story is also narrated.

"On the evening of that day, the first day of the week, the doors being locked where the disciples were for fear of the Jews, Jesus came and stood among them and said to them, 'Peace be with you.' When he had said this, he showed them his hands and his side. Then the disciples were glad when they saw the Lord. Jesus said to them again, 'Peace be with you. As the Father has sent me, even so I am sending you.' And when he had said this, he breathed on them and said to them, 'Receive the Holy Spirit. If you forgive the sins of any, they are forgiven them; if you withhold forgiveness from any, it is withheld.'" (John 20:19-23).

What will we see in this chapter? We will recount the first appearance of Jesus to His apostles (and to His other disciples) when ten of them were gathered (since Thomas was not there). John describes this part of the story in more detail than Luke; John writes that there were two visits of Jesus to the meetings of the apostles (and other disciples of His). In this chapter, I will talk about the first appearance, while in the next I will talk about the second appearance. A week later, Thomas was present at the subsequent occurrence.

In Luke 24:33-42 the first apparition is also described, the one in which Thomas was not present, and according to Luke's narration, this apparition occurred just when Simon Peter was recounting the experience of his encounter with Jesus, and at the moment in which the disciples of Emmaus arrived, who also told what they had experienced. It was on that stage, when they were all gathered there and telling what they had seen; on that same Sunday night (the same Sunday on which the Lord had risen, Luke 24:13) Jesus appears to them.

Some Bibles capitulate these passages as "The Appearance to the Ten" and others as "The Appearance to the Eleven"; However, the truth is that, if we read the biblical account carefully, we realize that it does not say how many disciples there were. There were certainly not ten, since there were the disciples of Emmaus, and probably many other disciples, among whom were possibly Matthias, Joseph, called Barnabas, Stephen, and perhaps also the women who saw Jesus.

In the Jewish week, there is only one day that has a name, Sabbath (Saturday), the last day of the week. The Sabbath is the day instituted by God when He rested after the creation (Genesis 2:2). The next day for them is the first day after Saturday (for us, Sunday); then the second day after Saturday (Monday), and so on.

Let us now look back at the time when these events occurred. It says in John 20:19 that the disciples were gathered at sunset, which usually occurs around 7 pm. They were in Jerusalem, the first day of the week (Sunday). Likewise, these events took place around 30-33 BC, in the month of Nisan (March-April), on the 17th day of the month.

"On the evening of that day, the first day of the week, the doors being locked where the disciples were for fear of the Jews, Jesus came and stood among them and said to them, 'Peace be with you.'" (John 20:19).

In this verse, we can notice that the disciples were scared and hiding due to possible persecution against them (and against all those who professed to follow Christ). While they were talking about these things, they were terrified, with the door closed, afraid that the Jews or Romans would find them and bring harm to them. They feared being crucified or facing persecution themselves.

Christ had appeared to the women, to the disciples of Emmaus, and to Simon Peter. As a result of these testimonies, the other disciples started to believe in the resurrection of Christ. The disciples' words in Luke 24:34 confirm that "The Lord has truly risen and has appeared to Simon!"

What is surprising about this is that: these men, despite knowing that Christ had risen, were still afraid. In this chapter, we will explore the topic that will be discussed. We must all ask ourselves: Who do I fear? Do I fear men, Satan or God?

As long as we are alive, we must not be afraid of men. This life is temporary and so is this body. We all have our time to be born, and our time to die. No matter how long anyone lives on this earth, we will never escape this body of death. Christ had already warned His disciples —and warns all of us— that in this world they would have trouble and persecution for following Him.

> **"'Now we know that you know all things and do not need anyone to question you; this is why we believe that you came from God.' Jesus answered them, 'Do you now believe? Behold, the hour is coming, indeed it has come, when you will be scattered, each to his own home, and will leave me alone. Yet I am not alone, for the Father is with me. I have said these things to you, that in me you may have peace. In the world you will have tribulation. But take heart; I have overcome the world.'"**
> **(John 16:30-33).**

In their conversation with Jesus in John 16, His disciples told Him they believed He had come from God. And Christ said to them: "Do you now believe?" And it was as if He were telling to them: "Do you really believe? Do you guys really think you are believers? Let's see if it's true that you believe my words. Let's see if you believe that I have come from God. In other words, it is as if Christ were saying to them:

"You still do not believe (although you claim to believe); you are not yet prepared to obey me until death. You profess your belief in me verbally, but when push comes to shove, you will abandon me and leave me to face it alone. You will be scattered, and will not remain with me, and you will do so out of fear. But I tell you this so that, when it happens, you will remember my words. With me by your side, you will experience peace, as you will be under the protection of the Father. If you remain in me, I will guide you, because there is no king, no soldier, no priest, no demon, nor anyone who can do absolutely anything against you without my consent."

And He warned them:

> "...In the world you will have tribulation. But take heart; I have overcome the world." John 16:33b

Christ told them this from the beginning of His ministry:

> "Blessed are those who are persecuted for righteousness' sake, for theirs is the kingdom of heaven. Blessed are you when others revile you and persecute you and utter all kinds of evil against you falsely on my account. Rejoice and be glad, for your reward is great in heaven, for so they persecuted the prophets who were before you." (Matthew 5:10-12).

Christ always taught His disciples the truth from the beginning of His ministry: He showed them the true cost of following Him. He never hid from them that they will suffer because of Him. But He told them (paraphrased): "have strength, resist, trust in me, have peace."

While Christ was with them, they believed they were invincible. They felt so protected by Jesus that even Peter tried to kill one of the soldiers when they went to arrest Jesus, although he failed and only cut off one of his ears (John 18:10-11). Peter was not afraid when Jesus was with him, because he was confident in Christ. But Christ was taken from them, so fear took over their lives. They feared the persecution and the true cost of following Jesus.

In Matthew 8:24-27 the story is about a storm that arose in the Sea of Tiberias. The disciples were desperate and thought they were going to drown. Then Christ, in the middle of all this chaos, was fast asleep. They then woke up Jesus, and He calmed the storm immediately. So, we too must also awaken Christ in our lives, so may we have peace when the storm comes. If Christ is asleep in me, that is, if I do not believe He has the power to bring peace in my life in the middle of a storm, it is because I have not believed His words.

We should live in the fear of the Lord, and my fear should be reserved only for Him. That is, my trust, my reverence, and my life, should be placed only in God and not in anyone else: not in my finances, not in my house, not in my status, not in my assets, not in my family. Only He can give us all things, and He can take away all things.

Everything could be taken from us in this world and the systems of this world we live in, but no one can take away the salvation we have in Christ, and the peace we now have with God (Romans 8:38-39). In any circumstance, God will never allow you to undergo a greater trial that you cannot endure (1 Corinthians 10:13). All the trials that we may go through on this earth, no matter how hard they may be, should not be an occasion to doubt our God; rather, we must fully trust Him and never doubt that God is always watching over us and has complete care of our lives.

> **"Because you have kept my word about patient endurance, I will keep you from the hour of trial that is coming on the whole world, to try those who dwell on the earth." (Revelation 3:10).**

We can live in fear of losing our job, in fear of not having enough finances, losing our house, suffering from an illness, not passing an exam, or not being able to meet a goal; frightened because of demons or an evil spirit, of a coming hurricane, etc.

Fear paralyzes us and does not allow us to progress in our faith. Fear makes us hide so we won't be confronted, hurt, or martyred. Fear clouds our vision, takes over us, and makes us forget what God has said in His Word.

> **"Therefore do not be anxious, saying, 'What shall we eat?' or 'What shall we drink?' or 'What shall we wear?' For the Gentiles seek after all these things, and your heavenly Father knows that you need them all. But seek first the kingdom of God and his righteousness, and all these things will be added to you." (Matthew 6:31-33).**

The only One we really must fear is not the one who kills the body, but the One who can not only kill the body but also -and this is the most terrible- He can throw both the soul and the body into hell forever. Christ said: "And do not fear those who kill the body but cannot kill the soul. Rather fear him who can destroy both soul and body in hell" (Matthew 10:28).

Who is the One who can do this? Only God can judge us to eternal damnation, He alone is the Judge of our souls. The fear of God is the beginning of wisdom (Proverbs 1:7). If we fear God, we will want to honor His name above all else, even if it costs us everything we have. Now, if we fear men, they will be our God, and that fear will make us succumb to men's evil will and not God's will. In this case, Jesus' disciples were paralyzed by fear, hiding, not knowing, or understanding that God had many plans for them and the extension of Gospel of Christ.

"On the evening of that day, the first day of the week, the doors being locked where the disciples were for fear of the Jews, Jesus came and stood among them and said to them, 'Peace be with you.'" (John 20:19).

Why did Christ say "Peace to you" to his disciples? Christ stood before them and said "Peace to you" because they would no longer have to fear death. From that moment they could be confident that God had absolute control of their life and death. They could now be confident that each test they faced would be for God to shape their character to mimic Christ's.

It was as if Christ was saying to them: "Have peace, trust, rest in me. You will certainly be persecuted, but do not give rise to fear. Have peace, remember that you are my sheep and I am your Shepherd; I will take care of you, and my purpose will be fulfilled in you"

The beautiful thing about being a child of God is that we have a heavenly Father who knows absolutely everything; He knows everything that is in our hearts. He has perfect knowledge of the past, the present and the future; He is almighty, and He sent His Son to die for us, so that we would never doubt that He loves us.

God was present when you were born, when you graduated from elementary school; on every birthday, on every accident, on every illness, on every job loss; every time one of your family members died; every time you partook of food; on all your vacations. He was present in all your pains. God has always been present and has never left you alone, even before you met Him, He was already there, and He knew you.

Brethren, we will all be tested while we are in this fallen body. So, our faith must rise above trials and temptations. And here, what Christ is saying to them is this: "Look at me! I died, and I rose again! I conquered death, and now you have peace with God, your lives are safe in me, through my sacrifice on the cross! 'Peace to you.'"

"But he was pierced for our transgressions; he was crushed for our iniquities; upon him was the chastisement that brought us peace, and with his wounds we are healed." (Isaiah 53:5).

The worst thing that could happen to us on this earth is that they persecute us, hurt us, mistreat us and murder us. Christ already went through these trials, and He was resurrected in glory. Therefore, that is also the divine promise that we have from Him: that we will have peace with God and the guarantee of eternal life with Him forever.

"But they were startled and frightened and thought they saw a spirit. And he said to them, 'Why are you troubled, and why do doubts arise in your hearts? See my hands and my feet, that it is I myself. Touch me, and see. For a spirit does not have flesh and bones as you see that I have.'" (Luke 24:37-39).

After this, Christ rebuked the disciples gathered there, just as He did with the disciples at Emmaus. It is as if Christ asked them: "Why do you doubt? Why don't you believe in Me? Why are you afraid? Where is your faith in me? Where are those brave disciples who said a few days ago that they would give their lives for me?"

Christ tells them (paraphrased): "Touch me, feel me, look at my hands and my feet, it's me. I am not a spirit, look, I also eat bread, like you do; I am real, I have risen". The disciples could feel the Lord, and they saw Him eating, all this was a proof and did not let them have the slightest doubt that He was real; therefore, after this experience, they would never doubt again that He was alive.

Disciples of Christ! Brothers in Christ! Whatever you must go through on this earth, it is nothing compared to the spiritual treasure we will have living in the presence of our God for eternity. Be strong in the Lord and may your trials be a blessing that help you be shaped in the image of Christ!

The Glorified Body

"On the evening of that day, the first day of the week, the doors being locked where the disciples were for fear of the Jews, Jesus came and stood among them and said to them, 'Peace be with you'". (John 20:19).

Now I want to focus on the glorified body of Jesus. Observe that the passage says that Christ appeared in their midst while the door was locked. John writes this in his Gospel, and he was witness of this. Luke doesn't mention this detail, but Luke wasn't with them when it happened. Perhaps it was John himself who had closed the door, and possibly that is why he was able to emphasize this important fact.

When we die as believers in Christ, our souls go to paradise (Luke 23:43), a place of rest in the presence of God; We will be there until the coming of the Lord. The first resurrection will be for eternal life, which will occur when the Church is caught up to be reunited with Christ, according to passages such as Revelation 3:10, 2 Corinthians 12:2, 1 Thessalonians 4:15-17, 2 Thessalonians 2:1-17, etc.; and also, at that moment, all of us who are in Him (those who still live on earth), will be transformed into a glorified body to be able to dwell in God's presence.

Anyone, except Jesus, has been resurrected in a glorified body. However, at the resurrection of the dead (when Jesus comes for his Church), both those who have died in Christ and those of us who remain then will be given a glorified body, and with this new body will live in God's presence forever (Revelation 20:4-5). Meanwhile, those who die without Christ, at the end of the millennium, will also be resurrected; The Bible calls this resurrection "the second resurrection." This last resurrection will be for judgment. For the damned also will be given a different body, this body will withstand the horrors of the lake of fire or hell for eternity (Revelation 20:11-15).

Let us now carefully examine what our glorified body will be like.

1. It will be similar to Jesus' body. Our glorified body will be like that of Jesus. This body will withstand seeing Jesus in all His glory and splendor. We will not see God the Father in all His glory, for no one can see God the Father in this way and live (1 John 4:12). However, we will be able to see the majesty and glory of Christ, who
is the visible image of our Father. Christ Jesus is the manifestation of the invisible God, and we will see and touch Him (Colossians 1:15-17).

> "Beloved, we are God's children now, and what we will be has not yet appeared; but we know that when he appears we shall be like him, because we shall see him as he is." (1 John 3:2).

2. They will be physical bodies (that can be touched, not spirits). Christ asked the disciples to touch Him. He desired for them to confirm that His body was made of actual flesh, not merely a spirit. (Luke 24:39). This body does not need food to live, because God is its sustenance; He can eat, for mere pleasure, but will not need to be fed to survive.

Also, when God makes the new heavens and earth, things that John talks about in Revelations 21, the new Jerusalem will come down from heaven, just as John saw in his vision. This is the wonderful City that is reserved for the redeemed. And in this City, John said by the Spirit, there will be no sea (Revelation 21:1). Therefore, the earth will not need water to sustain itself. However, the Bible speaks of a sea of glass (Revelation 4:6). The glorified body that God will give us may not require oxygen or hydrogen (the components of water). God Himself will fully support this body.

3. They will be bodies with superhuman abilities. Christ passed through walls (John 20:19), and suddenly disappeared (Luke 24:31). Likewise, there was something in the glorified body of the Lord that made His appearance different, and that is why His disciples could not recognize Him immediately, either changing His appearance or by changing their perception on Him:

a) It took the disciples of Emmaus hours to recognize Him (Luke 24:13-35)

b) His disciples did not recognize Him when He appeared to them at the Sea of Tiberias (John 21:12).

c) Mary Magdalene did not immediately recognize Him either (John 20:11-18)

4. They will be bodies given by God. Our bodies will be of divine origin, prepared to serve God for eternity.

> "But God gives it a body as he has chosen, and to each kind of seed its own body." (1 Corinthians 15:38).

5. They will be bodies without the human needs that we now have. There will likely be no need to sleep or rest. We will be able to work without fatigue or hardship. As children of God, reigning with Him for eternity, we will enjoy many divine characteristics.

> "It is sown in dishonor; it is raised in glory. It is sown in weakness; it is raised in power." (1 Corinthians 15:43).

6. They will be eternal bodies without sexual desires. Our resurrected bodies will be similar in honor and glory to those of God's angels. In the presence of God for eternity, we will experience the most beautiful and joyful pleasure, with no need for sexual desire; and this pleasure will last for eternity. There is no enjoyment in the entire universe that surpasses this.

> "But those who are considered worthy to attain to that age and to the resurrection from the dead neither marry nor are given in marriage" (Luke 20:35).

7. All parts of our being will be glorified. The Bible speaks of two parts in the human being, the spirit or the soul and the body. There are several theories regarding how these two elements are related; However, we can be sure of one thing: that there is, in addition to the physical body, something invisible within us. The following verses are just an example of this, 1 Corinthians 15:45; 1 Samuel 1:15; Job 7:11; Matthew 12:18.

When we are resurrected, our souls and spirits will also be glorified; Therefore, there will no longer be the possibility of us being influenced by the desires of this world.

> "It is sown a natural body; it is raised a spiritual body.
> If there is a natural body, there is also a spiritual body."
> (1 Corinthians 15:44).

8. Our bodies will be immortal and incorruptible. The body we now have ages with time, it gets sick and wears out. We are literally dying from the moment we are conceived. The Bible says that this body must die to be resurrected in glory (unless it is transformed at the coming of the Lord). Just as a seed that is sown must die for a plant to be born, this mortal body will need to die before being resurrected by the Lord in a glorified body.

> "So is it with the resurrection of the dead. What is sown is perishable; what is raised is imperishable. For this perishable body must put on the imperishable,
> and
> this mortal body must put on immortality."
> (1 Corinthians 15:42,53).

9. This new body will be luminous or radiant. Christ radiated light when he was transfigured; the same was true of Moses and Elijah (Matthew 17:2). When Moses was in the presence of God for 40 days on Mount Sinai, after he came down, his face was resplendent (Exodus 34:35).

> "Then the righteous will shine like the sun in the kingdom of their Father. He who has ears, let him hear."
> (Matthew 13:43).

10. We will keep our own identity, but we will have a new name. When Christ was transfigured, Moses and Elijah were present, and for some reason, Jesus' disciples knew who they were. Jesus continued to be the same person and identity even after resurrecting.

> "And God raised the Lord and will also raise us up by his power." (1 Corinthians 6:14).

> "He who has an ear, let him hear what the Spirit says to the churches. To the one who conquers I will give some of the hidden manna, and I will give him a white stone, with a new name written on the stone that no one knows except the one who receives it." (Revelation 2:17).

The Power of the Holy Spirit

Now we will see how Christ empowers or equips these men with the most important gift they will receive in their lives to be able to truly follow Christ from now on: He gave them the Holy Spirit.

> "And when he had said this, he breathed on them and said to them, 'Receive the Holy Spirit. If you forgive the sins of any, they are forgiven them; if you withhold forgiveness from any, it is withheld.'" (John 20:22-23).

Now I will ask you to transport yourself for a moment to that scenario. Imagine that you are there and that you are one of Jesus' disciples. It is a Sunday, three days have passed after the death of Christ, and you are one of those who are locked in that place full of fear. Jesus, the long-awaited Messiah, has died, and you, along with the other disciples, are blamed for stealing the body.

You are terrified of being martyred and feel helpless. The Roman government is against you, and so is the priestly body of Israel. They have no weapons or any way of defense. They are a small group, no more than 120 people.

You have a desire to believe and follow the message of Jesus, but you feel like the world is coming down on you. Your thoughts are overwhelmed, and you see no way out of this situation. Suddenly, the message of the resurrection arrives, and a ray of hope started to shine.

The women saw Him, Peter saw Him, and now the disciples of Emmaus. But, even so, they do not see a reliable way out, they remain afraid, with the doors closed and paralyzed.

Suddenly, in this very stressful situation, the Light of the world appears in the midst of everyone, the Creator of heaven and earth, the beginning and the end, the Alpha and the Omega, the Creator God, the Lamb of glory, the true King of kings and Lord of lords.

Jesus appeared before them and said: "Peace be with you", that is, there is nothing to fear. Jesus understood what you are experiencing, and He appears to you to tell you the same. He showed His disciples His hands and His feet; and in this way, they appreciate the martyrdom that He had just experienced, and also -this is the most important thing for you and the rest of the disciples- to affirm their hearts and give them confidence that He has complete control over life and death. "Come, touch me," Jesus told them, "see me eat, see that I am real"… Let us now return from that scenario.

Something began to happen with these men full of fears and doubts. Suddenly their faith began to rise. They began to have hope. Christ had noticed these unfaithful, unbelieving men, full of fears, and prepared them for a great commission: a task that required supreme faith, and unwavering trust in God.

In their strength, these men had failed Christ again and again. And in their own wisdom, they had often gone against the teachings of Jesus, so much so that Christ himself rebuked Peter, saying: "Get behind me, Satan!" (Matthew 16:23). These were men who were easily deceived by the enemy and did not need much to become corrupted, therefore, they needed a continuous and supernatural support. They needed strength and courage that could not come from within them.

Doing this work in their own strength was impossible, therefore, they needed someone to make the impossible possible. They needed supernatural strength and faith to overcome all the trials that would come into their lives. What was to come was many years of tribulation: they would have to suffer and endure the unbearable, even to the point of martyrdom, for the Lord's sake. So, the Bible says:

> **"And when he had said this, he breathed on them and said to them, 'Receive the Holy Spirit.'" (John 20:22).**

We find here the mention of the Holy Spirit of God. The term Trinity, referring to the Father, the Son, and the Holy Spirit, is often used in theological texts. The Father is said to be the first person of the Trinity, the Son is the second person, and the Holy Spirit is designated as the third person of the Trinity. However, in my opinion, the fact that the Holy Spirit is mentioned as the third person of the Trinity, in the minds of many believers, could cause the enormous importance of the Spirit of God to be significantly diminished.

Placing the Holy Spirit in a third position may suggest that his role is seen as lesser than that of the Father and Jesus. When we think of the Trinity, we must visualize God the Father, God the Son, and God the Holy Spirit as one God, they are all in the first place. Together they are God, they are one. None is first, none is second, and none is third. The three of them are all at the forefront, equally deserving of worship, respect, significance, glory, grandeur, and authority.

Among the Trinity, there is no envy, discord, strife, or desire for power. Among the Trinity, neither the Father, the Son, nor the Holy Spirit, none of the three persons is more worthy of glory than the others. They are the Creators of the universe, they together made everything that exists. They together created mankind:

"Then God said," Let us make man in our image, after our likeness. And let them have dominion over the fish of the sea and over the birds of the heavens and over the livestock and over all the earth and over every creeping thing that creeps on the earth." (Genesis 1:26).

Many believers talk about the Holy Spirit as if He were a manipulable person. I would consider that to be a blaspheming thing to do, which is to command God to do what we want. This worm of a man, as King David said of himself, this corruptible man, how will he order God what he has to do? Could I order Him to do my will? Does God live for our service? No, certainly not, the reality is that we are at His service, because He is God. So, no one could ever manipulate the Holy Spirit, because He is as much God as Jesus and the Father are.

Everyone who has been saved has been sealed with the Holy Spirit, and the seal of the Holy Spirit is our evidence of salvation. He is our passport to heaven who ensures our entry there. If we have been washed with the blood of Christ, we have been sealed with the Spirit and have entrance into the presence of God. But let us keep something in mind: God does not live where there is sin, His temple is sacred, and we, being temples of the Holy Spirit, are sanctified by Him. Christ bore the price of our sin, and now we are sanctified by the beautiful and glorious presence of the Spirit of God.

Sin was conquered by Christ and brought to a definitive end (1 Peter 4:1); therefore, the precious blood of Christ sanctifies the children of God for the dwelling of the Holy Spirit in them. Marvel in this thought: mortal body is the dwelling place of the Spirit of God. The Spirit of God does extraordinary work in us, rebuking us of sin, guiding us along the right path, helping us make wise decisions, comforting us, encouraging us, giving us joy and peace, and sanctifying us completely (1 Thessalonians 5:23).

Just as Christ forgave sins and healed the sick; and just as Christ was never defiled by sin, but on the contrary, He sanctified what was unclean, in the same way the Spirit of God continually purifies, sanctifies, vivifies, and rectifies those who put their faith in Christ.

Nothing can make God unclean, absolutely nothing. His presence is so holy that he is the one who sanctifies; The unclean cannot contaminate him, he is always victorious. For those who are filled with the Spirit, sin cannot dominate or control their lives. There is no place for sin in the life of a Christian. And if the Christian has any contact with sin because he walks on this earth, God gives him the power to overcome it and not fall into the temptations of the devil and the flesh. When a Christian stumbles, it is not due to a lack of resources but a choice to ignore them and give in to their sinful cravings. It is the power of the Holy Spirit who acts in the believer to make him always victorious over sin if we humble ourselves before him. We should never love or enjoy our sins but hate them and love living in God's righteousness.

In John 20:22 Christ equipped His disciples with the most powerful weapon they could ever receive, that is, God himself living in them. God himself scanning every thought, dictating every step, and guiding every step of their lives. Throughout the book of Acts, we witness the Holy Spirit leading the Lord's disciples at every step.

Today we have the Bible. The Bible was inspired by the Holy Spirit to guide the believer, so that we would know the will of God, and live with full certainty. Even those of us who are not learned in the Scripture, the Christian can be sure that, if he prays to the Lord, the

Spirit will make known the deepest thoughts of God the Father and of Jesus in due time.

> **"These things God has revealed to us through the Spirit. For the Spirit searches everything, even the depths of God." (1 Corinthians 2:10).**

The Holy Spirit has the infinite and eternal ability to reach the depths of God and understand Him. The Holy Spirit can perfectly reveal God's will to us because he is God Himself.

His majesty, his glory, his dignity, his grace, his mercy, his goodness, his wisdom, and his power, all are equal to God the Father, and Jesus. If the grace of the Holy Spirit were not infinite and eternal, how are we now alive and not condemned to death? He observes every sinful thought that crosses our minds and patiently leads us to renewal. His work is tireless and constant. Without the work of the Holy Spirit no one could come to Jesus, no one could accept Christ in their heart, no one could remain in Christ, nor please God the Father.

Every Christian necessarily needs the Holy Spirit to accept Christ and live like Him. He is the one who guides unbelievers to believe, and who convinces the hearts of those who rebel against God.

> **"Therefore I want you to understand that no one speaking in the Spirit of God ever says 'Jesus is accursed!' and no one can say 'Jesus is Lord' except in the Holy Spirit." (1 Corinthians 12:3).**

It is impossible to come to Christ without the Spirit of God revealing Jesus to us. Only the Spirit of God can guide us to Christ. This is why Christ said:

> **"But whoever blasphemes against the Holy Spirit never has forgiveness, but is guilty of an eternal sin" (Mark 3:29).**

We can see clearly in this passage that those who blaspheme or curse the Holy Spirit and attribute the works of the Holy Spirit made through Christ as the works of the devil don't have salvation, since it is precisely the Holy Spirit who convinces people or their sin and leads them to repentance to be saved. Likewise, the evidence that the Holy Spirit dwells in us is faith, we believe in Christ because of the Holy Spirit; and if anyone does not believe in the work of Christ, they also deny the work of the Spirit of God.

The Holy Spirit is the one who shows us Christ, is the one who bears witness to him, who reveals our sin, our need for repentance, salvation and reveals us the truth, that Christ is indeed the Holy Son of God. He is the one who opens our spiritual eyes to see, our ears to hear and makes us able to understand the spiritual revelation and significance of the Word of God.

"But when the Helper comes, whom I will send to you from the Father, the Spirit of truth, who proceeds from the Father, he will bear witness about me." (John 15:26).

So, everyone who believes in the Word of God does so because they have believed in the testimony of the Holy Spirit, who has inspired all the Bible. We could even state that the Holy Spirit is the true Author of the Word of God.

WE SEE IT AT WORK THROUGHOUT THE OLD TESTAMENT:

a) In Exodus 31:2-3 He is active in Bezalel, who was filled by the Spirit of God to assist in building the tabernacle.

b) The Holy Spirit convinced even the enemies of God to do his will. This occurred, e.g. with Saul (1 Samuel 19:23), who, even when he persecuted David, prophesied in the name of God, and the Spirit of God came upon him.

c) He came upon the false prophet Balaam, who sold himself to prophesy against Israel. However, after being rebuked —and this is perhaps unique in history— by a donkey, the Spirit of God came upon him, and he could not speak a curse against the people of God (Numbers 24:2).

d) He is present in Genesis during the creation of the universe (Genesis 1:2).

God promised that He would pour out His Spirit on all flesh, that is, on all those who believed in Him. Through the prophet Joel, God predicted that He would fill the hearts of many, and multitudes from all over the world would come to Him for repentance of sins. The glory of God would be seen by all and manifested through people. The power of the Holy Spirit would be present in the entire world.

"And it shall come to pass afterward, that I will pour out my Spirit on all flesh; your sons and your daughters shall prophesy, your old men shall dream dreams, and your young men shall see visions." (Joel 2:28).

Jesus entrusted the care of His church to the Holy Spirit until His second coming. This means that Christ recognized and fully trusted in the Spirit of God, who is powerful to sustain the redeemed, so that not even one of His sheep, of His bride, of His Church, would be lost if it remains under His careful protection. The Holy Spirit is able to preserve those whom Christ died for perfectly.

"Nevertheless, I tell you the truth: it is to your advantage that I go away, for if I do not go away, the Helper will not come to you. But if I go, I will send him to you. And when he comes, he will convict the world concerning sin and righteousness and judgment: concerning sin, because they do not believe in me; concerning righteousness, because I go to the Father, and you will see me no longer; concerning judgment, because the ruler of this world is judged." (John 16:7-11).

Jesus said that part of the work that the Holy Spirit would do would be this: convince the world of sin, justice, and judgment. That is to say, without the Spirit of God, no one can recognize his sin. No one is capable of acknowledging their faults before God, and if this does not happen, it is not possible for a person to believe in Jesus. Consequently, they cannot be justified by their works, and will be eternally condemned. Any person who does not repent before God is guilty of eternal judgment.

"And when he had said this, he breathed on them and said to them, 'Receive the Holy Spirit.'" (John 20:22).

There is debate as to what exactly these words mean, whether Jesus is speaking in a prophetic sense or whether they actually received the Holy Spirit at that moment. However, we can be sure of one thing: without the Holy Spirit, there is no spiritual life. Adam's body was brought to life when God breathed the breath of life into him (Genesis 2:7); now the disciples, through the Holy Spirit, were receiving spiritual life through the breath of Jesus, our Lord. Having made his perfect sacrifice on the cross and now resurrected from the dead, He moved these men from darkness to light, from lies to truth, from blindness to seeing, from death to life. After this the disciples would have the Holy Spirit working in them, guiding them to do the work of God on earth.

Forgiveness of Sins

Another important question we must ask ourselves is this: Who can forgive sins?

"If you forgive the sins of any, then they are forgiven; if you withhold forgiveness from any, it is withheld." (John 20:23).

What does this mean? Do we have the authority to forgive sins? Nowhere in the Scriptures do we read that the disciples forgave anyone's sins. In none of the NT epistles or the book of Acts do we read that the disciples declared to anyone: "Your sins are forgiven" as Jesus did. No one other than Jesus did this. Let's look at these passages where Jesus forgives people's sins:

• Jesus forgave the sins of Mary of Bethany (the sister of Lazarus, whom Jesus raised from the dead), when she poured perfume on his feet (Luke 7:48).
• Jesus forgave the sins of a paralyzed man, who was lowered from the roof of a house when brought in by his friends (Matthew 9:2).

Even the Pharisees hated Jesus because he claimed to have the authority to forgive sins, which for them was blasphemy, since only

God has the authority to do this (Mark 2:7). The apostle John himself testifies that only God has the power to forgive sins.

"If we confess our sins, he is faithful and just to forgive us our sins and to cleanse us from all unrighteousness." (1 John 1:9).

The Bible commands that we confess our sins to God. Only he can cleanse our sins and guilt. However, although men cannot forgive sins, we can seek help from the Church of God. Essentially, we have the opportunity to be a part of a close-knit community of believers, a discipleship group consisting of seasoned individuals in the faith, who provide us with encouragement. We can confess our sins to the pastors of the local church to receive spiritual help from them and be restored. The reason for doing this is not to receive forgiveness from these human beings (as imperfect as we are), but because confessing our sin helps us heal spiritually.

The first step to achieving repentance is confession. Repentance has to do with a turn in the opposite direction to our walk, and this has its root in the conviction of the Holy Spirit and in confession, either to God in private or in front of a group of friends in faith, who help each other to remain in Christ; in fact, the confession should be to God and fellow believers (ideally). God did not create us in Christ to walk alone. The Church's purpose is to support and care for one another with love and compassion.

"Therefore, confess your sins to one another and pray for one another, that you may be healed. The prayer of a righteous person has great power as it is working" (James 5:16).

It is very difficult to walk the Christian life alone, without the support of a church or mature brothers or sisters in the faith, people who guide us and guide us through the Word when we are in sin. Sin blinds us, and only the word of God can bring light.

Having said all this, what did Jesus mean by "those who forgive their sins will be forgiven"? Let's see the context.

> "Jesus then said to them again: Peace be with you; As the Father has sent me, so I also send you. After saying this, he breathed on them and said to them, 'Receive the Holy Spirit'" (Luke 24:21-22).

Christ here is sending His disciples (His church) into ministry; However, before sending them out, He gives them the Holy Spirit, who would convict the world of sin through the preaching of the Word of God. This is the context of the text.

Soon they would be empowered to bring the Word of salvation to others; and all those who repented and believed the Word would receive forgiveness of sins, while those who did not bear fruit of repentance, their sins would be retained. Christ is saying here that the Church could identify those who have truly believed by their fruits, and those who have not believed, also by their fruits. A true believer who walks in faith can usually be distinguished from one who has not yet been forgiven because of their fruits. For those in whom a true change of heart has taken place, the fruits of the Spirit of God will manifest them; in those who do not, (due to his lack of repentance) their fruits will also give testimony that they persist in their sins (even if they try to distort the Word of God to try to justify themselves).

What Jesus said to his disciples in Luke 24:21-22 is very similar to what He said in this other passage:

> "I will give you the keys of the kingdom of heaven, and whatever you bind on earth shall be bound in heaven, and whatever you loose on earth shall be loose in heaven" (Matthew 16:19).

In this passage Jesus gives authority (the keys) to his Church, to intercede and pray to the Father, so that, through the will of God, miracles and wonders may occur on earth. God is the one that does everything, and we can't do anything in our strength and power, it is His power that heals the sick and saves the lost. However, the Church has been given the authority to intercede with the Father, so that the will of God may be made a reality on earth.

Given this, the glory of all the good that happens on earth does not belong to us, for His is the kingdom, the power and the glory

(Matthew 6:13). It is the Holy Spirit who does the work, but we can intercede with the Father, so through the Holy Spirit, God's will be done on earth, which is, that the sins of the world be forgiven, because that is why He sent His Son to die in the cross for those who repent. If the Church does not fulfill this mission —in addition to preaching— then the sins of humanity will not be forgiven. As John Wesley once said, "God does nothing but through prayer."

Let's look at this other passage that also talks about the forgiveness of sins:

> **"Is anyone among you suffering? Let him pray. Is anyone cheerful? Let him sing praise. Is anyone among you sick? Let him call for the elders of the church, and let them pray over him, anointing him with oil in the name of the Lord. And the prayer of faith will save the one who is sick, and the Lord will raise him up. And if he has committed sins, he will be forgiven. Therefore, confess your sins to one another and pray for one another, that you may be healed. The prayer of a righteous person has great power as it is working" (James 5:13-16).**

We see here how James writes that those who are sick and suffering, and those who walk in sin, need the support of their church, and their pastors. They need people to care for their souls, not because they have the authority to forgive the sins of their soul, because they can help an ill person and through divine direction, prayer, and by the love shown by their church family, may they then be lifted by God, and then their sins may be forgiven through the repentance of their heart.

These who come to the disciples of the Lord, that is, to the Church, seeking healing or salvation, demonstrate with their humble attitude evidence of repentance; and they also demonstrate their faith, and so show evidence of forgiveness of their sins. By the way, unbelief is a sin before God. So, if God promises in this passage the salvation of the sick person for whom the elders of the church pray, and the anointing with oil being a sign that the ill person has decided to consecrate their life to the Lord, and so they shall repent with all their heart (because otherwise, this would be an obstacle to for their salvation), if God has promised this, it is then understood that the sick person has believed in God's promise. God promised to save those who repent, he doesn't promise to heal all who are sick.

As I have been demonstrating, a man, no matter how consecrated he is to God, does not have enough holiness to forgive a person's sin, nor can this forgiveness be achieved through repetitions of prayers, nor through the good works that someone may perform (no matter how excellent they may be). For a person to achieve forgiveness of their sins the only thing he needs to do is expressed in the following verse:

"The sacrifices of God are a broken spirit; a broken and contrite heart, O God, you will not despise." (Psalms 51:17).

Only a truly repentant, humbled, and broken heart before God will attain His favor and obtain His forgiveness. Do you want God to hear your prayer? Observe what Jesus says regarding the attitude we need to have when we pray:

"But when you pray, go into your room and shut the door and pray to your Father who is in secret. And your Father who sees in secret will reward you. And when you pray, do not heap up empty phrases as the Gentiles do, for they think that they will be heard for their many words" (Matthew 6:6-7).

Let us seek the face of God in private, where no one sees us, where no one hears us, and pour out our hearts before his presence, because only he can forgive our sins and cleanse us from all evil.

CHAPTER
IX

THOMAS' DISBELIEF

"Now Thomas, one of the twelve, called the Twin, was not with them when Jesus came. So the other disciples told him, 'We have seen the Lord.' But he said to them, 'Unless I see in his hands the mark of the nails and place my finger into the mark of the nails, and place my hand into his side, I will never believe.' Eight days later, his disciples were inside again, and Thomas was with them. Although the doors were locked, Jesus came and stood among them and said, 'Peace be with you.' Then he said to Thomas, 'Put your finger here, and see my hands; and put out your hand and place it in my side. Do not disbelieve, but believe.' Thomas answered him, 'My Lord and my God!' Jesus said to him, 'Have you believed because you have seen me? Blessed are those who have not seen and yet have believed'" (John 20:24-29).

In this chapter, we learn about a man who has perhaps been judged beyond his due by most Christians in history. Thomas has been known for centuries as "the unbeliever, the doubter"; although he was an apostle of Jesus, he didn't receive and believe the testimony of all the disciples who were present at the first appearance of the Lord. This event has made Thomas a universal symbol of unbelief and earned him the nickname of "doubting Thomas".

However, we should not make Thomas the icon of doubt or disbelief, nor say that this is the characteristic that best represents him, rather, disbelief goes beyond Thomas: it is present in many of us who say we are believers. If we trace this apostle's interactions in the Gospels —although he appears only in a few interactions— we could get a better idea of his character.

Thomas, the Apostle

Jesus selected him to accompany him on his ministry journey. (Mark 3:13-19). Jesus' ministry was growing, and likewise, the number of His followers, and of all the disciples who followed Christ, He selected twelve individuals to instruct them on a more intimate level. Of those twelve, He had closer contact with three of them, which were Peter, John, and James (Mark 13:3; Matthew 26:37; Matthew 17:1). So, Thomas, although he was an apostle, he was not one of Jesus' most inner circle.

Most of the disciples were from Galilee, except for Judas Iscariot, who was probably from Kerioth, a city south of Jerusalem in Judea. Within the region of Galilee was Nazareth, which was probably one of the worst cities in Israel, probably the worst in Galilee.

This is why everyone —even the disciples themselves— were surprised that Jesus was from Nazareth. The people of Galilee were considered peasants, uneducated people, farmworkers, fishermen, humble people, common people. They were not typically considered people worthy of being disciples of the Pharisees, Sadducees, Herodians, etc., since there were typically no renowned people coming from Galilee. Nazareth was despised even by the Galileans themselves.

At the beginning of Jesus' ministry, Philip sought Nathanael, and, "Nathanael said to him, 'Can anything good come out of Nazareth?' Philip said to him, 'Come and see.'" (John 1:46).

It was extremely difficult to think that, from a city as humble as Nazareth, a city considered (apparently) as the scum of Israel, and from where nothing good could come, was the city where the holiest being that has walked this earth grew up: Our Lord Jesus Christ. If we look closely, none of the apostles that Christ chose were highly educated;

none of them were teachers of the law, nor did they have any special gift.

None belonged to the sect of the Pharisees, the scribes, nor were they renowned politicians. There was no prince among the disciples. These men were rather common people, from the populace, people who typically never aspired to greatness. These men were just ordinary people like you and me, like most of those who will read this book.

These were the men Christ chose to carry His message to the world. There was no plan B, plan C or plan D. Christ only had plan A, which was for His church to spread and be established through the ministry of these simple men. Christ taught these men in a special way. Christ chose them, because He knew the plan He had for them, and the work that through the Spirit of God they were going to carry out. The foundation of the world's Christian faith was placed in the hands of these unsophisticated men.

They were sinners, and they recognized it; however —on the other hand— upon reading the Word of God we see that the apostles were not very humble, they sought the best positions in the kingdom of Jesus (Matthew 20:20-21); also, they lacked mercy and love for the sinner (Luke 9:54). They needed to be transformed into the image of God, just like you and me.

Christ was going to have maybe 16 to 18 months to train these men for the most difficult task of their lives. A task that in the end would demand a price of blood and sacrifice, this was the cost of following Jesus. God did not choose the best that there was in Israel, He chose people who might seem insignificant to the world, people from whom little could be expected, and from whom no one would ever think they would be capable of accomplishing something great. They were ordinary men, and from a low social class.

He chose fishermen; He chose Matthew, a publican or tax collector (these Jews considered traitors). The publicans were considered to have very low morals and a terrible reputation because they had sold themselves to the Romans for money and extorted their own people. He chose Simon, the Zealot (Simon was possibly an assassin who had dreams of being a revolutionary fighting against the Roman government).

In this group, there could be no influence peddling (so that someone could gain power). The apostles were not powerful men or with great achievements, they were not "elite socialites or high-class men", or considered socially prominent. They didn't have friends in high society to help them carry out the call of Jesus. It is worth noting that carrying out the church's mission as set by Christ does not involve seeking a prominent social status or striving for success in society. This is why Paul said:

"But God chose what is foolish in the world to shame the wise; God chose what is weak in the world to shame the strong; God chose what is low and despised in the world, even things that are not, to bring to nothing things that are, so that no human being[a] might boast in the presence of God." (1 Corinthians 1:27-29).

If God chose you, it is because you are weak, poor, in need, and everything you think are your strengths are probably your weaknesses, and everything you think are your weaknesses may be your strengths. Peter's weakness was that he was always very quick to speak, and slow to think. However, we can admire something about him: he was not afraid of making mistakes, but rather he had great enthusiasm to please God.

Just as Peter at one moment spoke a great truth (Matthew 16:16), he would say something horrendous as well (Matthew 16:23). He was very emotional, and very impulsive; but God used this character to put Peter as head of the Jerusalem church. God used all of Peter's weaknesses, used them to build his character, and used them to advance the Gospel.

God chose us because we are weak so there is nothing for us to glory ourselves or boast about so that no one says that it is because of their intelligence, wisdom, or knowledge that the work of God advances. There is a popular saying: "Tell me what you boast about, and I will tell you what you lack" [tell me what you boast about, and I will tell you in which area you should humble yourself].

Our greatest strengths must be broken so that our weaknesses shine and God receives the glory. The greatness of believers is not in riches or earthly power but in their humility and love for our Lord. This is why Christ said:

"But Jesus called them to him and said, 'You know that the rulers of the Gentiles lord it over them, and their great ones exercise authority over them. It shall not be so among you. But whoever would be great among you must be your servant.'" (Matthew 20:25-26).

How did Christ choose His apostles? Several of them, such as Peter, Andrew, and Matthew, were invited by Christ to follow Him while He was preaching; but we do not have specific data on others, only their names appear on the list of the twelve selected.

"The names of the twelve apostles are these: first, Simon, who is called Peter, and Andrew his brother; James the son of Zebedee, and John his brother; Philip and Bartholomew; Thomas and Matthew the tax collector; James the son of Alphaeus, and Thaddaeus" (Matthew 10:2-3).

"And when day came, he called his disciples and chose from them twelve, whom he named apostles: Simon, whom he named Peter, and Andrew his brother, and James and John, and Philip, and Bartholomew, and Matthew, and Thomas, and James the son of Alphaeus, and Simon who was called the Zealot, and Judas the son of James, and Judas Iscariot, who became a traitor" (Luke 6:13-16).

A noteworthy observation is that the evangelists organized the list of apostles into groups of four. So, there were three groups of four disciples. In the first group, Peter is always mentioned first and was the main leader of all the apostles, along with Peter, Andrew, his brother, and the sons of thunder (Mark 3:17), John and James (who He was the first apostle martyr [Acts 12:2]).

In the second group Phillip goes first, and next to him Bartolomé (Natanael); then Matthew and Thomas. Finally, in the third group, James (son of Alpheus) is mentioned as the main one; then to Simon, the Zealot; Judas, son of James and Judas Iscariot.

All the disciples believed in Christ as the Messiah and thought that the kingdom of God had finally come to earth. However, there is enough evidence to think that they were haughty at heart, proud; they wanted the best seats, they loved the fame that Jesus had and being seen with Christ (the miracle worker); but none of them humbled themselves to wash the feet of others at the last supper. They all professed to love Jesus; however, at the moment of crisis, when Christ was captured and then hung on the cross, they abandoned Him.

No disciple in the Bible is recorded as believing that Christ would be resurrected. Not even Mary, his mother, thought this was possible, and she is not even mentioned until after the resurrection, at Pentecost.

We already learned that Mary Magdalene and the other women did not believe in the resurrection of the Lord until they saw Jesus alive. The disciples at Emmaus did not believe until their eyes were opened when Jesus broke the bread. Not even Peter -the apostle of greatest faith among them [the one who walked on water, like Jesus]- believed without having seen, and none of the rest of the disciples were completely convinced that Christ had risen until He appeared before them. Everyone, absolutely everyone, was unbelieving, and did not believe in the resurrection of the Lord until they saw Him alive; and even Matthew records an even more surprising fact:

"And when they saw him they worshiped him, but some doubted" (Matthew 28:17).

This means that there were even some disciples who, seeing the resurrected Christ with their own eyes, nevertheless doubted. The human disbelief is something so strong that only with the help of the Holy Spirit can we overcome it.

Thomas was no exception; his disbelief was no greater than that of the other disciples. If it's a contest regarding disbelief, everyone takes the prize. No one dared to confront the Sanhedrin or the Romans to prevent Christ from going to the cross; everyone was full of fear, they all fled and went into hiding. Among the frightened disciples was Thomas.

To grasp the meaning behind the passage discussing Thomas's unwavering doubt, despite the other disciples confirming Christ's resurrection, we must delve deeper into the character of this apostle. John MacArthur wrote a book called 12 Ordinary Men. I suggest checking out this engaging book, where the author dives into the depths of the apostles' hearts by drawing on biblical evidence and historical records. The information discussed in this chapter is largely derived from the study book.

Thomas, the Ordinary Man

Who was Thomas? He was also known as Didymus, a word that means twin in Greek. The New Testament does not reveal the identity of his twin, and no details are provided.

Where was Thomas at Jesus' first appearance? Through a closer examination of his personality, we may be able to determine Thomas' location and emotional state when confronted with Jesus' death.

It is interesting to note, firstly, that only the Gospel of John records the episode of Thomas' unbelief, and in general, it is the only Gospel that records the sayings of this apostle in the Bible. Neither Matthew, Luke, nor Mark recorded Thomas' words.

The first sentence of Thomas recorded in the Bible is in the story of Lazarus. In John chapter 10 we read that Christ's ministry was flourishing; At that time, he ministered in Judea (a region of Israel near Jerusalem); But when being in Judea, due to Jesus' comments regarding his identity (since he identified himself as the Son of God, making himself equal to God), the Jews wanted to stone him. However, he left there, and together with his disciples, crossed the Jordan. It was at that point in his journey that he heard that his friend Lazarus, the brother of Mary of Bethany, and Martha, was seriously ill. Bethany was two miles from Jerusalem, and the Jordan River was about 21 miles from Jerusalem. The biblical passage in reference says the following:

> "Now a certain man was ill, Lazarus of Bethany, the village of Mary and her sister Martha. It was Mary who anointed the Lord with ointment and wiped his feet with her hair, whose brother Lazarus was ill. So the sisters sent to him, saying, 'Lord, he whom you love is ill.' But when Jesus heard it he said, 'This illness does not lead to death. It is for the glory of God, so that the Son of God may be glorified through it.' Now Jesus loved Martha and her sister and Lazarus. So, when he heard that Lazarus[a] was ill, he stayed two days longer in the place where

he was. Then after this he said to the disciples, 'Let us go to Judea again.' The disciples said to him, 'Rabbi, the Jews were just now seeking to stone you, and are you going there again?' Jesus answered, 'Are there not twelve hours in the day? If anyone walks in the day, he does not stumble, because he sees the light of this world. But if anyone walks in the night, he stumbles, because the light is not in him'" (John 11:1-10).

Christ loved Lazarus. He had a special love for this family. In those days, Lazarus fell ill and his illness was fatal. However, Christ told His apostles that this illness would be so that God would be glorified. Christ knew that this situation, no matter how difficult it was, would not end in tragedy, but rather it would be so that the power of God would be demonstrated, and so that everyone would realize that He has power over life and death.

So, instead of immediately coming to the aid of His friend, Christ planned to stay two more days before going to Lazarus [who by then was already dead]. During that period, Jesus' followers were experiencing the tense atmosphere in Judea, particularly in the vicinity of Jerusalem. They had been threatened with death just a week or two ago, and they had withdrawn from there because the Jews had the firm intention of stoning Jesus; However, what was difficult for them to understand was that Jesus wanted to return to that place. That is why the disciples asked him with fear and amazement: "Rabbi, the Jews recently tried to stone you, and are you going there again?" (v. 8).

It's as if they were saying to Him: "Couldn't you heal him from here? Why would you expose yourself to totally unnecessary danger?" And then they added: "And you're going there again?" (V.8), as if to say: "Aren't you afraid of dying?" Basically, these words were an attempt by the disciples to give Christ "wise and prudent advice": "You must hide; we are all afraid of going back, and you should be too. We will all be in danger of death, and there is no need for that, we are safe here."

We see here that the disciples had not learned to listen to the voice of Jesus. Even Peter, the brave disciple, who said to Christ: "Lord, if it is you, command me to come to you on the water." (Matthew 14:28), this time he remained silent. Surely, he himself was also afraid of going back to Judea.

Given this, Christ's response was surprising. He did not hesitate as to where He would go; He walked in light, not in darkness and had complete certainty of the perfect will of the Father; He knew the purpose for which He had come to earth. Christ never feared death while He walked as one of us, nor did He do things in secret. He is the light of the world, and in Him there is no darkness.

> **"After saying these things, he said to them, 'Our friend Lazarus has fallen asleep, but I go to awaken him.' The disciples said to him, 'Lord, if he has fallen asleep, he will recover.' Now Jesus had spoken of his death, but they thought that he meant taking rest in sleep. Then Jesus told them plainly, 'Lazarus has died, and for your sake I am glad that I was not there, so that you may believe. But let us go to him." (John 11:11-15).**

It is seen in this passage once again how the disciples did not have enough trust in Christ, and how they let their fears fill their hearts. They looked for any excuse not to return to that land —to the region of Judea— for fear of persecution and death. Jerusalem and Bethany were in the region of Judea, and Bethany was just two miles from Jerusalem. They did not want to go there and tried in every way to convince Jesus not to go.

Sometimes, in our own prayers or requests to God, we act in a very selfish way, and perhaps, we do not even realize it. It is as if the disciples said to Christ: "He does not need you, your power, your presence, your grace, and your eternal love. Better, Lord, let us stay here where we are safe."

If Christ had listened to their selfish request, humanity would not have seen one of the Lord's most impressive miracles while on this earth. He wanted to teach them not to fear. He wanted to teach them who they should trust: the one who has power over life and death. This is precisely where Thomas is first recorded speaking in Scripture.

> **"So Thomas, called the Twin, said to his fellow disciples, 'Let us also go, that we may die with him.'" (John 11:16).**

We see that the idea that the disciples had was this: If we return to Judea, we will die. It was here that Thomas -and not Peter- is the one who takes the initiative, and basically says: "Come on, let's follow Jesus unto death if necessary. I want to be where Christ is, and if we have to die, let's die." Thanks to Thomas's intervention, the disciples, still afraid, decided to obey the voice of Christ.

This man loved Jesus, and he did not live under the illusion that following Him would be easy. He preferred to die with Christ than to depart from Him. In this context we could perhaps think that Thomas was a pessimist, one who sees the worst scenario in everything; instead of an optimist would say: "Come on, God will save us from death!"

For Thomas, returning to Judea meant dying, but he preferred to die with Christ rather than live apart from Him. We could perhaps get the idea, based on this interaction, that Thomas tended to see the worst in each circumstance; He might have been like those who always see the negative in everything (and not the positive). However, we can see the faith that is revealed here: Thomas was willing to die for the Lord. Would we have this faith that Thomas expressed knowing the danger that both Jesus and His disciples would face? This danger later became more real to them when Jesus died and was the reason they fled. Let us ask ourselves now: Are we willing to follow Christ until death?

Thomas showed us with his life and testimony the words of Paul when he said: "For me to live is Christ, and to die is gain" (Philippians 1:21). From Thomas' words, we can learn to be brave enough to honor Jesus no matter the cost. It is very comfortable to live a Gospel that does not demand anything, one that we live only in the church, with our families; without suffering the persecution that following Christ entails. It's a fact that living a life in line with Christ's teachings and worshiping God authentically might lead to facing persecution at some point. Christ said:

> **"Blessed are you when others revile you and persecute you and utter all kinds of evil against you falsely on my account. Rejoice and be glad, for your reward is great in heaven, for so they persecuted the prophets who were before you." (Matthew 5:11-12)**

In Thomas, I see the love he had for Christ. However, he was a pessimist, he said, "Come on, let's die with Him." He was sure that if they returned to Judea, it would only be to find death. He saw the negative side of things, but even in his pessimism, in his negativity, Thomas followed Christ and led the other disciples to do the same.

So, there are also some in the kingdom of God. These are good at seeing the worst-case scenario, but at the same time, they are faithful, they love God with all their hearts, and God uses them to direct others to do His holy will.

Thomas's second interaction is recorded in John 14, but let's look at the preamble, John 13. John chapter 13 tells what happened at the Last Supper, during the Passover, a few hours before the crucifixion. Let us remember that a few days before this dinner, Christ made His triumphal entry into Jerusalem (John 12: 12-19). The disciples were probably empowered and hopeful thinking that Christ would soon take the kingdom and soon begin to reign over Israel.

In John 13 it is mentioned that Christ washed the feet of His disciples, including those of Judas, the traitor, and openly exposed him as such. That same night, Jesus told them that they would have a new commandment; He told them: "that you love one another: just as I have loved you, you also are to love one another." (v.34). At that moment, Jesus also predicts Peter's denial, and in the midst of all this, Christ tells them:

> "'Let not your hearts be troubled. Believe in God; believe also in me. In my Father's house are many rooms. If it were not so, would I have told you that I go to prepare a place for you? And if I go and prepare a place for you, I will come again and will take you to myself, that where I am you may be also. And you know the way to where I am going.'" Thomas said to him, 'Lord, we do not know where you are going. How can we know the way?' Jesus said to him, 'I am the way, and the truth, and the life. No one comes to the Father except through me'" (John 14:1-6).

This is the preamble or context of one of the most famous verses in the Bible, John 14:6. In this section, Jesus is talking about His departure, that they will no longer see Him, and that He would go back to God. Christ tells them that He will prepare dwellings for them, and then He will return for them. Clearly, Christ states here that He is the only way to the Father.

While Christ was saying all this, one of the disciples apparently only heard the part in which the Lord said: "I have to go and you will not be with me." Here we know a little more about Thomas' heart. He is the only one of the disciples who dared to ask Jesus about His departure. This information began to cause an internal panic in him: Christ would separate from him (them)! Here, again, we can consider the pessimistic character of the apostle Thomas, which is denoted once again. He did not listen to what Christ would do at his departure (prepare a place for them), but he was more concerned about knowing how he would be able to find him.

He viewed himself as a lost sheep, vulnerable to the dangers of the world, now that Jesus, the Good Shepherd, would no longer be by his (their) side. Thomas did not want to be separated from Jesus in any way. Thomas' greatest fear was that Christ would leave and that he would be separated from Jesus forever. He preferred to go with Jesus and die than to separate from Him; and now that Jesus says He is leaving, Thomas probably felt like he was about to lose the direction of his life. Thomas's questions reflect great anxiety in his thoughts.

Thomas' greatest fear came true in John 18, when Christ was arrested and then crucified. This man, the one who was willing to die with Christ, who did not want to be separated from Him at all (and who expressed that this was his greatest fear), did not know that in a few hours what he feared most would occur (when Christ was arrested and crucified).

His soul was confused. He was scared, helpless, lost, without direction. The words of Christ had turned him into a sheep without a shepherd. He did not know where Christ would go, and he did not know how to seek Him. Thomas felt alone, hopeless, emotionally destroyed. He was a man who, although pessimistic, loved Christ intensely and his worst nightmare was that the Lord would leave him (them).

We can imagine the intense pain Thomas had when Christ was crucified. This fact surely broke Thomas' heart (since, by nature, pessimists tend to suffer more than optimists). For the pessimist, pain and suffering is intensified. Pessimistic people usually do not see the solution to their problem, they tend to withdraw into themselves, and become more depressed than others. These people do not want to be bothered or talked to, because nothing you say can take them out of their suffering. It appears as if Thomas didn't want to talk about the events of Jesus death with anyone. Like he went to suffer all alone.

Jesus' initial encounter with the disciples stemmed from his intense suffering, suggesting that he may have simply desired solitude; that very likely he just wanted to be left alone. By examining the resurrection accounts closely, we can observe that Mary, the mother of Jesus, was absent both at the tomb during Christ's resurrection and during His appearances to the disciples. It is quite possible that both (Mary and Thomas) were inconsolable over the Lord's death, and simply wanted to be alone.

Now let's go back to John 20 and look at Thomas through this lens. Let's look at Thomas with eyes of compassion: he was a man who thought he had lost his greatest treasure, who, in his pessimism, refused to entertain any idea or hope to end his suffering. In his pessimism, he likely did not want to create a false hope in his heart, he did not want to believe that Jesus had risen for fear that it was not true.

> **"Now Thomas, one of the twelve, called the Twin, was not with them when Jesus came. So the other disciples told him, 'We have seen the Lord.' But he said to them, 'Unless I see in his hands the mark of the nails, and place my finger into the mark of the nails, and place my hand into his side, I will never believe.' Eight days later, his disciples were inside again, and Thomas was with them. Although the doors were locked, Jesus came and stood among them and said, 'Peace be with you.' Then he said to Thomas, 'Put your finger here, and see my hands; and put out your hand, and place it in my side. Do not disbelieve, but believe.' Thomas answered him, 'My Lord and my God!' Jesus said to him, 'Have you believed because you have seen me? Blessed are those who have not seen and yet have believed.'"**
> **(John 20:24-29).**

Now, knowing a little more about Thomas' character, perceiving the love he felt for Christ, and his pessimistic and depressive tendency, and his anxiety at the thought of losing Christ, we can understand why he was not present at the beginning. We can understand that what he felt was not only disbelief, but also a true love for Christ and a great desire to be with Him again.

Thomas was emotionally isolated; he did not want to believe the possibility of a miracle like this. We can see his pessimism when he says, "Unless I see the nail marks in his hands and put my finger where the nails were, and put my hand into his side, I will not believe " (John 20:25). He didn't want to believe so as not to have false hope. Likewise, Thomas was not satisfied with what others said, he wanted to experience for himself that Christ had risen.

He wanted to be sure of this reality: that his Lord and Savior was alive. Despite saying that he would not believe if he did not see him for himself, despite his refusal to believe, and his pessimism, Thomas did not turn away from Him, and the disciples' words moved him to return with them. Despite his pessimism, deep in his heart, he did want what they told him to come true. We know this, because if he were truly so unbelieving, what was Thomas doing with the other apostles eight days after Christ's first appeared to them?

Despite seeing everything negative, and with little hope; Despite not believing the testimony of the disciples, once again, his actions demonstrate how much he loved Jesus. Despite saying that he did not believe with his mouth, he returned to the disciples and this time did not depart from the group.

Let us now look at the love and grace that Christ shows Thomas. Let us observe the delicacy with which Christ treats him. Christ does not come and harshly rebuke him. He cares for his heart, shows him grace, and allows Thomas to be convinced that he is real. Just as Christ was patient with the unbelief of the other disciples; Just as he showed grace and patience with those at Emmaus, so he also showed it with Thomas.

Christ gave Thomas exactly what he needed. Jesus restored his faith. After convincing Thomas that He is real, and He is alive, then Christ rebukes his unbelief and motivates him to believe in His words.

What is the number of times Christ needs to reveal himself for us to believe? When are we going to leave our pessimism behind to truly follow Jesus? When will we stop seeing everything dark or obscure with no end to our suffering? The cure for our lack of faith and trust. The antidote that kills bitterness, and dispels our doubts is, and forever will be, the manifestation of our beautiful, glorious, majestic, powerful, loving, and holy Lord Jesus Christ.

A person may be living apart from Christ, in the depths of their sin, and live in the vilest spiritual situation that could be experienced, but if he or she is a sheep of Christ, the Lord will leave the ninety-nine and go look for him or her. He will look for them wherever they may be (Matthew 18:12). We have a Good Shepherd who loves his sheep, and no matter how far they have fallen, he will do everything necessary to bring them back to the fold. It is God's will that not one of his sheep should be lost (John 6:39). Therefore, each of us must walk in the light of the Word of God. Christ said:

"Let not your hearts be troubled. Believe in God; believe also in me. In my Father's house are many rooms. If it were not so, would I have told you that I go to prepare a place for you? And if I go and prepare a place for you, I will come again and will take you to myself, that where I am you may be also" (John 14:1-3).

No true Christian should show disbelief in the Word of God, since this is a serious sin before God, from Genesis to the book of Revelations, we see the dire consequences of this. However, we can trust that if we remain in prayer and supplication before the Lord; if we continue to follow and obey His Word and hold fast to it, the Lord will send His Spirit to strengthen our faith, and will lead us to see with our own eyes what we need to see and will lead us to hear with our ears what we need to hear, so that our faith be strengthened in Him.

And as for you, dear reader, no matter what your tribulation is, cast all your worries unto the Lord. If you are a disciple of Jesus, He has prepared a place for you, so that where He is, you also may be with Him forever. Just wait and trust, believe His Word, because it's truth.

Although times of difficulty and persecution come; although fears assail us, and we suffer losses. Even if our eyes are filled with tears, let us always put our faith in the words of Christ, who has prepared an eternal home for all of us who love Him. That is why nothing —for all eternity— could ever separate us from the Lord (Romans 8:35-39).

Our Lord Jesus came to accomplish his work. He transformed a pessimist like Thomas into a man filled with the Holy Spirit who did great things for the kingdom of God. Tradition says that Thomas took the Gospel to India, and that he died there around 72 AD. Tradition says that he was murdered by a Hindu priest on December 21st, accused of insulting one of their deities and leading many to follow the

Christ. There are still churches whose founding is attributed to the apostle Thomas.

Thanks to the love and patience of the Lord, this man, being a pessimist and unbeliever, was so radically transformed by the Lord that he became one of the greatest examples of faith this earth has ever had. This is the transforming power of God in the human heart. Now, if God used an ordinary man, like Thomas was, He can also use any of us if we love Him as much as Thomas loved Him.

Chapter

X

The Appearance in the Sea of Tiberias

"After this Jesus revealed himself again to the disciples by the Sea of Tiberias, and he revealed himself in this way. Simon Peter, Thomas (called the Twin), Nathanael of Cana in Galilee, the sons of Zebedee, and two others of his disciples were together. Simon Peter said to them, 'I am going fishing.' They said to him, 'We will go with you.' They went out and got into the boat, but that night they caught nothing. Just as day was breaking, Jesus stood on the shore; yet the disciples did not know that it was Jesus. Jesus said to them, 'Children, do you have any fish?' They answered him, 'No.' He said to them, 'Cast the net on the right side of the boat, and you will find some.' So they cast it, and now they were not able to haul it in, because of the quantity of fish. That disciple whom Jesus loved therefore said to Peter, 'It is the Lord!' When Simon Peter heard that it was the Lord, he put on his outer garment, for he was stripped for work, and threw himself into the sea. The other disciples came in the boat, dragging the net full of fish, for they were not far from the land, but about a hundred yards off. When they got out on land, they saw a charcoal fire in place, with fish laid out on it, and bread. Jesus said to them, 'Bring some of the fish that

you have just caught.' So Simon Peter went aboard and hauled the net ashore, full of large fish, 153 of them. And although there were so many, the net was not torn. Jesus said to them, 'Come and have breakfast.' Now none of the disciples dared ask him, 'Who are you?' They knew it was the Lord. Jesus came and took the bread and gave it to them, and so with the fish. This was now the third time that Jesus was revealed to the disciples after he was raised from the dead." (John 21:1-14).

In this chapter we will study about the appearance of Christ to the disciples in the Sea of Tiberias. Here we will find another beautiful example of the wonderful love of God, and the grace Christ shows towards us. Not only the Lord paid the price for our peace, but He, through the Holy Spirit, takes us by the hand in every step of our lives, carving His work in us and forging our character, guiding us with infinite love and patience.

After the first appearances to the disciples on Easter Sunday (this day there was multiple appearances: "Mary Magdalene, the women, the Emmaus disciples, Peter and most of the disciples together), it was a silence of eight days. Then, after that time, Thomas was present, and the Lord appeared again. Surely the disciples expected Christ to appear again, but a considerable amount of time must have passed, so much so that they perhaps thought Christ would not return again.

After His resurrection, Jesus appeared repeatedly over forty days (Acts 1:3), before ascending to heaven. Therefore, the third appearance of the Lord to the disciples occurred between the eighth and fortieth day after his resurrection. Maybe it had been about one, two, or three weeks since his last appearance (we do not know). Without a doubt, we know that it was the third day when Christ revealed himself to the disciples.

They were initially near Golgotha (the place where Christ was crucified in Jerusalem). When the angel who had appeared to the women at the tomb had told them: "But go, tell his disciples and Peter that he is going before you to Galilee. There you will see him, just as he told you." (Mark 16:7).

Christ had already told them this before dying: "But after I am raised up, I will go before you to Galilee." (Matthew 26:32). It was thus that the angels reminded them of the same thing that Christ had already told them. What did the disciples do? They obeyed, and after the second appearance they went to Galilee; and this is where we are now.

They were obeying the voice of Christ to go and wait in Galilee. They did not know specifically where they should be waiting; but it is very likely they were in Capernaum in Peter's house waiting for a few reasons, Peter was the leader of the group and Capernaum was the base of Jesus Ministry, where he moved to when he left Nazareth (Matthew 4:13). It is most likely that days went by, and they did not know exactly what to do, but we know that they paid attention and obeyed. Let's read the first verse of our passage again:

> **"After this Jesus revealed himself again to the disciples by the Sea of Tiberias, and he revealed himself in this way" (John 21:1).**

After the last apparition, the next one occurs here, in the Sea of Tiberias. We don't know exactly what city the disciples were in, but we may have a pretty good idea about where they actually were.

Why is it called the Sea of Tiberias? There is a city called Tiberias that remains in Israel to this day. It is located on the southwestern coast of the Sea of Galilee, and was named in honor of the second Roman emperor Tiberius Caesar Augustus (14 BC-37 AD), who was Augustus Caesar's successor. Today it has a population of around 45 thousand people.

The city was founded by Herod Antipas, who was the king who ruled in Israel when Jesus exercised His ministry. Antipas was the son of King Herod the Great, the one who ruled when Jesus was born, and who led to the slaughter of the children in Bethlehem (Matthew 2:16).

The city of Tiberias was also the capital of Galilee; a cosmopolitan city, full of Gentiles and Hellenistic Jews, that is, Jews who had adopted Greek culture. The prestige of this city was so great that the Sea of Galilee became known also as the Sea of Tiberias; however, there is no indication that the disciples were in that city.

If we read the passage where Jesus calling Peter is mentioned, then we will have an idea of where he used to fish. This was a city located northwest of the Sea of Tiberias or the Sea of Galilee. From the Gospel of Mark, we know that Peter lived in Capernaum (or very close to it).

> "And they went into Capernaum, and immediately on the Sabbath he entered the synagogue and was teaching. And immediately he left the synagogue and entered the house of Simon and Andrew, with James and John." (Mark 1:21,29).

Near the town of Capernaum was the town of Gennesaret, the place where Peter was initially called by Christ (Luke 5:1-11). The sea of Galilee was also called lake of Gennesaret (Luke 5:1) which name means "Garden of the prince, or valley of riches" in Greek. Between these two cities there was an approximate distance of three miles (almost five kilometers), and it is very likely that this was the place where Peter and these disciples went to work given Jesus hadn't appeared to them, since Peter and Andrew, and John and James normally worked there, and it was the place where they had their fishing business before becoming disciples of Jesus.

They perhaps went to Peter's house to wait for Christ, and since Christ did not appear, Peter decided -like the disciples of Emmaus- to return to his old life and start working, even after seeing Jesus resurrected. Perhaps, he felt unworthy to follow Christ due to his sin, his betrayal; being an impulsive and impatient man, he did not want to wait for God's time.

> "Simon Peter, Thomas (called the Twin), Nathanael of Cana in Galilee, the sons of Zebedee, and two others of his disciples were together. Simon Peter said to them, 'I am going fishing.' They said to him, 'We will go with you.' They went out and got into the boat, but that night they caught nothing." (John 21:2-3).

Only seven of the disciples were together at this time and mentioned in the passage. Peter, being restless, impatient and the leader of the group, decided to return to work fishing. Peter stopped waiting on Christ, but the reality is that he was battling something greater in his heart. He probably felt that he was not worthy to continue this walk of faith. How could he continue to be the head of the group after having betrayed his Lord?!

Has something like this ever happened to you? You are afraid to stand before God because you feel unworthy because of the sin you have committed. You want to flee from His presence, and you would rather continue your old life than have to appear before God and show your shame, your lack of love for Him, your indignation and affront before God.

> **"For everyone who does wicked things hates the light and does not come to the light, lest his works should be exposed." (John 3:20).**

Sometimes, we believers do not want to come to the light, and we go through times of spiritual dryness until the Holy Spirit guides us again to cry out to God. Peter had already seen Christ three times so far, and Christ had not mentioned anything to him regarding his betrayal. The weeks had passed and Peter ruminated in his mind about what he had done. He was fighting an internal battle that he dared not even mention.

The Apostle Peter was very ashamed because of his sin; he likely felt unworthy of the Lord. After boldly declaring that he would never do such a thing, he realized he had failed. Peter had said the very day before the crucifixion "Lord, I am ready to go with you both to prison and to death" (Luke 22:33). It was then that he returned to the beginning, to the same place where he was called. To the same place where Christ began His ministry; that place where —by order of the Lord— the miraculous catch occurred. That was the day when Peter believed in Christ as his Lord and his God.

> **"But when Simon Peter saw it, he fell down at Jesus' knees, saying, depart from me, for I am a sinful man, O Lord." (Luke 5:8).**

Peter had already been following Christ for three years, and he was still a sinful man. This disciple was the one who was closest to Christ, received the most rebukes, was the most exalted, and was taught the most by Him. This was the leader of the group of apostles, who said that he would never deny Him (Matthew 26:33). The one who believed himself to be stronger and more believing than everyone else. Now he does not feel that he can lead the group, to be the courageous man he thought he was, nor to carry out the task that Christ had entrusted to him.

Similar to the disciples of Emmaus, Peter also resumed his old life and job. Peter was returning to the same work Christ had called him. And his friends, perhaps either with a similar feeling of restlessness or not wanting to leave Peter alone, followed him. Their actions indicated a return to worldly pursuits, forsaking a life devoted to serving God. Let us now see how Christ called Peter:

"While walking by the Sea of Galilee, he saw two brothers, Simon (who is called Peter) and Andrew his brother, casting a net into the sea, for they were fishermen. And he said to them, 'Follow me, and I will make you fishers of men.' Immediately they left their nets and followed him." (Matthew 4:18-20).

This man had let go of his old way of living and providing for himself and his family, uprooted his life completely to follow Jesus; and after that event, the only fish he had caught was to pay taxes; fish that, by the way, Christ himself commanded him to fish (Matthew 17:24-27). Already Peter had left this life, he had been called to be a fisher of men (Matthew 4:19), to leave his old life behind to live for the Gospel of Christ. However, Peter, being a very emotional man, was greatly affected by his denial of Jesus. He intended to dedicate his life to Christ, but now he questioned if he even deserves the title of disciple.

What happens when a church leader falls into sin? What happens in the community? And if we talk about the secular world, what significance does it have for a head of state to become immoral and corrupt? The chief executive of a business, etc.? If a soldier dies in war, there are more soldiers; but if they kill the general of these soldiers, the impact on that war will be much greater: the experience, and tactics of a general are more difficult to replace. If a person is fired, it is not as serious as if the owner decides to close the business, since everyone who works in that company would be out of work.

We can see how his denial, his lack of trust in God, his fear of death, and giving his life on the cross with Christ that night if it was necessary, affected Peter's leadership, his lack of faithfulness to Christ and consequently dragged down another six other disciples with him. Peter led them down the same sinful path. They stopped waiting in Christ and returned to their old life.

This serves as a stark illustration of the devastating outcomes that can arise from a deficiency in leadership within a community, a household, or a place of worship. Those under such leaders tend to be carried along by their example for better or worse. We have been called to be the salt of the earth and light of the world (Matthew 5:13), but when we separate ourselves from God, we become insipid or tasteless salt that cannot preserve anything. Instead of being a lamp on a table that would shine a light on the entire room, we become a hidden light that allows darkness to prevail (Luke 11:33).

If a Christian separates from the Lord this will have consequences on his family (because now they will not see the Gospel throughout their life); it will have consequences on his work (because instead of bringing his colleagues closer to Christ, they will close their hearts to the Gospel), etc. Brothers and sisters, when any follower of Christ turns away from the truth, he will end up being a stumbling block to others. If this person continues professing to be a Christian —living a worldly life— his life will not only, not bring glory to God, but will thereby be debasing and defiling the precious and Holy Name of the Lord.

If any of us profess to be a believer but walk, talk, dress, etc., like a worldly person; and if this person acts as the world acts and thinks (drinking, dancing inappropriately, cursing, committing adultery, hearing ungodly music, etc.) then this person (consciously or unconsciously) will be leading other people down the path of perdition since they would be showing with their life that there is no difference between be a believer or non-believer. If any of us profess to have faith in Christ, but then returns to the world, he will lead others into hypocrisy, spiritual coldness, and will be a stumbling block to those walking in darkness and who need to see the light of the Gospel.

This is not something that can be taken lightly. For Christ, it is a serious fault for a leader to divert his sheep from the truth, since this will have eternal consequences. Let us observe how great the warning that Christ gives to those who cause others to stumble or turn away from the Gospel:

> **"But whoever causes one of these little ones who believe in me to sin, it would be better for him to have a great millstone fastened around his neck and to be drowned in the depth of the sea. Woe to the world for temptations to sin! For it is necessary that temptations come, but woe to the one by whom the temptation comes!" (Matthew 18:6-7).**

Pretending to be believers while living without Christ drives others away from Him. When a person lives day to day without seeking to honor God and then goes to church on Sundays just because he has this tradition (even though his heart is hardened by sin), such a person will only bring spiritual harm to everyone around him. As I already mentioned, in his attitude, Peter dragged Thomas, Nathanael, John, James, and two other disciples, who, by the way, caught absolutely nothing throughout the night.

Do you know why they didn't catch anything? Because they turned away from Jesus. Just as their nets were empty, their hearts were empty, therefore, the work of their hands would not be blessed, and their life would not prosper. They had turned away from Christ, and since they had already stopped being fishers of fish to be fishers of men, their efforts were doomed to fail.

Christ said in John 15:5 that apart from Him, we could do nothing; this was precisely what these disciples were trying to do: work without the Lord. Therefore, they worked in vain all that night, and their work was fruitless. The apostles needed to work for the kingdom of God so that souls would receive an eternal benefit, not for material things (fish).

Peter and the disciples went back to their previous life after witnessing the resurrected Jesus firsthand, seeing him, touching him, and hearing his voice.

> **"Just as day was breaking, Jesus stood on the shore; yet the disciples did not know that it was Jesus. Jesus said to them, 'Children, do you have any fish?' They answered him, 'No.' He said to them, 'Cast the net on the right side of the boat, and you will find some.' So they cast it, and now they were not able to haul it in, because of the quantity of fish" (John 21:4-6).**

One positive thing we can mention about these men and their work is their persistence. They spent the whole night trying again and again, trying to produce something for their labor, but they had no profit. When it was already dawn, Christ spoke to them from the beach, from afar, and asked them for a fish. This looks like the story of Matthew 4 is almost being repeated when Jesus told these fishermen that they would be fishers of men. Now the risen Christ reminds them where He had taken them from. One word from Jesus was enough for the power of God to be unleashed, and immediately they caught many fish, 153, to be exact.

There were at least 18 kinds of fish in the Sea of Kinneret (the Hebrew name for the Sea of Galilee, which probably means "harp shaped" in Hebrew, given the Sea of Galilee has a harp shape). However, three groups of fish were most commercialized at that time. The sardine [gr. *opsaria*] (a small fish), was the most abundant fish in the Sea of Galilee. The second group was the *musht* (Galilean tilapia), a fish that weighed about four to five pounds [2 kg] (also called "St. Peter's fish", and still exists in the Sea of Galilee today). The third group was the largest fish, the binny, or barbel (*barbus longiceps*), and these reached about 30 inches (76 cm) and weighed up to 15 pounds (7 kg).

Considering the physical prowess of the men who helped retrieve the net filled with fish and the boat's size, it is likely that the disciples managed to catch the musht and binny, the two most prevalent types of fish. They were six men, they caught 153 fish, and they could barely get the net out; therefore, if we consider that the catch was of mushts, we would be talking about around 750 pounds (340 kg) of fish; and if it was the binny, it would be about 2,000 pounds (900 kg). So, if the catch had been only for this last type of fish, then the boat would not have survived without sinking. Hence, it is highly probable that the catch included both varieties of fish, yet we cannot definitively confirm this.

In this story, one can sense the patience and love of Christ toward these men. Christ, who knows the end from the beginning, knows exactly the end of this story. He had full confidence that they would achieve their purpose on this planet. The grace and mercy that Christ shows to these men is the same that we must have with others, with those brothers in Christ who turn away to return to their old life, and who need to be reminded again and again from where Christ brought them out of.

We all come to Christ in different ways, at different times and circumstances; but we all need the same grace, patience, and love with which Christ treats these men. We can never forget the Lord's ministry of restoration. He never forgets any of his sheep, but He goes and restores them, corrects them, and returns them to the fold. We should have a heart that grieves for sin, not only our own, but that of others; and refrain from seeing ourselves as holier or more righteous, choosing instead to demonstrate humility and compassion. That day were they, tomorrow maybe I who falls away from Christ.

How many of us are quick to judge? How many of us have lacked grace when a brother has fallen into sin? Frequently, when one brother makes a mistake, the rest are quick to pass judgment without any compassion (although those who judge him are also in sin, although they could have the appearance of mercy). People reject fallen brothers; gossip destroys their hearts, and no one reaches out to restore them.

> **"And as they continued to ask him, he stood up and said to them, 'Let him who is without sin among you be the first to throw a stone at her.'" (John 8:7).**

It is up to the church council, pastors, and elders to pray and decide on the suitable discipline. We, the sheep or flock, must love and show grace to our fallen brethren. Let us not talk behind their back, but instead unite in prayer for the fallen so that he may be restored. Let us not talk behind their back, but instead unite in prayer for the fallen so that he may be restored. Let's do it with sincerity of heart, knowing that we could be the ones who are in their shoes. Not all those who have fallen repent, and there indeed are those who prefer to leave the church, perhaps realizing that they were not of us (1 John 2:19); However, there will be those who manage to be restored.

If Christ did not reject these sinners who turned away from the way to return to their old life, why should we reject and accuse a brother who turned away from the way? This is precisely when they need us the most to help them return to the path of faith because that is God's will.

> **"Then Peter came up and said to him, 'Lord, how often will my brother sin against me, and I forgive him? As many as seven times?' Jesus said to him, 'I do not say to you seven times, but seventy-seven times'" (Matthew 18:21-22).**

We have to follow the example of Christ, who always showed grace to His disciples, even when they were not on the right path, even when they strayed from Him. He always guided them to accomplish their work on this earth, and He continues to do the same with us, because Jesus is the same yesterday, today, and forever (Hebrews 13:8).

> **"So if you are offering your gift at the altar and there remember that your brother has something against you, leave your gift there before the altar and go. First be reconciled to your brother, and then come and offer your gift." (Matthew 5:23-24).**

Forgiving your brother means that you will never again consider what they committed against you; that is, you will not demand justice or revenge; You will not have any more ill thoughts against them, and you will show love towards the offender (even if he or she does not reciprocate in the same way). It doesn't mean that —necessarily— you and the offender will be best friends from then on, but it does mean that, in your heart, there won't be even a hint of resentment against him/her. Shortly before dying, Christ prayed for sinners saying: "Father, forgive them, for they know not what they do" (Luke 23:34).

What happens if your brother, boss, friend, or spouse, they ask for your forgiveness, but they come back and does the same thing? Should I continue to forgive them?

> **"Pay attention to yourselves! If your brother sins, rebuke him, and if he repents, forgive him, and if he sins against you seven times in the day, and turns to you seven times, saying, 'I repent,' you must forgive him." (Luke 17:3-4).**

This is the heart of Christ; He always shows continuous grace and forgiveness towards us. Don't we continually sin against Him, and always come asking for forgiveness? Can you imagine hearing Christ's response towards us, telling us that He has already forgiven us way too much?

If we could see the book of God (Revelation 20:11-12) with the list of our sins, we would all be surprised to see the enormous number of faults: thoughts, actions, attitudes, and words. All of those things have been offenses against God. If we think about it, what if that whole long list of sins was read before us? Would we deserve to be condemned for it? Of course! Therefore, only His continued grace and forgiveness can free us from such condemnation. It's due to the Lord's continued forgiveness which is the reason for our sustained salvation.

> "That disciple whom Jesus loved therefore said to Peter, 'It is the Lord!' When Simon Peter heard that it was the Lord, he put on his outer garment, for he was stripped for work, and threw himself into the sea. The other disciples came in the boat, dragging the net full of fish, for they were not far from the land, but about a hundred yards off. When they got out on land, they saw a charcoal fire in place, with fish laid out on it, and bread. Jesus said to them, 'Bring some of the fish that you have just caught.' So Simon Peter went aboard and hauled the net ashore, full of large fish, 153 of them. And although there were so many, the net was not torn. Jesus said to them, 'Come and have breakfast.' Now none of the disciples dared ask him, 'Who are you?' They knew it was the Lord. Jesus came and took the bread and gave it to them, and so with the fish. This was now the third time that Jesus was revealed to the disciples after he was raised from the dead." (John 21:7-14).

Then Jesus appeared to them without knowing it was Him and asked them for a fish. They had tried to catch something all night, but they had caught nothing. So, He ordered them to cast the net to the right side, and the fish they caught in the net were very many. At that moment, John said: "He is the Lord!" Then Peter put on his clothes, jumped into the sea, and swam to Jesus. When they reached the shore, Jesus was already preparing a fish for them, and asked them for more.

The disciples did not recognize Him physically; however, they did not dare ask Him, "Who are you?" because they knew He was the Lord. Here we see Peter's typical temperament, always wanting to be ahead of everyone. He didn't care that his friends were left with the job of hauling all those fish. He didn't care about the large amount of money that represented; all he wanted was to go to where his Jesus was.

Why did Peter put on the clothes and then jump into the water to swim? I think a good reason would be that he did not want to appear before Jesus half-naked. Once again, we see Peter's character shine: he always wanted go ahead of everyone.

We can also observe that Jesus ordered the disciples to go and bring more fish, and Peter —once again— is the one who goes and goes first to get the fish, and it seems that the others did not show such initiative. We can see that they all believed it was Jesus, but they couldn't recognize him because of His physical appearance. Furthermore, we also see that the way Jesus spoke to them at the beginning was the way an old man speaks to younger people since He calls them children. This was not a common term He used during His ministry to refer to His disciples (the only other time He spoke to them like this was in John 13:33).

These men were tired. They had worked all night, and their work had been fruitless until Jesus appeared on the scene. They hadn't had a meal and were most likely quite famished at that particular moment. Therefore, they needed sustenance, and then Christ appeared to them and with this appearance and this miracle He was telling them that he was their sustenance. It is as if he were telling them: "Here I am, making you breakfast so you can regain your strength. To show you that you depend on me. If you follow my voice and obey my words, then I will be you sustenance and prosper your ways. I have commanded you to win souls (Matthew 4:19), and if you bring the Gospel to them, they will hear your message, many will be saved, and you will not have to worry about material sustenance."

"But seek first the kingdom of God and his righteousness, and all these things will be added to you." (Matthew 6:33).

We must seek first the kingdom of God, and He will bring the fish into our nets, so that we may have the spiritual sustenance of our souls. As children of God, we cannot trust that, through our own strength, we will achieve our provisions since God is the one who gives us everything we need. It is not through our intelligence, nor through our wisdom, or our education that we achieve our wealth, it is God who gives us everything we need.

These men were busy, searching all night for their own earthly provision. However, although they tried for many hours, they could not catch anything. So, as children of God, if we have believed and trusted in Him, and honor Him in our ways, He has promised to always sustain us and give us everything we need.

> "Therefore I tell you, do not be anxious about your life, what you will eat or what you will drink, nor about your body, what you will put on. Is not life more than food, and the body more than clothing? Look at the birds of the air: they neither sow nor reap nor gather into barns, and yet your heavenly Father feeds them. Are you not of more value than they? (Matthew 6:25-26).

Just as it happened with the disciples at Emmaus, Jesus took the bread, reminding them that He is the bread of God that came down from heaven. Christ is that bread that gives eternal life (John 6:35), who gave His life for us. Christ reminded His disciples that they should never forget the price He paid for their (and our) freedom.

The Restoration of Peter

The disciples were in Galilee, in the Sea of Tiberias or Sea of Galilee. So, Simon Peter, feeling unworthy of fulfilling the calling for which he was entrusted by Christ and morally incapable of following Him due to his betrayal -although deep down he loved Jesus- was sure that he did not love him enough to surrender to Him for life (at least at that moment).

This was for Peter his darkest moment, the lowest point in his life since he started to follow Christ (about three years ago), especially after he had promised that he would never deny Him, and that he was even willing to die for Him. Peter saw Jesus's most difficult moment on earth, shortly before His martyrdom. He was the one who had witnessed most of the appearances of Christ, and this was for Him now the fourth appearance of the Lord. Christ Jesus had appeared to Peter personally, sometime that first Sunday of the resurrection, after appearing to the women (Luke 24:33).

There was no doubt that Peter was convinced of the reality of Jesus' resurrection. He had seen, touched, embraced, and eaten with the resurrected Christ, with God himself in human form, and Peter, knowing this, decided to step away from the ministry, and dragged six others with him.

Christ appeared to them in the Sea of Tiberias, and for the second time He performed the miracle of fishing, and this time He does it to remind them where Christ took them out from. He reminds them of the ministry He had given them and what He had called them to do. Christ had called these men to be fishers of men and not fish. He called them to leave their old life for this new life; That was the reason for their failure that night, because despite being expert fishermen, that night they had not caught a single fish. Let us now read the continuation of the third encounter of Christ by his disciples.

"When they had finished breakfast, Jesus said to Simon Peter, 'Simon, son of John, do you love me more than these?' He said to him, 'Yes, Lord; you know that I love you.' He said to him, 'Feed my lambs.' He said to him a second time, 'Simon, son of John, do you love me?' He said to him, 'Yes, Lord; you know that I love you.' He said to him, 'Tend my sheep.' He said to him the third time, 'Simon, son of John, do you love me?' Peter was grieved because he said to him the third time, 'Do you love me?' and he said to him, 'Lord, you know everything; you know that I love you.' Jesus said to him, 'Feed my sheep. Truly, truly, I say to you, when you were young, you used to dress yourself and walk wherever you wanted, but when you are old, you will stretch out your hands, and another will dress you and carry you where you do not want to go.' (This he said to show by what kind of death he was to glorify God.) And after saying this he said to him, 'Follow me.' Peter turned and saw the disciple whom Jesus loved following them, the one who also had leaned back against him during the supper and had said, 'Lord, who is it that is going to betray you?' When Peter saw him, he said to Jesus, 'Lord, what about this man?' Jesus said to him, 'If it is my will that he remains until I come, what is that to you? You follow me!' So the saying spread abroad among the brothers that this disciple was not to die; yet Jesus did not say to him that he was not to die, but, 'If it is my will that he remain until I come, what is that to you?' This is the disciple who is bearing witness about these things, and who has written these things, and we know that his testimony is true. Now there are also many other things that Jesus did. Were every one of them to be written, I suppose that the world itself could not contain the books that would be written." (John 21:15-25).

After working all night, Jesus prepared breakfast for them; they ate, and we now see how Jesus set Simon Peter as an example for his fellows. The time had finally come for Peter to face what in his heart had separated him from Christ. Let us remember the night when Peter betrayed Christ with the following verse:

"And the Lord turned and looked at Peter. And Peter remembered the saying of the Lord, how he had said to him, 'Before the rooster crows today, you will deny me three times'. And he went out and wept bitterly" (Luke 22:61-62).

Let's imagine that moment: Christ had been unjustly arrested and tried, and Peter, present among those who judged Christ, and being terrified of the same fate, denied him three times. At that precise moment, Jesus' gaze must have penetrated his soul. This look from Jesus was as if He were saying: "Oh, Peter, I told you that you were going to deny me." Peter must have felt like a knife went through his chest.

The one who believed that he was the strong one, the great one, the leader, the one who usually acted hastily, the only one who dared to go in where Jesus was being tried, sneaked in on his own strength and skills, was now suddenly realizing how weak, small, and sinful he really was. This must have been the most disappointing moment in Peter's life.

Peter, seeing Jesus' suffering, did nothing but betray and deny Him, just as Judas had done; and he did it for fear of losing his own life. When he heard the rooster crow, he went out and cried bitterly. Peter had sinned many times and, in many ways, but we never see him crying like he did that day. He had not been broken by his sin yet, nor had he recognized the depth of the wickedness of his heart.

Peter believed he really loved Christ, but here we see the extent of his love for Christ by that time. Jesus was demonstrating to Peter that his professed love was still insincere, despite his earlier claims. Peter had not yet realized that he had not totally surrendered to God.

Still hurting for having betrayed the Lord, and still feeling very ashamed, Peter, despite his strong desire to follow Jesus, doubted his ability to succeed. Peter's betrayal makes him realize —once and for all— that the love he felt for the Lord at that moment was not greater than the love he had for himself, since he had tried to preserve his life rather than lose his life for Christ. Now, let us ask ourselves: What is our calling? How much should we love Christ? How far should our devotion to Him go?

"Then Jesus told his disciples, 'If anyone would come after me, let him deny himself and take up his cross and follow me. For whoever would save his life will lose it, but whoever loses his life for my sake will find it.'" (Matthew 16:24-25).

Peter wanted to earn his life instead of giving it up for Christ; however, instead of gaining it, he lost it because his heart turned away from the Lord. Peter did not want to die, and his selfish instinct made him safeguard his life, that is, he denied the Lord to "save his life". Peter, at that time, did not understand that, if he wanted to be a true disciple of Jesus, he had to lose his life, since it is Christ who is in control of our lives, and we will not die until God calls us to His presence. Therefore, he could have borne witness to Christ and God would surely have delivered him, but even if he wouldn't, he would have died with Christ. Let's now look at another detail.

"When they had finished breakfast, Jesus said to Simon Peter, 'Simon, son of John, do you love me more than these?' He said to him, 'Yes, Lord; you know that I love you.' He said to him, 'Feed my lambs.'" (John 21:15).

Jesus had changed Simon's name, and he was now called Peter (John 1:42). Simon means "one who listens" in Hebrew, while Peter or Cephas means "stone or rock". If we observe, we will realize that on many occasions Christ used the name Simon (or Simon Peter), to represent Peter's old nature, when he did not act correctly. It is the equivalent today of our parents calling us by our full name to warn us about something or correct us for doing something wrong or being disobedient.

An example is Mark 14:37 where it says: "And he came and found them sleeping, and he said to Peter, 'Simon, are you asleep? Could you not watch one hour?'". It is as if Christ called him Simon when he was showing his sinful nature, his old nature; and Peter when he was acting correctly.

Another interesting thing is that Jesus, having finished breakfast with the disciples, took Peter and went with him for a walk. So it was that Jesus and Peter met alone. However, John followed them closely, listening to the conversation (this is probably why John is the only one who recounts this conversation in his Gospel).

> "When they had finished breakfast, Jesus said to Simon Peter, 'Simon, son of John, do you love me more than these?' He said to him, 'Yes, Lord; you know that I love you.' He said to him, 'Feed my lambs.' He said to him a second time, 'Simon, son of John, do you love me?' He said to him, 'Yes, Lord; you know that I love you.' He said to him, 'Tend my sheep.' He said to him the third time, 'Simon, son of John, do you love me?' Peter was grieved because he said to him the third time, 'Do you love me?' and he said to him, 'Lord, you know everything; you know that I love you.' Jesus said to him, 'Feed my sheep'" (John 21:15-17).

Here we will see the restoration, the calling, and the assigned task of Christ to Peter. Also, we see the call to us believers in what Christ says to Peter. These questions are not just for Peter, it is for us too.

Many of us sympathize with Peter because he tangibly represents way in our walk with God. Just like many of us, Peter, from the beginning, has felt that he loved Jesus more than what he truly did. He believed himself stronger than what he was. He had believed that he could do more than he really could, and because of this, time and time again, Peter failed in his service to Christ, even ending up denying Christ at the moment of his Lord's greatest crisis.

Now, although he had seen the resurrected Christ, Peter, due to his denial, saw himself as an unredeemable sinner, and that, because of this, he was unworthy of forgiveness or of carrying out the ministry that Christ had given him. Here we see Christ's calling him to love, sacrifice, and obey God above all else in this world.

Following Christ, loving Him and sacrificing everything for Him, is not easy (although it seems that way to many people). The cost to follow him is a complete surrender and totally sacrifice of our lives for Him. We must lose our life to gain Christ (Matthew 15:25), that is, we must die to our old self to truly be alive in Him (Philippians 1:21). The cost may be that we lose everything we have because of our faith, that our own family hates us, and that we may even be left alone in this world (Matthew 10:34-37). The cost of following Christ can even be persecution and death.

Following Christ means taking up our cross and following Him (Matthew 16:24). The cost of following Christ is our entire life. It is an extreme call to follow a man, who, being a human being, claimed to be God on earth, the Creator of all that exists. Following Christ is a call to be slaves to Him out of love (1 Timothy 4:6), and to imitate His example of sacrifice to the end (Ephesians 5:1).

In his humanity, our beautiful God, our Lord Jesus, suffered hunger, thirst, scarcity, poverty, tribulations, temptations, persecution, rejection, humiliation, and contempt. As a child, a teenager and then a grown man, he lived like everyone else. He spent the first 30 years of His life in anonymity, as a total unknown; living in one of the poorest and most despised cities in Israel. Throughout His life, He suffered countless persecutions, until He was finally martyred and died on a cross for us.

Why did He do it? He did it for love; because those who truly love sacrifice themselves and give themselves up for love above all else. So, when you truly love someone, your own life doesn't seem so important to you. Why do you think loving God is the first and greatest commandment? (Matthew 12:30).

Your love for God must surpass your love for everything else - your spouse, kids, possessions, time, holidays, and most importantly, your sins. Your genuine love for God and your sincere devotion to following Him are evidenced by your earnest pursuit of Him, your attentive ear to His words, and your complete obedience to His will (John 14:15). Christ gave his life for us because he loved us unto death. Who would not easily give his life for their child? In John 15:13 it says, "Greater love has no one than this, that a man lay down his life for his friends," that is, for those he loves". We can see that love is an extremely powerful motivation.

When our love for God is genuine, it influences our choices, inspires us to follow His teachings, and He leads us with His Spirit. Love is what leads us to serve God above all else. To love God is not an option, is a commandment: we are to love God with all our heart, soul, and strength (Matthew 22:37-39). Love is what leads us to seek

God even when we fail. The Bible does not call us to follow God out of legalism, nor out of fear, but out of love.

This is the true first love that Revelation 2:1-7 speaks of. In that passage Jesus praises the Ephesians church for their works, for being faithful to his Word, for rejecting false preaching, and for suffering for his Name's sake; but He only had one thing against them:

"But I have this against you, that you have abandoned the love you had at first." (Revelation 2:4).

The First love is not the feeling one has when first becoming a believer. It is not a feeling inside. It is not an emotion that lasts a few months and then disappears; that is a simplistic belief and a total misinterpretation of the meaning, and very different from what the true love of God is. The church at Ephesus had stopped loving God above all things and had become like the Pharisees: legalistic in their hearts, and an Orthodox Church, great doctrine but no love for God. They did things well, and obeyed only because the Bible says so; however, due to their lack of love for God, the church was on the path to its own destruction, since its heart was leaning towards the love for the world rather than towards the Creator; therefore, their worship was not a true worship to God.

I remember listening to one sermon, in which Pastor John MacArthur, speaking on the topic of love, said: "This is like a husband saying to his wife: 'Honey, I will be faithful to you, I will do everything that falls to me as your husband. I will love our children, I will provide for our family, and I will never leave home, I will not divert my heart by seeing other women, but the truth is that I do not love you.'" What a terrible emptiness this would cause in his wife if this man was only with her to fulfill his duties.

How do you think this woman will feel sleeping every day next to a faithful husband who provides everything for her, but who does not love her? It would mean that every kiss and every hug from this husband is just an act, a farce. This is what God tells the church at Ephesus, that their worship of Him is just a false performance of a heart that has turned away from Him. This service will not be acceptable to God, nor does it reflect genuine love.

Peter was a man who needed a complete restoration of his heart because of sin and brokenness. Of all the evil that he had done before, nothing had destroyed Peter's heart more than his having denied Jesus. Nothing in the past had caused him to turn away from the Lord, and now, not even the fact of having seen the resurrected Christ was enough for Peter to give up his idea of returning to his old life (although he knew that by doing this he would be turning away from Christ).

We do not know whether the other disciples knew of Peter's denial at the time; and if they did, perhaps it was something that they simply kept in their hearts, because they knew that, in one way or another, all the disciples (except for John) had betrayed the Lord. They had all been disobedient, but Christ took Peter as an example.

We see in the passage that Christ asked Peter three times if he loved Him. Jesus wanted to confirm Peter's love for Him; He also wanted there to be no doubt left in Peter's mind that his denial had been forgiven. Christ knew well that this was what Peter was struggling with.

Simon, son of Jonah, do you love me? This is the question that should always be asked of a disobedient believer. Everyone who walks in disobedience has a basic problem: they have decided to love something or someone above God. That is why Christ asks Peter something like: "Are you prepared to leave your career, your nets, your business, your sin, your unbelief, and leave your entire life to follow me above all?"

The Peter's response to the first two times that Christ asked him if he loved him, was this: "Lord, you know that I love you." The word Christ used when asking Peter if he loved him, in Greek, is the word "Agape".

Three words are translated as love in Greek, namely, Agape, Philia, and Eros. The word "agape" is unconditional love. It is a love that has nothing to do with how the other person treats you, whether the other person offends you or not, nor does it depend on what they offer you. This is God's love for us, his adopted children, and the love we should have for Him too.

"Philia" is the love for a friend. It is a brotherly love that, when conditions change, or if that person offends us, we could easily end our friendship. This is a love that is subject to change. Eros is the physical love or desire. This is the love that films with sexual content promote today, and that could be within a connotation of lust; this love is not necessarily sinful, since is also expressed in a marriage relationship.

If we combine these Greek words with the English language (as an illustration) we would say that Christ asked Peter: "Do you agape me?", and that Peter answered: "I *Phileo* you." Peter was responding to Christ with a lower level of love, that is, with the love that someone has for a friend, a conditional love that depends on the circumstances. This was precisely the love he had shown to Christ when he denied Him: when circumstances changed, he also changed his love for the Lord. Peter, out of fear of death, had shown a *Phileo* type of love, which was the love he had shown for Jesus at that moment in his life.

He had shown that he loved Jesus, but as long as his life was not in danger. That is why Peter did not dare to respond to Jesus that he loved him with agape love, with unconditional love, the love with which God loves us because he knew that he had not loved Christ in this way. Peter, before his denial, was quite capable of saying that he loved Christ that way, and he would have said it without a second thought; He even said that he would follow him to death (Matthew 26:33).

Why did Christ ask Peter that question? Because we sacrifice and give everything for the ones we love. Without Peter acknowledging his sin, repenting, and wholeheartedly loving Jesus with all his mind, soul, and strength, he would never have been able to sacrifice himself.

Love for God above all leads believers to serve Him with joy and rejoicing, even to the point of being willing to become martyrs for His sake. This was the case of Polycarp (70-155 AD). He was burned at the stake for the Lord's sake. Polycarp was the leader of the Smyrna church and was burned alive for refusing to offer incense and worship the Roman Emperor Antonius Pius. Polycarp was a martyr at the age of 86.

If we realize, that what most characterizes the world in which we live —since the fall of Adam and Eve, is the lack of love or, rather, hatred towards God and all his representatives on earth. Consciously or unconsciously, the world rejects everything that God asks of it. They do not want to hear, or know about God (John 3:20); and if the world is comforted by its sin, it then persecutes those who confront it.

In the world, love for the self prevails. We only think about our desires, passions, goals, achievements, assets, families, treasures, and what the world loves most which is its sin, all of this in the world is above God, and his Word. The Bible reveals the nature of mankind in the present times.

> "But understand this, that in the last days there will come times of difficulty. For people will be lovers of self, lovers of money, proud, arrogant, abusive, disobedient to their parents, ungrateful, unholy, heartless, unappeasable, slanderous, without self-control, brutal, not loving good, treacherous, reckless, swollen with conceit, lovers of pleasure rather than lovers of God" (2 Timothy 3:1-4).

As we see, what characterizes unbelievers is the lack of love towards their neighbor. These are lovers of themselves, and lovers of pleasures more than lovers of God, and all the other sins that they practice are a consequence of their lack of love for God. This is the place Peter found himself in, which led to his betrayal of Christ; and many of us can relate to Peter, even as long-time believers.

Many boast and believe themselves to be more than they are. Others are ungrateful to those who have served them, hate what is good, desire what God hates, and are easily puffed up by material things.

When Christ asked Peter for the third time, "Do you love me?" How did the apostle answer Jesus? He replied: "Lord, you know everything." Peter appealed to Christ's omniscience to tell Him how much He really loved Him. He had to appeal to His omniscience, so that Christ would know Peter's true love for Him because the great love He had previously proclaimed to have for Him could not come out of His mouth.

Peter had declared his unconditional love for Jesus, a love that would not fear death; he had said that he was even willing to give his life for Christ. He had declared total surrender, obedience, and dedication for the Gospel, and his Savior, but he had failed.

> "Peter answered him, 'Though they all fall away because of you, I will never fall away.' Jesus said to him, 'Truly, I tell you, this very night, before the rooster crows, you will deny me three times.' Peter said to him, 'Even if I must die with you, I will not

deny you!' And all the disciples said the same." (Matthew 26:33-35).

After Christ prophesied to Peter that he and others would turn away from him during the persecution, at that moment, he felt so empowered and so strong, that he told Jesus, God made man, that He was wrong. It seems like Peter was telling him: "You are wrong Jesus, my love for you is unconditional!" His prideful spirit blinded him from heeding Jesus' warning.

Today, if a pastor were to publicly deny Christ, or distort the Gospel to avoid persecution when confronted by the law or by non-believers attacking him for preaching the Gospel, his reputation would most likely be discredited, and he would lose the respect of God-fearing believers. Today, Peter would probably have been rejected and disqualified from ministry. The brethren of the church would have judged him, condemned him, and finally cast him aside forever.

But this is not what Christ did. He took Peter, even though he was a man unworthy of God's calling: a sinful, treacherous, volatile, lying, changeable man, and turned him into a rock. Christ made Peter a transformed man and solid in faith. He did not stop being imperfect but he became truly faithful to Jesus. Christ did not reject Peter, even though his love for Him was not where it should be yet. Christ showed Peter how the power of God would be perfected in him, leaving behind his sin and weakness.

In this emotional state, while Peter was still broken and separated from Christ, the Lord ordered him to take care of his sheep. For the third and last time Christ now asks him, Peter, do you *Phileo* me? or Peter do you love me?

Now Christ puts into question Peter even using the lower level of love he was professing for Him. He had already asked him twice using the word Agape, but now Christ uses the word *Phileo*. It seems that Christ is now even questioning Peters' professed *Philial* Love. Peter's actions did not demonstrate even this kind of love for him.

"He said to him the third time, 'Simon, son of John, do you love me?' Peter was grieved because he said to him the third time, 'Do you love me?' and he said to him, 'Lord, you know

> everything; you know that I love you.' Jesus said to him, 'Feed my sheep.'" (John 21:17).

This third question from Jesus was the one that touched Peter's heart: he was saddened because Christ was even questioning his professed love for him. Three times, Christ urges Peter to feed his lambs and sheep. It was as if Christ told him: "No more fishing, your job is not to catch fish, your job is to be fishers of men, take care of my sheep and take the Gospel throughout the world. I've already gotten you out of this place, don't go back to your old life. Go and fulfill the purpose for which I call you."

> "Truly, truly, I say to you, when you were young, you used to dress yourself and walk wherever you wanted, but when you are old, you will stretch out your hands, and another will dress you and carry you where you do not want to go." (This he said to show by what kind of death he was to glorify God.) And after saying this he said to him, 'Follow me.'" (John 21: 18-19).

Incredibly, Christ declares to Peter here that he was going to be martyred for Him, telling him the type of death he was going to have. This expression of "you will stretch out your hands" was associated with the crucifixion. Christ told Peter basically, "You are going to die crucified like me. You are going to suffer like I also suffered."

A thought-provoking question arises: Why did Christ disclose to Peter the manner of his death? Christ showed Peter that precisely where he had failed now, in the future he would be victorious. In the area where he had sinned, he would later be a great champion: one day he would not be afraid of being crucified for the glory and honor of God. God used Peter's own denial to prepare his heart for what would come, and then he would not commit the same sin again.

Christ wanted to show Peter that the next time he was confronted with the same challenge he would no longer deny Jesus, but would be martyred and killed for the Gospel. Peter's failure served to restore his faith and trust in God. Christ was assuring Peter that He would give him the strength to walk a lifetime with Him and that He would certainly fulfill the ministry to which he was called.

History says that Peter died crucified during the reign of the Roman emperor Nero (around 64 AD); and tradition also states that he felt so unworthy to die as his Lord, that he asked to be crucified upside down. Where before there was fear of dying, now there was a willing heart, a heart like Jesus', willing to suffer what was necessary for the love of God. Peter lost the fear of dying for Christ and gained the crown of life by his death. After all this, for Peter —as with Paul— to live was Christ, and to die was gain (Philippians 1:21).

Having revealed the way he would die, Christ continued and said to him: "Follow me." In other words: "All you must do is follow me. Stop worrying, I will take care of transforming you, just follow me, obey me, and believe me."

"Peter turned and saw the disciple whom Jesus loved following them, the one who also had leaned back against him during the supper and had said, 'Lord, who is it that is going to betray you?' When Peter saw him, he said to Jesus, 'Lord, what about this man?' Jesus said to him, 'If it is my will that he remain until I come, what is that to you? You follow me!'" (John 21:20-22).

Peter realized that John was there, and said to Christ: "Lord, what about John?" Isn't John also going to die crucified or martyred? Am I the only one who will suffer this? Christ responded: "If I decide that John will live until my second coming, what is that to you?" I am talking to you, Peter, follow me, focus on me. Forget about the plan I have for John, or the other disciples. In the same way, we must set our eyes on Christ, and on doing God's will for us, which is different for every one of us.

"So the saying spread abroad among the brothers that this disciple was not to die; yet Jesus did not say to him that he was not to die, but, 'If it is my will that he remain until I come, what is that to you?'" (John 21:23).

This caused a rumor among the disciples, that John would live forever. It's incredible how simple it is to misunderstand or twist the meaning of God's word. Let us remember that John was the one who wrote this Gospel years later, and he was clear about Christ's message that the Lord —in this conversation he had with Peter— was simply using hyperbole.

> **"This is the disciple who is bearing witness about these things, and who has written these things, and we know that his testimony is true. Now there are also many other things that Jesus did. Were every one of them to be written, I suppose that the world itself could not contain the books that would be written."**
> **(John 21:24-25).**

The apostle John validates his own Gospel since it's his testimony. He testifies that what it's written is true, since he had witnessed and experienced all the things described in his Gospel. There are so many ways John could have ended his Gospel; however, he did so by narrating the conversation that Jesus had with Peter. And by doing so, he is telling us all that, even if we have sinned against God, He can restore us and fulfill His work in us. God can restore us and complete His will in our lives. Likewise, the apostle Paul says:

> **"And I am sure of this, that he who began a good work in you will bring it to completion at the day of Jesus Christ."**
> **(Philippians 1:6).**

The application of this verse is exemplified in the life of Peter, and I hope the words in this book have helped you see the perfecting work of the Lord in your life. If your entire life was documented from beginning to end, one could fill hundreds of libraries writing down every thought, and every story that has ever happened in your life.

If everything that Christ made were documented, there would be no space for the number of books on this planet, because He is eternal, and he belongs outside of time; Therefore, if all the things that He has done and that He will do were written down, the books resulting from such writings would not fit on a planet as ephemeral and small as ours. I pray that your faith would be placed in Jesus, in the true and only One worthy of receiving all glory and honor.

If your gaze is fixed on something else, or someone other than Christ, I urge you to take your gaze away from those distractions, look towards heaven, open your eyes, and cry out to Him. Always trust that He is listening and always present in our lives. He is continuously attentive to the cry of each one of us. Never doubt, even in the worst circumstances of your life, remember that Jesus went through the worst test of all and that his triumph on the cross has freed us from eternal judgment. Also, remember that everything in this world is transitory and temporary. God knows your needs; God knows your pain. However, God has you there for a reason. Let us fix our eyes on Jesus and look nowhere else.

"looking to Jesus, the founder and perfecter of our faith, who for the joy that was set before him endured the cross, despising the shame, and is seated at the right hand of the throne of God." (Hebrews 12:2)

Chapter

XI

THE APPEARANCE ON THE MOUNTAIN IN GALILEE

We have already seen multiple appearances of Christ after the resurrection, starting with Mary Magdalene until the appearance to the seven disciples at the Sea of Tiberias. We will now see when Jesus appears to the eleven disciples in Galilee. Now, Jesus appears to them on the mountain that He had commanded them to go to (after His third appearance at the Sea of Tiberias to the disciples). This mountain was somewhere in Galilee where Christ began His ministry.

The Bible mentions only two appearances of the resurrected Christ in Galilee. On the other hand, John mentions that the appearance at the Sea of Tiberias was the third appearance to the disciples (John 21:14) at which time only five of the apostles (those mentioned by name) were at the Sea of Tiberias and the names of the other two disciples are not known (John 21:2-3). Now we see that all the apostles were together waiting for Jesus; there were probably more disciples, and although the Bible does not say this clearly, we could assume that the women and other disciples of Jesus (like the disciples on the road to Emmaus, for example) were also present.

Previously we saw how Peter was confronted and restored by Jesus, and now they were all together on a mountain waiting to see the Lord

Jesus again. If we read these events on Mark 16:14-19, here we see a condensed summary of the events of the resurrection, given it does not detail each appearance as the other Gospels do.

Now, if we try to reconcile where we find these events which include Matthew 28:16-20; Mark 16:14-19; Luke 24:44-53 and Acts 1:6-11 (Where we see the transition of the Gospels to the formation of the Church). Upon a quick reading of these verses, they seem to contradict each other. However, in this chapter, we will see that the apparent contradiction does not exist. I suggest you spend a few minutes reading these passages to understand the events we will be discussing.

By studying these mentioned passages, we can see that the Gospel of Luke does not speak of the second appearance of Christ to the disciples individually, nor the appearances of the Lord in Galilee, but rather The Gospel of Luke summarizes the appearances from the first appearance to the disciples and then immediately goes to the description of the ascension of Christ.

When we read Luke, it would appear to indicate that everything happened in just a matter of a few days; however, Luke himself is the only one who states in the book of Acts that Jesus appeared to the disciples for 40 days (Acts 1:3). Same as Mark, who gives little information on these last appearances events, and from the Gospel of John we already saw how his Gospel ends with no mention of any further appearances of Christ after this. Therefore, the only Gospel that truly details the appearance of Jesus on the mountain of Galilee is Matthew.

Now we will dive into one of the most powerful commands given by Jesus to his disciples, the command that would cause the entire world to be touched by the Gospel. This command inspired these men to dedicate their whole lives to Christ.

> **"Now the eleven disciples went to Galilee, to the mountain to which Jesus had directed them. And when they saw him they worshiped him, but some doubted. And Jesus came and said to them, 'All authority in heaven and on earth has been given to me. Go therefore and make disciples of all nations, baptizing them in the name of the Father and of the Son and of the Holy Spirit, teaching them to observe all that I have commanded you. And behold, I am with you always, to the end of the age.'" (Matthew 28:16-20).**

The Gospel does not mention exactly what the mountain was called. According to tradition, it is Mount Tabor, and since the 4th century AD, this mountain has been recognized as the place of the transfiguration; it is possible that this was the mountain where they met Jesus (since it was a place known to them). Mount Tabor is located about 10 miles east of Nazareth, and about 30 miles southwest of Capernaum (the city where Peter lived). Capernaum was also where the disciples were probably staying when Jesus appeared to them at the Sea of Tiberias. This mountain is also on the way to Jerusalem, which is important, given that Jerusalem is where they later saw Christ for the last time before His ascension unto heaven.

When the disciples saw Christ, they immediately worshiped Him, but the Bible states that they had some doubts. What doubts could they be? They could not possibly doubt the resurrection because given they were all together worshiping and seeing the resurrected Christ. They could not doubt the power of Christ, for He showed them that He has power even over death. They could not doubt His words since everything He had previously said had been fulfilled.

Due to the context of what is happening (the mandate that Christ gives them now), they were probably unsure of what to do next; they probably felt unable to fulfill the mission that Jesus had given them.

After the resurrection, they departed from Jerusalem as instructed by Jesus, journeyed to Galilee, and then returned to Jerusalem again. Jesus had appeared to them from a time and always unexpectedly, after which he would disappear for a week or two. They were lost, and they were clueless about what exactly they were to do without the direct guidance of Christ. They were like lost sheep who couldn't find their way home. Some of the doubts they might have had were: What will we do now? What is the next step to take? Or perhaps they were thinking: *Am I going to be able to fulfill my calling in this ministry? Am I going to be able to follow Christ and carry out what he has commanded me to do?*

This order was not quite what they envisioned when they started to follow the Messiah. They expected positions of power, not persecution. They expected honor, not humiliation. They expected riches, not poverty. They expected abundant life, not death. All these things raised doubts about whether they really wanted this life, or if they would have the strength and will to carry out this task.

The doubt consisted of not knowing what to do. Indecision and lack of a clear path tend to create a lot of anxiety in our hearts. If you are uncertain about whether you will have a job tomorrow, or whether you will be able to provide for your family, this will cause great anxiety. Perhaps you doubt if you are qualified for the ministry God wants you to perform. Doubt according to the Oxford dictionary is: "hesitation or lack of determination when faced with various possibilities of choice about beliefs, news or facts."

I believe that there is not a person who at some point in their life has not doubted what decision to make. And what about you? Perhaps you had doubts when you began your walk with Christ, perhaps about things written in God's word that caused you to doubt His goodness, for example, why would God command the slaughter of children in the Old Testament? (1 Samuel 15:3-4) Why, because of the sin of a man like David, did God send a spirit that killed thousands of people? (2 Samuel 24:25), or if God is all-powerful, why doesn't He just save everyone?

There are many questions we could ask that could shake our faith if we do not know the God we serve and the purpose we have in this life. The opposite of doubt is certainty, confidence, and decision. This is how our faith in God should be, although we may not understand everything, we don't doubt His plans for us, we are confident, and we believe with certainty that He has decided to make us in the image of His Son.

"And I am sure of this, that he who began a good work in you will bring it to completion at the day of Jesus Christ." (Philippians 1:6).

These disciples, despite all the evidence given by Christ and the clear support He had promised them, still doubted whether they really wanted to do this task or whether they could carry out the ministry to which Christ was calling them. Let us remember that these disciples did not imagine that they would be sent into the world to preach, both to Jews and Gentiles, the good news of the resurrection. For them, they believed that Christ would come to reign right there and then. Even today, the Jews expect the Messiah to be a political liberator, like Moises or David.

I find it interesting that, as we examine our hearts, we find how uncertainty or doubt can overwhelm us even when we have Christ before us. It is incredible how, even having Jesus in front of us and seeing His resurrected body, our faith can still fail. And if this happened to these disciples, what would become of us who have never seen Christ with our physical eyes? What hope do we have?

Many people, even when seeing, do not believe, and even when they have irrefutable evidence before them, they doubt. The truth is that we are not omniscient, we do not know everything, and therefore, we cannot know with complete certainty if we will fulfill a mission entrusted to us. Peter doubted his ability to fulfill his ministry and follow Christ, therefore, he returned to his old life, and now some other disciples were also going through the same thing.

How many of us have doubted the Word of God? Have we ever doubted if we were truly saved? Our calling? Even when His Word is clear before us —as it was with these disciples— our sinfulness causes us to doubt. However, these disciples were obeying the voice of Christ, they were with Him, and they were there, trying to do the will of God. God does not call us to have all the answers, much less if we are just born-again Christians, new in the faith. However, he commands us to have faith, to believe that He is the one who will direct our steps to do His will.

This doubt (whether they were capable of carrying out the task that Christ was entrusted to them) was dispelled by the Lord when he told them: "All authority in heaven and on earth has been given to me."(Matthew 28:18). In other words, what Jesus was telling them was this: "I have control over you and everything that happens in the world." He has the authority and the power over good and evil on this planet and over the universe; over all creation.

The Old Power of Satan

It is interesting to think that biblically, Satan has the authority over this world (John 14:30; John 12:31-33; Ephesians 2:1-3). He is the prince of this world and has authority on this earth and the principalities that govern here, because that was the authority he usurped from Adam due to sin. However, he does not act by himself, nor does he have absolute power over the earth. He is unable to harm a follower of Christ unless God allows it. (Luke 22:31-32). Satan is required to seek permission from God before carrying out his plans.

Who created Satan? It was God. God gave the authority that was from Adam to Satan, Christ himself even referred to Satan many times as the prince of this world. However, being the prince of this world, he would have no authority above the King, Christ Jesus.

"The judgment of this world is already here; now the prince of this world will be cast out" (John 12:31).

He is also mentioned in John 14:30 and 16:11. Paul mentions him as the prince of the power of the air in Ephesians 2:2. When Christ was in the wilderness, Satan offered him all the kingdoms of the world on the condition that Jesus would worship him (Matthew 4:8-9). With these verses, we can realize the power that Satan has over all the nations of the world.

It should not surprise us then that what reigns in this world is sin, that rulers separate themselves from God, and do things contrary to God's law. We should not be surprised that they deny the Creator and exchange the truth of God for a lie. Satan is the one who has influenced this world using his ungodly tactics of deception and falsehood, seeking to destroy the image of God in every nation on this earth.

Satan influences nations to alcoholism, lying, perverse sexuality, adultery, jealousy, anger and strife, murder, lust, drugs, greed, selfishness, and homosexuality. In our days, Satan deceives people into thinking that God made a mistake about their gender and that they must work to change their sexual identity. With all this, Satan tries to cause the maximum destruction of the image of God in humanity so that it is as unholy as him and thus does not inherit eternal life (Galatians 5:16-21). Satan wants human beings to convert to his image and likeness. He knows very well that by filling our minds with perversion, the nations will hate God and bring condemnation upon themselves.

He uses every possible way to influence our hearts so that we follow the desires of the flesh: our own desires, our pleasures, the things we want, the temporary things that the flesh craves. The heart, because of its fallen nature (inherited from Adam and Eve), is deceitful and wicked above all things (Jeremiah 17:9); Therefore, when we do not have the spirit of God in us, it is very easy to listen to the voice of the enemy and obey him in everything he persuades us to do, which is something that shouldn't happen with the Lord's sheep who walk in obedience, since they recognize the voice of their Shepherd (John 10:27-28).

Satan influences all nations and almost all kings, presidents, or rulers of this world to do his will and rebel against God. They tolerate and promote social policies that allow sexual debauchery, divorce, the murder of babies or abortion, etc. The rulers and authorities of this world applaud sin and attack those who want to do good. Satan is not omniscient, but he uses the world's system so that darts or arrows hurt or invade our minds and separate us from God. This is how he incited David to sin against God, as we can see in 1 Chronicles 21:1, where he says: "Then Satan stood against Israel and incited David to number Israel" (1 Chronicles 21:1).

We cannot deny the authority and power that God has given Satan over this world. None of us humans have the capacity, strength, power, skill, wisdom, and intelligence that Satan has, which is why it is impossible for us, in our strength, to defeat him. For the same reason, no one without the Spirit of God can resist the temptation of sin; and so, what the system of this world offers will always seem extremely attractive to you.

It is as if David were going to fight Goliath with his own strength, without having God on his side. It would have been practically impossible for a teenager between 13 and 19 years old (1 Samuel 17:55-56) like David, who was not even old enough to fight in the war (Numbers 1:3), to defeat a three-meter-tall man with a stone from a nearby stream. Goliath was a giant skilled in battle, who made all Jews shake in fear and no matter how skilled David was, it was impossible for him to defeat him in such a way. This was the hand of God, not the hand of David.

Christ Proclaimed as the Lord of all Creation

Our triumph is not on our talents or capabilities but on God's Spirit who guides us. In Matthew 28:18 (along with other verses I have already mentioned in this book, e.g. John 10:10), Christ is saying to the disciples (paraphrase): "I now have all authority. Satan has the empire of death, but and I have the empire of life. Satan has come to kill, I came to save, Satan wants to destroy the image of God, I came to restore it."

That authority of Christ is not yet in full effect, since the prince of this world —Satan— is still loose and continues to do his evil in the world. Satan has not yet been imprisoned; however, a day will come when he will be. The book of Revelation says that Satan will be bound for a thousand years (this will occur at the second coming of Christ, according to Revelation 20:2-3).

Christ is like a president who has won the elections, but who is waiting for the day when He takes the reins of government, but the losing party will refuse to conceit, and He will take His ownership by force. This "official change" is already described in the Book of Revelation. In Revelation 5 we read what will happen on that glorious day in which Christ will finally remove the power of darkness from the devil, and a new government will come; a glorious government, with an Eternal King and High priest who will restore the world: that Lamb who is worthy to open the book, the book that has the certificate of ownership of the world.

"Then I saw in the right hand of him who was seated on the throne a scroll written within and on the back, sealed with seven seals. And I saw a mighty angel proclaiming with a loud voice, 'Who is worthy to open the scroll and break its seals?' And no one in heaven or on earth or under the earth was able to open the scroll or to look into it, and I began to weep loudly because no one was found worthy to open the scroll or to look into it. And one of the elders said to me, 'Weep no more; behold, the Lion of the tribe of Judah, the Root of David, has conquered, so that he can open the scroll and its seven seals." And between the throne and the four living creatures and among the elders I saw a Lamb standing, as though it had been slain, with seven horns and with seven eyes, which are the seven spirits of God sent out into all the earth. And he went and took the scroll from the right hand of him who was seated on the throne. And when he had taken the scroll, the four living creatures and the twenty-four elders fell down before the Lamb, each holding a harp, and golden bowls full of incense, which are the prayers of the saints. And they sang a new song, saying, 'Worthy are you to take the scroll and to open its seals, for you were slain, and by your blood you ransomed people for God from every tribe and language and people and nation, and you have made them a kingdom and priests to our God, and they shall reign on the earth." (Revelation 5:1-10).

Christ spoke to the disciples in the present tense. He told them that all authority had been given to him, and that is totally true. The prophecies in the Bible are often given in the present tense, or as an event that has already occurred since it is impossible for what has already been decreed by God not to happen. Therefore, what God has said is taken as if it was already granted as if it had been fulfilled today. God is the one who declares the end from the beginning (Isaiah 46:10), and here we see the day in which Jesus takes the reins of the government of this world which was declared to the apostle John.

John was the only one of the apostles who had the blessing of witnessing the day in which Christ would take the title deed to the earth to open it; and, at that moment, Christ took the earth as His property, decreeing afterward the judgments on the nations that would occur, before His coming.

When John was there, initially he was faced with the prospect that there was no one worthy of opening the book and untying the seals, and due to this, John began to cry. He knew how important it was for that book to be opened and that what the Lord said regarding the judgments of this world be fulfilled, because then the second coming of Christ would take place, and the Lord would finally be established as King over all forever. It was then that, amid this gloomy panorama, John saw a Lamb as if slain (sacrificed): This is the only one worthy of opening the book and loosening the seals (which are the judgments of God)! Thus, once this book was fully opened, Jesus would establish himself as the owner and supreme ruler of everything; He would come to reign and rule the earth with a rod of iron (Revelation 2:27), at his glorious coming.

Why do human beings, when they receive authority, abuse it? Because we do not use it for the glory of God but for our own glory; and in seeking our own glory, rulers destroy themselves and their people. In the books of 1 and 2 Kings, 38 kings are mentioned; of these only five pleased God in any way. Israel, the nation chosen by God, and it was entrusted with the Holy Scripture so that its citizens would follow the living God. However, they failed. And if these kings, who had the Word of God, failed, what would have become of the other kings of the earth who had no knowledge or revelation of the one true God?

Being able to do good, with all the power at their disposal, given by God to them, the kings mentioned in 1 and 2 Kings almost always did evil. The same story was repeated over and over (1 Samuel 8:11-22). Nowadays, it happens that in times of elections, the citizens place their faith in a man, and not in the God who lifts and removes kings. And then, when the chosen ruler has sat on the throne of authority, he glories and is arrogant. Humans were not designed by God to seek glory, and when they do, it only leads to pride in their hearts and a distancing from God.

Only One is worthy of receiving all glory and authority: the Lamb of God, Jesus Christ (Revelation 4:11). He is the only one worthy because He and He alone defeated death on the cross. There is only one who, having supreme power, was willing to live for 30 years in anonymity, and did not use His power to pursue any personal benefit. Likewise, during the three years of His ministry, He sought not His own glory but the glory of the Father. Also, there is only One who, having supreme power, submitted to the authority of this world, and fulfilled all the law that He Himself had given to Moses.

Christ is the only One worthy, and the only One who can say: "All authority has been given to me in heaven and on earth." Christ is the one worthy of opening the book, and he is the one worthy of worship. Even all those in heaven, and all the angels, bowed their knees before the Lamb as He opened the book. The title to the land was taken away from Satan.

Called to Make disciples

These men's doubts caused Jesus to assure them that He had been given all authority. And He says the same to us, so we have no reason to doubt whether we can fulfill God's purpose. Christ conquered the empire of death, He is the worthy slain Lamb of God, who sustains us with his right hand of power. This power given from heaven is the power of the Holy Spirit, and through that power, God will sustain us to do his work here. So, then, Christ says:

> **"Go therefore and make disciples of all nations, baptizing them in the name of the Father and of the Son and of the Holy Spirit, teaching them to observe all that I have commanded you. And behold, I am with you always, to the end of the age."**
> **(Matthew 28:19-20).**

Jesus gave this command to these common men, who had doubted their calling, even after seeing him resurrected! These men had deserted

Christ, they denied him, they abandoned him; However, with all that, Christ sent them to carry his message. Jesus commanded them to do what He had done throughout His ministry.

They were entrusted with the task of bringing the Gospel to the nations. This task was also entrusted to me, and if you have believed in Christ, it has also been entrusted to you. We were called by Him who has all authority, to preach the good news of salvation to the world.

> **"How then will they call on him in whom they have not believed? And how are they to believe in him of whom they have never heard? And how are they to hear without someone preaching? And how are they to preach unless they are sent? As it is written, 'How beautiful are the feet of those who preach the good news!'" (Romans 10:14-15).**

We must guide others who are beginning to walk the path of faith and allow ourselves to be guided by those already spiritually mature and learn from them. The task of making disciples is not only to preach to people to repent but also to teach them as an elementary school student is taught until they graduate eventually from college.

Every disciple must grow in faith, must strive to know the Word of God, how to live by it, love it, know what God has revealed to us through it, and be like Jesus by following His example. Christ is the model, and each of us, his disciples, should be imitators of Him. In 1 Corinthians 11:1 Paul said: "Be imitators of me, as I am of Christ." In other words, "in that which I am like Jesus, imitate me". A Gospel without works is a dead Gospel (James 2:18), and to teach others we have to live it first.

Christ embodied the Word of God to perfection, and through Him, we can clearly see how God wants us to live. Christ commanded all his followers to make disciples of all nations; That is, Jesus made the Church responsible for bringing the message of salvation to all parts of the world; However, He did not give them this mandate without giving them the power to fulfill it, because at the same time his church would have God's full support for this ministry. This is also why baptism is in the name of the Father, the Son, and the Holy Spirit, since the three persons of the Holy Trinity are involved in the salvation process. It is by the authority of God that the believer -without deserving the grace and forgiveness of God— is accepted as an adopted son of the Almighty (John 1:12).

As followers of Christ, our calling to make disciples extends to children, friends, and co-workers, even if we are not pastors, or we are functioning in a ministerial role. We are called to imitate Jesus and bring the Gospel of salvation. This is not only a "God bless you", it is not only praying from time to time for that person in need. This command does not mean simply letting co-workers know that you are a believer, posting Christian things on the internet, or telling your community and extended family that you now follow Jesus; This is certainly necessary, and is a sign that you are not ashamed of the Gospel. However, we must try to take advantage of the opportunities that God places in your way to tell others about Christ, so that they may believe, and then be discipleship.

Learn to Teach

We should all be students of the Word of God, and the reason is this: the command that Christ has given us is to teach others to observe all that He has commanded. Therefore, the command implies that, to teach, we first have to learn. It is necessary to scrutinize, pay attention, discern, and internalize the teachings of the Bible; spend hours on end dedicated to knowing God through what He has revealed of Himself, and then go and teach others. We can share our testimony without much knowledge of the Gospel yet; we are encouraged to do this given, so this is very powerful, but to make disciples and learn to understand the Word of God, may take many years, so we should continually invest time in growing in Christ, to share the Word faithfully and not teach false doctrine.

As a new believer, it's easy to be misled by churches that don't faithfully preach the Word of God. If we fail to examine ourselves, we can be led astray for years, causing our faith to become stagnant due to our lack of understanding.

No architect would dare give a class on anatomy to a group of doctors, just as a doctor would not dare give a class on how to design a building to architects. To be a teacher one needs preparation: that takes time, dedication, love, and passion for what he/she studies.

Paul told Timothy, "Do your best to present yourself to God as one approved, a worker who has no need to be ashamed, rightly handling the word of truth" (2 Timothy 2:15). This needs to be done diligently. Being diligent in the Word means reading it, memorizing it; but also listening to sermons, teachings, etc., everything that helps us fill ourselves with God's Word, so we can then use this to help fill others with the same love and passion for the Word of God. Diligence in the Word will enable us to disciple others regarding faith with love and grace. The apostle Peter said: "...always being prepared to make a defense to anyone who asks you for a reason for the hope that is in you; yet do it with gentleness and respect." (1 Peter 3:15b).

One of the reasons you are reading this book is because you are curious to learn more of the Word of God, and maybe get a different take or perspective on what's revealed already in the Bible that perhaps you hadn't thought of, and this was also the same curiosity the first disciples felt. Today, thanks to those disciples, because they obeyed Jesus' command to spread the Gospel, we too can enter the path that leads to eternal life; and like them, also carry the Gospel throughout the world. The price of carrying the Gospel has been high, and much blood has been (and will continue to be) shed, so that the seed of hope, salvation, and eternal life may be sown in many hearts. Christ backs up His Word, He backs up those who are brave to obey, love and follow Him, and give their lives to the service of God.

He said clearly: "And remember! I am with you always, until the end of age." Also, Jesus himself promised to send us a Comforter/Helper who would guide us into all truth (John 16:13). Even if we can't see, touch, hear, or feel Him, Jesus Christ will be with us every day forever throughout eternity. Our God will never leave us alone. He always honors His Word; Let us also honor His Holy Word, and may God put in us the burning desire to bring others to the feet of Jesus.

Chapter

XII

The Ascension

In this final chapter of the book, we will explore the last moments of Jesus on Earth before ascending to heaven. It's about the moment when Christ returned to His place of glory and majesty. The eternal God, who entered time for thirty-three years, returned to His throne, victorious over death and sin; He received the crown of life, and dominion over the earth. At that moment, we are also assured the hope of eternal life which rests in the resurrection of Christ.

Before beginning, I think it is important to note the differences between the Gospel of Mark, Luke, and Matthew regarding the issue of the ascension. If someone superficially reads the account of these three Gospels, they might assume again that there may be contradictions. However, in this chapter, we will see that these "contradictions" are part of the same story. Let us then compare the story of Mark and Luke, since we have already seen what Matthew and John say in the previous chapters.

MANUEL BELLO

Differences Between the Gospels Regarding the Ascension

> "Afterward he appeared to the eleven themselves as they were reclining at table, and he rebuked them for their unbelief and hardness of heart, because they had not believed those who saw him after he had risen. And he said to them, 'Go into all the world and proclaim the Gospel to the whole creation. Whoever believes and is baptized will be saved, but whoever does not believe will be condemned. And these signs will accompany those who believe: in my name they will cast out demons; they will speak in new tongues; they will pick up serpents with their hands; and if they drink any deadly poison, it will not hurt them; they will lay their hands on the sick, and they will recover.' So then the Lord Jesus, after he had spoken to them, was taken up into heaven and sat down at the right hand of God." (Mark 16:14-19).

In Mark chapter 16 we have the full account of the Lord's resurrection described, but Mark summarizes the events. In Mark 16:1-8 He talks about the women who brought spices to anoint the body of the Lord and how the angel appeared to them. Then in Mark 16:9-11, Mark mentions the Lord's appearance to Mary Magdalene and her testimony to her other disciples. Mark then mentions the Emmaus disciples in passing (vv. Mark 16:12-13), and finally describes the appearance to the eleven disciples (Not mentioning the first appearance to all the disciples)—without saying anything about Thomas specifically— and culminates with the brief mention that Jesus was taken to heaven. Mark does not mention the appearance of Christ in Galilee, at the Sea of Tiberias, or what happened on the mountain of Galilee. Therefore, if we read only Mark's account, we would have the impression that Jesus only appeared to His disciples once.

The Gospel of Mark summarizes the events that occurred during 40 days very briefly, and the stories included are shorter versus other Gospels. The Gospel of Mark provides a concise overview of the most important events rather than delving into specifics. We can denote in his Gospel key facts: Jesus was resurrected, there were witnesses, He gave them the mandate to preach the Gospel, He empowered them for the ministry, and then He went to heaven. This is basically what Mark summarizes in chapter 16.

THE RESURRECTION OF CHRIST

Mark 16:14 summarizes the first two appearances of Jesus to the disciples (occasions in which Christ rebuked them for their unbelief): when the Lord appeared to the disciples without Thomas (John 20:19-23), and when Thomas was present (John 20:24-28). Mark mentions these two events as if they were one; and after these two appearances, the disciples no longer doubted the resurrection of the Lord Jesus. Mark then moves on to the Great Commission, which Jesus may have spoken while the disciples were in Jerusalem, in the upper room, before the ascension (Acts 1:12), as recounted by Luke, or it could also be that he is summarizing what happened on the mountain of Galilee (Matthew 28:18-20), which could also have been the place where Christ commissioned his disciples to go and preach the Gospel.

Subsequently, Mark jumps to the ascension, giving the impression that it happened immediately after Jesus' first meeting with his disciples. However, in the book of Acts, written by Luke, we know that the ascension occurred on the Mount of Olives (Acts 1:12). Let's now look at what Luke's Gospel describes.

> **"Then he said to them, 'These are my words that I spoke to you while I was still with you, that everything written about me in the Law of Moses and the Prophets, and the Psalms must be fulfilled.' Then he opened their minds to understand the Scriptures, and said to them, 'Thus it is written, that the Christ should suffer and on the third day rise from the dead, and that repentance for the forgiveness of sins should be proclaimed in his name to all nations, beginning from Jerusalem. You are witnesses of these things. And behold, I am sending the promise of my Father upon you. But stay in the city until you are clothed with power from on high.' And he led them out as far as Bethany, and lifting up his hands he blessed them. While he blessed them, he parted from them and was carried up into heaven. And they worshiped him and returned to Jerusalem with great joy, and were continually in the temple blessing God" (Luke 24:44-53).**

In Luke 24:36-42 it is reported that Christ appeared to His disciples the first time (as well as Mark), and then, in vv. 44-49 it would seem that Christ gives them the Great Commission and then ascends to heaven (a narrative similar to that of Mark). We can then notice that Luke and Mark summarize all the events after the resurrection in a single story as if it were a single interaction; Luke here narrates the first appearance, the second, and that of the mountain of Galilee, to immediately continue with the ascension. Therefore, if we read the text without paying close attention, the accounts of Mark and Luke may seem to contradict those of Matthew and John. However, this is not so.

Unlike John 21 (which ends with Jesus' appearance to seven disciples at the Sea of Tiberias), Matthew 28 ends on the mountain of Galilee, with the Great Commission. Then we see Luke recounting a conversation that Jesus had with His disciples before the ascension to the Lord. He tells His disciples to remain in Jerusalem until they receive the Holy Spirit (Luke 24:49).

Connecting then the dots between the Gospels, we could deduce that the disciples were not in Galilee at this time that Luke describes, but had probably already returned from the mountain in Galilee and were now in the upper room in Jerusalem (Acts 1:12). That said, because Luke appears to be the only one to record with much more detail the story regarding the Ascension. We will end this book by focusing solely on Luke's account, given he wrote both the Gospel of Luke and the book of Acts, where we see best narrated the ascension of Jesus.

The Great Commission

> "Then he said to them, 'These are my words that I spoke to you while I was still with you, that everything written about me in the Law of Moses and the Prophets and the Psalms must be fulfilled.' Then he opened their minds to understand the Scriptures, and said to them, 'Thus it is written, that the Christ should suffer and on the third day rise from the dead, and that repentance for the forgiveness of sins should be proclaimed in his name to all nations, beginning from Jerusalem. You are witnesses of these things. And behold, I am sending the promise of my Father upon you. But stay in the city until you are clothed with power from on high.'" (Luke 24:44-49).

I have already commented in previous chapters about the interaction that Jesus had with the disciples of Emmaus; how Jesus explained to them everything that Moses, the Prophets, and the Psalms said about Him, that is, what the Old Testament says about Him. We saw how important it was for all this to happen since it had been a plan orchestrated by God before the foundation of the world (Ephesians 1:4).

Christ showed them the importance of his death and resurrection, as seen in the Old Testament. Many passages in the Old Testament speak of the Lord coming, but let's take as an example the book of Job (which is probably one of the oldest stories in the Bible, dating to Genesis to the period likely after the flood). Even in the book of Job, whose story could have taken place during the time in which Abraham lived or even before, we see already the longing of God for the establishment of a Mediator between He and men. A Mediator who could restore the relationship between fallen humanity and the Holy God.

> "Neither is there any mediator between us who might lay his hand upon us both. Let Him take His rod away from me, and let not fear of Him terrify me." (Job 9:33-34).

And this Mediator longed by Job eventually came, which was Jesus Christ, who, by his sacrifice and death for us, restored our relationship with God, and removed the death penalty (the result of divine judgment) that was against us (Romans 5:1). The resurrection is one of the most important events of the Bible since without it there would be no Gospel, we would all still be in our sins (1 Corinthians 15:13-17), and all the preaching—from the apostles until now—would have been in vain. Whoever denies the bodily and physical resurrection of Jesus automatically becomes a prisoner of eternal judgment, even if he believes everything else that is written in the Bible. The doctrine of the resurrection is a fundamental doctrine of the Word of God, and denying it is the same as continuing in sin and not being a true believer (Galatians 1:8).

The Concept the Disciples Had of a Leader

We know that even after the resurrection, the disciples did not have a clear idea of Christ's mission; They expected Jesus to become king of Israel at that moment, and free the nation from the yoke of Rome. They were also unaware of the purpose that God had for them: that they should go throughout the world to preach the Gospel. Until this moment, and throughout the time they walked with Christ in His earthly ministry, they did not expect to go to the pagan nations to preach. For the Jews, salvation was only for Israel, and for those Gentiles who agreed to become Jews. Despite this, Christ makes it clear that the message will start in Jerusalem and then would extend to the whole world.

Despite this, they struggled with this concept even after receiving the Holy Spirit; even after witnessing the conversion of thousands with the first sermon Peter preached after Pentecost (Acts 2:37-41). That is why God himself had to reveal to Peter that salvation was for the whole world (Acts 10:9-16). Peter had not understood that salvation was also for Gentiles until God sent him to preach in the house of a Gentile named Cornelius. It was in this Gentile's house that the Holy Spirit was poured out, and he and his entire home were converted. Finally, after this happened, Peter said, "...Truly I understand that God shows no partiality, but in every nation anyone who fears him and does what is right is acceptable to him." (Acts 10:34-35).

Christ never spoke about establishing an earthly kingdom until his second coming but of the proclamation of the good news of salvation to all who believe in Him. The good news is this: that God freely offers forgiveness of sins through Christ Jesus. That is, so that everyone who truly repents before God, who believes in the death and resurrection of Jesus, and who recognizes that He is the Savior who came to reestablish our relationship with God —through his grace— will receive forgiveness of sins (John 14:6).

A Spiritual Kingdom in the Human Heart

It is an unbelievable thought that God has loved us so much, that, being creatures, made by His hands and brought to life by His breath, but that because of our sin we were condemned to eternal judgment, that God Himself, in the person of His Son, decided to become a man and die for us on a cross. And not only that, but He has given us an undeserved title in His kingdom. Since we were children of the devil (1 John 3:10), Jesus, through His death, opened the door for us to be constituted children of God (John 1:12). Christ defeated on the cross that evil being, who is the father of lies and a murderer (John 8:44), abusive, accusatory (Zechariah 3:1-2), immoral, deceiver (Acts 13:8-10); to that being who is full of hate, who ruled as king in our lives, whom we adored with so much love, being just as liars, fornicators, murderers, immoral, adulterers, blasphemers and blind to our own sin as him; and although we may have believed to be good, we were dead in our sins (2 Timothy 3:1-5).

We are not all children of God until we are born again, for the word says in John 1:12 "But to as many as received him, he gave the right to become children of God, that is, to those who believe in his name."

There is no salvation outside of Christ, and if we leave this world without having accepted the gift of salvation, the reality is that we will spend eternity in a place of eternal torment and suffering (Revelation 20:10). But the fear of this punishment is not what should move us to approach Him, but should be our love for him and the desire to be with Him forever. Therefore, our desire to be with Christ for eternity motivates us every day to honor the heavenly Father above all else. And even if hell did not exist, a true believer would honor the Heavenly Father anyway.

Luke 24:47 says that the name of Jesus would be preached to the nations for the forgiveness of sins. Here, the word nations is translated from the Greek *ethnos*, the root of the Latin word ethnicity. Christ is saying here that the message of salvation would be preached to all ethnic groups in the world. To every language, race, tribe, people, and nation in the world.

The Vision of Jesus: A Different Vision

The ascension of Jesus is described mainly in three places: in the Gospel of Mark, Luke and the book of Acts of the Apostles. If we were to read only the passage in Matthew 28 (where Jesus gave them the great commission while they were on the mountain of Galilee), one would think that after this Christ ascended to heaven; but Matthew does not speak of the ascension. Jesus ascended to heaven from Judea, from a place near Bethany (Luke 24:50), near where Lazarus was resurrected; and according to Acts 1:12, Jesus ascended on the Mount of Olives, near Jerusalem. The distance between Bethany and the Mount of Olives is only 1.6 km (1 mile).

How can we be sure that this was the fifth appearance of Jesus to his disciples (this time in Jerusalem)? Because Christ told them in Luke 24:49 to remain in the city until they had received the Holy Spirit, and after that, he led them to the outskirts of the city. In Acts 1:13 we read that the disciples were staying in an upper room in Jerusalem (where they returned after the ascension).

> **"So when they had come together, they asked him, 'Lord, will you at this time restore the kingdom to Israel?' He said to them, 'It is not for you to know times or seasons that the Father has fixed by his own authority. But you will receive power when the Holy Spirit has come upon you, and you will be my witnesses in Jerusalem and in all Judea and Samaria, and to the end of the earth.'" (Acts 1:6-8).**

In Acts 1:4 we see the instruction not to leave Jerusalem until they had received the promise of the Father, that is, the baptism in the Holy Spirit. The conversation likely occurred when Jesus discussed the Great Commission with His disciples, similar to the dialogue in Acts 1:4-6 and Luke 24:49. When we review the Gospel of Luke, He describes the very same topic in Luke 24:49, connecting then the conversation between this Luke's last chapter and Acts chapter 1 (it seems to be the same one).

We can believe that the disciples never imagined that Christ would take over two thousand years to return, as has happened until today. They expected Jesus to leave and return soon, while they were still alive. Therefore, they asked: "Will you restore the kingdom of Israel at this time?" Conversely, this also indicates that the disciples' primary focus was on the political restoration of Israel rather than spreading the Gospel globally. Their goal was for Israel to regain its sovereignty and become a prominent world leader.

The spiritual blindness that exists without the guidance of the Holy Spirit is immense. Without the Holy Spirit, it is impossible to discern spiritual truths even if the resurrected Jesus himself speaks to us face to face (as was the case with the apostles). Christ's plan went far beyond the small territory of Israel. At that time, the total area encompassing the land of Israel was perhaps 15-20 thousand km^2. While the surface of the earth is about 150 million km^2. The vision of the Lord was 10 thousand times greater than what the disciples had.

A Global Task

Everyone tends to think locally. We think about the culture and social context where we live, and this is normal. Now, if today it is difficult to think globally (even with all the technology and advances in the globalization systems that have taken place in recent decades), it is difficult to imagine the very small vision that the disciples of Christ had at that time; and even greater if we talk in terms of evangelization. For example, if I live in the United States, it is difficult to feel burdened for the salvation of people who live in South Africa, Mongolia, Tanzania, Thailand, Indonesia, etc. Unvisited locations and unknown countries that rarely cross our thoughts. The truth is the world for us is immense, and we can't take on the whole world. Our local church has the great responsibility of lifting the name of Christ in its own social and cultural context, and in the historical moment in which they live. This is our priority: to honor God in our local community or wherever He calls you to live and serve.

Nevertheless, I am of the opinion that missions hold significant importance, and it is the duty of local churches to collaborate with the propagation of the Gospel by aiding believers who have chosen to dedicate their lives to this crucial task. Going to the mission field is not a calling for every believer, since, if it were so, the churches would be empty, and all the pastors would go on to missions. However, those who are not called to this ministry must consider supporting those who are, in prayer and provisions. But one thing is certain: it is the responsibility of all Christians in a local church to share the Gospel with their community and serve as role models of faith for those around them.

Christians are usually preoccupied and guided by the constraints of time, location, and the societal issues they encounter in their daily lives. This can be seen in the letters to the seven churches in Revelation 2 and 3. Christ called His disciples to be missionaries wherever they were. Whether in their house (Jerusalem); with their closest neighbors: Judea; or with their most hated enemies: Samaria; and, finally, to all the ends of the earth, that is, wherever we are we must raise the flag of the Lord Jesus.

It is necessary to show humility with our words and actions that we serve the King of kings and Lord of lords. And because of this, a question now arises: Why did Christ command us to preach so firmly, and just before leaving this earth? Why is this command given now and not long before (while He walked with the disciples doing the ministry)?

It is because the time has come in which the power of God was about to descend upon them. The seal that guarantees our entry into heaven (Ephesians 1:13), and that guides us to all truth (John 16:13-15). The

Spirit of God is the one who would make it possible for the Gospel to have the impact it has had, since only with the power of the Holy Spirit will people be able to believe the message of the Gospel.

Before this, it was impossible for them [and us] to carry out such an impossible task. Without the Holy Spirit, we would all be led into lies, and the Church could not exist. The Spirit of God is the one who directs us to Christ, and then, in all our journey towards the heavenly homeland.

The Mount of Olives

After this and now ready to ascend back to heaven, Christ took the disciples outside the city, to the Mount of Olives. Let's now read this encounter:

> "And he led them out as far as Bethany, and lifting up his hands he blessed them. While he blessed them, he parted from them and was carried up into heaven. And they worshiped him and returned to Jerusalem with great joy, and were continually in the temple blessing God" (Luke 24:50-53).

> "So when they had come together, they asked him, 'Lord, will you at this time restore the kingdom to Israel?' He said to them, 'It is not for you to know times or seasons that the Father has fixed by his own authority. But you will receive power when the Holy Spirit has come upon you, and you will be my witnesses in Jerusalem and in all Judea and Samaria, and to the end of the earth.' And when he had said these things, as they were looking on, he was lifted up, and a cloud took him out of their sight. And while they were gazing into heaven as he went, behold, two men stood by them in white robes, and said, 'Men of Galilee, why do you stand looking into heaven? This Jesus, who was taken up from you into heaven, will come in the same way as you saw him go into heaven.' Then they returned to Jerusalem from the mount called Olivet, which is near Jerusalem, a Sabbath day's journey away." (Acts 1:6-12).

THE RESURRECTION OF CHRIST

In these two passages Luke wrote different parts of the same ascension story. Why would Jesus have chosen the Mount of Olives to ascend to heaven from there? This was the place where David went up crying; sad and humiliated (wearing his head covered and his feet bare) because of the betrayal of Absalon, his son (2 Samuel 15:30). This was also the place Jesus frequented to pray (John 8:1). It was also in this place where Jesus prayed before going to the cross, in Gethsemane, which is located at the foot of the Mount of Olives (Matthew 26:30). Likewise, this was a place where Jesus used to teach His disciples (Mark 13:3) and the place where Jesus gave the disciples the signs of the end times (Matthew 24:3-4). It is truly remarkable that this was the exact location from where Jesus ascended to heaven (Acts 1:12).

Jesus gave his disciples his blessings and ascended to heaven in their presence. Many think that the Mount of Olives is probably the place where more than 500 people witnessed the resurrected Jesus (1 Corinthians 14:4-7). But the Bible does not categorically say where it was that these 500 people saw Him alive.

While their eyes were fixed on the sky, two angels appeared with white garments, which represent purity and holiness, and said to the disciples: "And while they were gazing into heaven as he went, behold, two men stood by them in white robes, and said, 'Men of Galilee, why do you stand looking into heaven? This Jesus, who was taken up from you into heaven, will come in the same way as you saw him go into heaven'" (Acts 1:10-11).

Here we find an interesting reason why the Mount of Olives was important to Jesus: this is the same place where Jesus will return when He comes to reign over the earth. The angels said that just as we watched Him depart, we will witness His return. The prophet Zechariah had already prophesied this event when he predicted that Jesus would return to earth as King and place His feet on the Mount of Olives. Here we see a sign of the second coming of Jesus in the Old Testament.

> **"Behold, a day is coming for the Lord, when the spoil taken from you will be divided in your midst. For I will gather all the nations against Jerusalem to battle, and the city shall be taken and the houses plundered and the women raped. Half of the city shall go out into exile, but the rest of the people shall not be cut off from the city. Then the Lord will go out and fight against those nations as when he fights on a day of battle. On that day his**

feet shall stand on the Mount of Olives that lies before Jerusalem on the east, and the Mount of Olives shall be split in two from east to west by a very wide valley, so that one half of the Mount shall move northward, and the other half southward. And you shall flee to the valley of my mountains, for the valley of the mountains shall reach to Azal. And you shall flee as you fled from the earthquake in the days of Uzziah king of Judah. Then the Lord my God will come, and all the holy ones with him. On that day there shall be no light, cold, or frost. And there shall be a unique day, which is known to the Lord, neither day nor night, but at evening time there shall be light. On that day living waters shall flow out from Jerusalem, half of them to the eastern sea and half of them to the western sea. It shall continue in summer as in winter. And the Lord will be king over all the earth. On that day the Lord will be one and his name one." (Zechariah 14:1-9).

Although Jesus had the freedom to ascend to heaven from any part of Israel, he specifically chose this location because it is where he will return when he comes back for his second coming, just as the angels predicted that he would return in the same manner he left. This passage is a wonderful and impressive vision of the coming of the Lord. This is the same vision mentioned in Revelation 19:11-14. Christ descends from heaven together with His saints dressed in garments of the finest linen, white and clean, to fight against the kings of the earth and the antichrist (19:19). The sun will be darkened, the moon will give no light, and the stars will cease to be (Matthew 24:29, Revelation 21:23), and the Lord will be King over all the earth (Revelation 19:11-16).

Christ, the Only One Worthy of Opening the Book and Undoing its Seals

Who else but God —who knows the end from the beginning— can make us see and understand this precious truth? I think the important thing about His ascension is that He clearly reminds us of the amazing promise of His return. Our God lives outside of time. For God, one day is like a thousand years, and a thousand years is like one day (2 Peter 3:8-10). We see this when we think about the moment of the ascension. When we read the book of Revelation, we find the climax and the continuation of this story. The moment when the hour of judgment arrives and is about to be fulfilled. But there is a problem: the seals of the book (God's judgments) need to be opened first, and the Lamb of God has not arrived. Let's look at the passage:

> "Then I saw in the right hand of him who was seated on the throne a scroll written within and on the back, sealed with seven seals. And I saw a mighty angel proclaiming with a loud voice, 'Who is worthy to open the scroll and break its seals?' And no one in heaven or on earth or under the earth was able to open the scroll or to look into it, and I began to weep loudly because no one was found worthy to open the scroll or to look into it."
> (Revelation 5:1-4).

It's incredible to imagine this moment. Imagine the deep suffering that John felt at this moment. He had a great desire for these seals to be opened, and possibly the same desire as those who witnessed this portentous scene. Here was before John what he had been waiting for: that God would finally avenge His enemies, send judgments on humanity, and Jesus would descend to reign over the earth with His saints gathered to Him. As John looked at this, there was no one worthy that could open the seals. This was for John of serious concern. He has been working now for the kingdom of God for decades expecting to see that Christ would be worthy of this honor. Had he labored in vain all these years? Was it all a hoax? Where is the Lamb he has given his life for?

> "And one of the elders said to me, 'Weep no more; behold, the Lion of the tribe of Judah, the Root of David, has conquered, so that he can open the scroll and its seven seals.' And between the throne and the four living creatures and among the elders I saw a Lamb standing, as though it had been slain, with seven horns and with seven eyes, which are the seven spirits of God sent out into all the earth. And he went and took the scroll from the right hand of him who was seated on the throne." (Revelation 5:5-7).

No one was worthy on the scene, but suddenly a sacrificed Lamb appeared. There was no one worthy, and now the root of David appeared; there was no one worthy, and suddenly, the One they murdered appeared, who also rose from the dead, and who forty days later ascended to heaven (1 Corinthians 15:3-7; Acts 1:3). At least 50-60 years had passed since Jesus had ascended to heaven; and perhaps John thought something like this, "If Christ died, rose again, and ascended to heaven, how come there is no one worthy? Has my preaching been in vain? Is there no salvation for the world? Where is the Jesus I saw ascend to heaven many years ago?" It's possible that these thoughts weighed heavily on John's heart, pushing him to the brink of despair and leading him to cry openly.

However, God exists outside of time; that is why I believe we see John (who by then would be about 80-90 years old), seeing this event as if time had never passed. John witnessed the victorious arrival of the slain Lamb in heaven right after witnessing His ascension. It is almost as if only a few moments had passed between Christ's ascending and the moment He began to open the seals.

The resurrection stands out as a fundamental doctrine in our faith. Without the resurrection there is no Gospel, no ascension, and no one who opens the book and takes possession of the earth. If Christ had not defeated death, Christ would not return, and our faith would have no meaning because without the resurrection we would still be in our sins. But, glory to God! Christ was resurrected! Therefore, He has given us this great promise —which fills our hearts with hope— "I am coming quickly" (Revelation 22:20).

What Stops the Return of Jesus

There is only one thing that holds back the return of Jesus, and it is not satan, nor the antichrist, nor the apocalypse. Many may mock us by saying: "Two thousand years have already passed. Where is Christ? Do you still believe in that fable? Where is Jesus who is not coming?" Let us thank God that he has not come yet, because if Christ had returned before the 1st. July 2005, I would have remained in my sins and not been saved. This is what I believe holds the return of Jesus.

"Knowing this first of all, that scoffers will come in the last days with scoffing, following their own sinful desires. They will say, 'Where is the promise of his coming? For ever since the fathers fell asleep, all things are continuing as they were from the

beginning of creation.' But do not overlook this one fact, beloved, that with the Lord one day is as a thousand years, and a thousand years as one day. The Lord is not slow to fulfill his promise as some count slowness, but is patient toward you, not wishing that any should perish, but that all should reach repentance." (2 Peter 3:3-4, 8-9).

Peter, writing to the church, says that it is not that Jesus is late in coming, but that what scoffers consider delay is a sign of His patience and goodness. He does not want anyone to perish; therefore, He waits patiently for everyone to come to repentance. This is what prevents Christ from returning. He is waiting for all His Church to be completed, and all His children to come to Him. But of course, that does not mean that everyone in the world will repent; by the way, millions of people have already died without Christ, and thousands more die every day. We can be assured in our God and remember that the Bible also says:

"And this is the will of him who sent me, that I should lose nothing of all that he has given me, but raise it up on the last day." (John 6:39).

"Even as he chose us in him before the foundation of the world, that we should be holy and blameless before him. In love he predestined us for adoption to himself as sons through Jesus Christ, according to the purpose of his will" (Ephesians 1:4-5).

If we join the passage from 2 Peter 3 with these others, we can understand that Jesus has not returned yet because of God's patience. Because He, by His grace, has waited for all those who in the future would believe in Him, those whom He chose before creating everything that exists, those whom He predestined out of love to adopt as children, those whom God the Father gave to His Holy Son, Jesus, as a Gift so that none of them would be lost (but would resurrect them on the final day), for love of these future believers, the Lord has not yet returned. But soon He will return. We don't know who all those believers are, but God does know each one of them by name. He won't lose not even one of His children, not one of His sheep, and nothing in heaven, on earth, or anything that exists can separate us from His amazing love. Once the last child of God has accepted His calling, Jesus will return to reign with all the believers on earth.

> **"For I am sure that neither death nor life, nor angels nor rulers, nor things present nor things to come, nor powers, nor height nor depth, nor anything else in all creation, will be able to separate us from the love of God in Christ Jesus our Lord."**
> **(Romans 8:38)**

I recommend you to keep on reflecting, yearning, and contemplating Christ. May the power of his resurrection fill you with joy and rejoicing. Rejoice in thinking that the sting of death no longer has dominion over us (1 Corinthians 15:55) and that our walk-in faith is not in vain. If you have believed don't fear death, after your eyes have closed on this earth because you will open them instantly in heaven and see our glorious Jesus welcoming you to heaven, just like Stephen saw him sitting on his throne welcoming him with open arms (Acts 7:55), so he will receive all of those who have placed their faith in Him, and they will come into his presence forever. Have faith in the one who triumphed over death! His resurrection assures us that we will one day rise again and be with our beautiful and glorious God, King, and Lord. Amen.

****

I hope this book has been a blessing to you. I can tell you that writing it has changed my life. I have come to appreciate in a new and enriching way the love that Christ has for each of us, thanks to God. He opened my eyes to appreciate the immense sacrifice of His death and see the great value that the resurrection has in the life of every believer. Our Christ has risen, and we too will rise with Him. Let there be no doubt in your heart that He who ascended into heaven, who promised to return, will one day descend from heaven, and the dead in Christ will rise first, and those who are alive will be taken to meet Him in heaven.

May God bless you and guide you along the path of truth. May the passion and love for God and His Word be stronger than your desire for sin. May God guide you to humble your heart before the Almighty. I urge you to never turn your heart away from Christ (by returning to the path that leads to perdition). Love God with all of your heart, and never let the world deceive you, for the ways of this world only give rubbish: anything in this world is nothing compared to the wonderful presence of our Jesus.

The devil will always offer you happiness, freedom, and gratification, but remember he is a liar. Sin is always something temporary, and it will always leave you with a great void. Apart from God, we are nothing, we can do nothing good or fruitful. God offers us a more excellent way: the path of true love, justice, peace and, joy in His presence. A narrow path that leads to life, where there is fullness of joy and a fountain of water springing up to eternal life. And whoever drinks this water will never thirst again. I ask God that your faith may be strengthened and that a flame may be lit in your heart that will never be extinguished by the desires of this world.

If you have finished this book and were encouraged, transformed, touched, and confronted by it, and helped enrich your love for Christ, renew your walk with God, and grow in your faith, then consider sharing it with others who may also need to understand the importance of the resurrection of Jesus, and who also need to know that our Christ is not dead, but is alive and reigns forever. He reigns sitting on a high and sublime throne, ruling over everything, and always attentive to those who cry out wholeheartedly to Him day and night. May our deepest desire, day to day, be to live in the presence of our Lord and long for the return of our beloved Jesus and the day we will finally see Him face to face.

> **"He who testifies to these things says, 'Surely I am coming soon.' Amen. Come, Lord Jesus! The grace of the Lord Jesus be with all. Amen." (Revelation 22:20-21).**

www.ingramcontent.com/pod-product-compliance
Lightning Source LLC
Chambersburg PA
CBHW070051080526
44586CB00013B/1011